BRIDGING THE CONSTITUTIONAL DIVIDE

Joseph V. Hughes Jr. and Holly O. Hughes
Series on the Presidency and Leadership

James P. Pfiffner, General Editor

A list of other titles in this series appears at the back of this book.

BRIDGING THE CONSTITUTIONAL DIVIDE

Inside the White House Office of Legislative Affairs

Edited and with an Introduction by
Russell L. Riley

Texas A&M University Press : College Station

First edition

This paper meets the requirements of ANSI/NISO Z39.48-1992
(Permanence of Paper).
Binding materials have been chosen for durability.

Library of Congress Cataloging-in-Publication Data

White House Congressional Affairs Symposium
(2003 : White Burkett Miller Center)
Bridging the constitutional divide :
inside the White House Office of Legislative Affairs /
edited and with an introduction by Russell L. Riley. — 1st ed.
p. cm. — (Joseph V. Hughes Jr. and Holly O. Hughes series on the
presidency and leadership)
Includes bibliographical references and index.
ISBN-13: 978-1-60344-149-0 (cloth : alk. paper)
ISBN-10: 1-60344-149-2 (cloth : alk. paper)
1. Executive-legislative relations—United States—Congresses.
2. United States. White House Office. Office of Legislative
Affairs—Congresses. I. Riley, Russell L. (Russell Lynn), 1958–
II. Title. III. Series: Presidency and leadership (Unnumbered)
JK585.W46 2003
352.2—dc22
2009023282

This book is dedicated to the memory of

Richard E. Neustadt

—a generous teacher.

I would rather make choice to know certainly
what talk he had in his tent
with some of his familiar friends,
the night fore-going the battell,
than the speech he made the morrow
after to his Armie and what he did
in his chamber or closet,
than what in the senate or market place.

MONTAIGNE

CONTENTS

LIST OF PARTICIPANTS

White House Congressional Affairs Symposium, September 12–13, 2003

ASSISTANTS TO THE PRESIDENT FOR LEGISLATIVE AFFAIRS

William L. Ball III (Ronald Reagan, 1986–88)

Charles M. Brain (Bill Clinton, 2000–2001; deputy, 1998–2000)

Max L. Friedersdorf (Gerald Ford, 1974–76; Ronald Reagan, 1981–82, 1985–86; also part of Richard Nixon's legislative affairs team, 1971–74)

John Hilley (Bill Clinton, 1996–98)

Frederick McClure (George H. W. Bush, 1989–92; also a special assistant for Ronald Reagan, 1985–86)

Frank Moore (Jimmy Carter, 1977–81)

Lawrence Stein (Bill Clinton, 1998–2000)

LEAD INTERVIEWERS

Richard E. Neustadt, Douglas Dillon Professor of Government Emeritus, Harvard University

Russell L. Riley, Associate Professor and Research Fellow, Miller Center of Public Affairs, University of Virginia

James Thurber, Professor of Government and Director of the Center for Congressional and Presidential Studies, American University

James Sterling Young, Emeritus Professor of Government, Randolph P. Compton Scholar, and Director of the Presidential Oral History Program, Miller Center of Public Affairs, University of Virginia

OTHER ACADEMIC PARTICIPANTS

James Ceaser, Professor of Politics, University of Virginia

John Gilmour, Associate Professor of Government, College of William & Mary

Karen Hult, Professor of Political Science, Virginia Tech University

Stephen Knott, Assistant Professor and Research Fellow, Miller Center of Public Affairs, University of Virginia

Sidney Milkis, James Hart Professor of Government and Co-Director of the American Political Development Program, Miller Center of Public Affairs, University of Virginia.

Eric Patashnik, Associate Professor of Politics, University of Virginia

Charles Walcott, Professor of Political Science, Virginia Tech University

Stephen Wayne, Professor of Government, Georgetown University

Philip Zelikow, White Burkett Miller Professor of History and Director, Miller Center of Public Affairs, University of Virginia

PREFACE

This book is the record of a two-day symposium on White House congressional relations held at the Miller Center of Public Affairs, University of Virginia, on September 12–13, 2003. It is primarily a transcribed group oral history, featuring the spoken recollections of seven former heads of the White House Office of Legislative Affairs, spanning the presidencies of Richard Nixon to Bill Clinton. All former chief congressional liaisons were invited to be with us; over half of those then living appeared. The symposium was also attended by a number of invited scholars of American politics, including several distinguished experts on presidential-congressional relations who moderated the proceedings and helped to refine the topics under discussion. Among their number was the then dean of presidential studies, Professor Richard E. Neustadt—whose own White House experience went back to Harry Truman—in what we believe to have been his final public appearance in the United States just before his death the following month in England.

The purpose of the symposium was to create an occasion for candid reflection among Democrats and Republicans alike about the nature of modern presidential-congressional relations. The result is a front-row seat to presidential history as recounted by those who lived it.

This symposium was sponsored and organized by the Miller Center's Presidential Oral History Program, which in 1981, under the direction of James Sterling Young, began conducting in-depth elite oral history interviews with those who previously occupied senior positions in the White House and the cabinet. Since its inception, the program's main course of activity has been single-administration interviews, capturing in confidence each former official's recollections of his or her time with a given president—including systematic examination of the Carter, Reagan, George H. W. Bush, and Clinton presidencies.[1] Upon the conclusion of a given presidential project, the program then opens to the public the archive of cleared transcripts on that White House, releasing (according to the standard canons of oral history procedure) those materials authorized by the interviewee. Confidentiality in the conduct of these interviews has assured the highest possible degree of candor by the respondent in speaking for history into the tape recorder.[2]

A group oral history, however, offers two advantages over the Presidential Oral History Program's standard fare. First, the proceedings can be openly conducted, and the contents can be made available to the public more quickly, as with this edited volume. The second great virtue of a group oral history session is that it permits a cross-fertilization of ideas among people who shared the same responsibilities over time in the White House, opening up possibilities for cross-administration comparisons that are seldom possible in solo interviews. Most of the participants in this symposium have, in fact, recorded individual oral histories about the specifics of their own time in the White House.[3] But our intent in organizing this symposium was to look beyond the particulars of any single president or party at larger questions of governance and institutional relations.

This book purposely preserves the spontaneous character of the symposium. The tone is thus informal and conversational. We tried—successfully, as I think this volume will show—to stake out a happy middle ground: to create a relaxed environment for the sharing of common experiences and the relating of favorite tales while maintaining a focus on fundamental issues. Thus, these discussions enlighten in two ways: they provide us a revealing glimpse into the inside, usually hidden, business of Washington, and they afford us the considered reflections of a thoughtful group of political veterans.

What appears in these pages is authentic data about American politics, some related directly to key questions of contemporary scholarship. For example, political scientists working on formal models of institutions will find beneficial the discussions that follow about veto strategies, the issuance of executive orders, and the scarcity of anything that can be meaningfully called a "legislative agenda." But there are also in these pages a lot of good stories, such as Max Friedersdorf's wonderfully painful account of being ordered to confront a congressman accused of stealing White House silverware from a Nixon state dinner. It is an episode that even the most sophisticated model of presidential-congressional relations fails to apprehend, and yet it illuminates something essential about the human element of American politics. If our conceptions of political science are sufficiently broad to benefit from this tale, as well as from the thoughtful analysis about the ways of Washington offered by these well-placed sources, there is much raw material in these pages to be mined profitably.

The core purpose of the Miller Center's Presidential Oral History

Program is a public service: to generate and to make available for the broadest possible educational use original data about the American presidency in the form of the candid recollections of those who know the White House best. Although as the editor of this volume I do provide an authored introduction and brief commentaries after each session, these are intended to comprise only a single illustrative lens through which to view these rich original materials. It is not at all false modesty to suggest that these authored contributions are several orders of magnitude less important than the transcripted conversations themselves. Indeed, the bedrock principle of the Presidential Oral History Program is that our scholars can best foster public understanding of the nation's politics by making sure that the words and wisdom of those who served in Washington are preserved and made available to as wide an audience as possible. The broader marketplace of ideas should ascertain how this evidence is best interpreted—that is, how it confirms or undermines any theories of American politics to which it has relevance. My primary hope is that the transcripted conversations will be read profitably—perhaps even *enjoyed*—by a wide audience of people interested in American politics *wie es eigentlich gewesen*, and that this published record will be broadly cited in a wide variety of political science and historical literatures as a source of original data about American politics over the last half century. The direction those interpretations take is, insofar as this editor is concerned, immaterial. Let a hundred flowers blossom

Finally, a word here about the editing of these transcripts. The usual rule for editing oral history interviews is the less, the better. The goal is to maintain as closely as possible fidelity to the original spoken word. (Indeed some oral history purists eschew transcriptions at all, because any conversion from oral to written form involves a loss of literal authenticity.) A different, much more liberal standard has been used here. The goal in producing this volume has been to convert the content of these spoken discussions into a relatively easy read, with an emphasis on clarity in the substantive content. This has meant taking much greater liberties in editing the verbatim account of the original transcript than is typical of most oral history work.

To be sure, the vast majority of this text precisely mirrors the original spoken record. But, as anyone who has labored over a transcripted conversation will readily understand, there are challenges in dealing with such simple problems as flawed syntax, false starts, vague pronoun references and cross-talk, plus plain instances of misspeaking. Normally the intention of the speaker is relatively easy to determine by the listener, so edits have been made where necessary to comport with that intent. This more aggressive editing has been necessary here to make sure that the idiosyncrasies of spoken English in a group setting do not impair the reader's ability to follow these discussions.[4] However, anyone for whom the nuances of verbal phrasing might be critical or determinative is urged to consult the original video of these sessions, also available through the Miller Center.

The unusual character of this book means that its production truly has been a group effort. My greatest thanks go to the seven former White House officials who agreed to speak about their experiences on the record; this volume would have been impossible without their contributions. Special recognition is due to Fred McClure, who helped plan the symposium and gently nudged a few others to join us. I also wish to thank here the group of academic participants, both the moderators and those on the periphery of the discussions, who helped to refine our questioning. Charles O. Jones was unable to attend but offered sage guidance in advance of the proceedings.

That the symposium happened at all is because of the vision of James Sterling Young and Philip Zelikow, who, respectively, brought presidential oral history to the Miller Center and breathed new life into it. Jim deserves credit, too, for seeing the possibilities in group oral history. Governor Gerald Baliles and Sidney Milkis have provided essential leadership for carrying on this tradition today. I also want to recognize here the fine work of Lorraine Settimo, who stepped in on a temporary basis as an administrator to organize, flawlessly, the symposium. As we have found repeatedly over the years, comfortable people make better interview subjects. My thanks also go to Katrina Kuhn and Jane Rafal Wilson for their invaluable assistance with the postsymposium piece of this work.

I remain enormously grateful to both James Pfiffner and Mary Lenn Dixon for their enduring confidence in an unconventional book. Their support ultimately made the long hours of revision tolerable. Two anonymous readers for the Press helped me greatly to refine my own contributions and to take a stronger editorial hand to ensure that the participants' conversational English did not obscure their wisdom. Special thanks, too, are due to Thom Lemmons and Noel Parsons for their editorial support in aid of these two efforts.

Finally, words of gratitude are meager compensation for my family—Monique, Joseph, and Cathryn—who live daily with the sacrifices required when a father and husband tries to write. For their forbearances, this is their book, too.

BRIDGING THE CONSTITUTIONAL DIVIDE

1

BRIDGING THE CONSTITUTIONAL DIVIDE

An Introduction

The peculiarities of the American political system can be mystifying to foreign observers because our government does not feature a unitary sovereign. Rather, at the center of the American government is a *process:* an ongoing competition between the legislative and executive branches to direct the nation's public affairs. Critics as far back as the American founding derided this design as awkward and unwieldy, lacking the simple elegance of models featuring a single leading institution. Instead, our founders crafted what some at the time ridiculed as a "heterogeneous phantom," a government in which the predominance of power moves, in a protean way, between clusters of ever-changing actors in an ongoing interplay of compromise and consensus.[1] Although the model has worked remarkably—some would say miraculously—well for over two hundred years now, there is still something of the phantom in the inner workings of American politics, which can bewilder even the best-trained observers. "I know of few things harder to state clearly and within reasonable compass," wrote one close nineteenth-century student, "than just how the nation keeps control of policy in spite of these hide-and-seek vagaries of authority. Indeed, it is doubtful if it does keep control through all the roundabout paths which legislative and executive responsibility are permitted to take." And if it fails, continued Woodrow Wilson bluntly, "How is the schoolmaster, the nation, to know which boy needs the whipping?"[2]

This book is an effort to demystify that core governing process by consulting the observations of a group uniquely well qualified to comment on it: those who have run, for more than thirty years, the White House's Office of Legislative Affairs. These are the presidents' chief lobbyists, people charged with working to win from an independent national legislature the policy preferences of a president with no formal call on its allegiance. Their job has been, then, to try to establish unity of purpose within a separated system, to translate the intentions of the nation's chief executive into the direction of the nation's government. How they accomplish this, or attempt to accomplish this, is the central subject of the book that follows.

The proceedings of this symposium thus provide the reader a rare opportunity (apart from the imaginary experience of television's *The West Wing*) to enter the White House vicariously, to step into the world where the president lives and works. "This is not the way we conventionally view the office," observed Richard E. Neustadt in the preface to his classic text on presidential power: "Ordinarily we stand outside it, looking in." Neustadt's purpose in writing his book was to show how distorted a vision of American politics we get by relying on that outside perspective, and thus he asserted the virtues of viewing "the Presidency from over the President's shoulder, looking out and down with the perspective of his place."[3] The essence of presidential power becomes evident only from this vantage point. When Neustadt offered observations about the unique challenges of the American presidency, he did so informed by his own experience as a presidential aide, standing shoulder-to-shoulder with Harry Truman. The nuts-and-bolts accounts of the presidency provided in this volume provide a glimpse of what it is like to be in that position. And, if Neustadt was correct, that proper perspective is the necessary starting point for understanding, properly, presidential power.[4]

Indeed, three of the most vexing challenges each president must confront appear in striking relief in these pages because they are so relevant to the president's relations with Congress—and so central to the life of the aide charged with managing the president's congressional affairs. The first challenge relates to the president's position as only one among several actors authorized by the Constitution to share the power of the state; the second relates to the need by the president to assemble, empower, and manage a professional staff to help him fulfill his multiple responsibilities, including congressional relations; and the third relates to the vast diversity of the branch of government nominally under the chief executive's direction, but whose unity of purpose is not a fact to be asserted but a goal to be aspired to.

The main *constitutional* fact of life for the president—and the very reason for the congressional liaison's existence—is the sharing of powers by separated institutions in the national government. No public policy question of any real weight can be truly settled in the American system unless there is basic agreement by the president and Congress and at least the tacit blessing of the third branch, the judiciary. That division has to be accommodated by Washington's public policy makers as an essential predicate for action.[5]

It is this constitutional context that Bryce Harlow, who was a founding father of the congressional liaison(CL) office in the 1950s, addressed when he declared that the CL's job involved "building bridges across the yawning constitutional chasm . . . fashioned by our power-fearing fathers."[6] Harlow highlighted the framers' intention "to keep Congress and the president at a safe distance from one another in the interest of human liberty."[7] Institutional separation—at once frustrating and requiring collective action by the legislative and executive branches of the government—is not just a vestigial remnant of a parchment Constitution. It remains at the very core of how American politics functions—or fails to function.

Harlow's "constitutional chasm" is the product of a larger political culture that places a high value on separation and independence. There is within the United States a lasting ambivalence about a powerful central government, and thus separation is built into the very fiber of the constitutional order. What the framers of the American Constitution produced was a reflection of this fundamental reality. The maintenance of the Constitution in its essential forms for over two hundred years is evidence that a fear of centralized authority has, but for some occasional departures to confront system-threatening crisis, endured.[8]

Part of the genius of the American system was the founders' success in perpetuating this devotion to fragmentation. As Madison indicated in *Federalist* No. 51, the Constitution's framers successfully connected "the interest of the man . . . with the constitutional rights of the place," setting up a system in which officeholders naturally become jealous guardians of their constitutional prerogatives. "Separated institutions sharing powers" survives as much because of the self-interested behavior of elected officials in asserting their constitutional prerogatives as because of any liturgical reverence among the polity for the framers' handiwork or because of the rulings of a Supreme Court charged with refereeing the Constitution's boundaries.[9] The independent assertion of these institutional prerogatives across the government has thus assured that a multiplicity of views will typically have to be accommodated before the course of government policy is firmly settled, diminishing the prospect that any single actor can manipulate the power of the state to intrude on human liberty.

Where the early critics used the word *heterogeneous* to indict this divided system, modern-day detractors substitute *inefficient* or, more bluntly, *messy*. There have long been efforts by those worried about such messiness to overcome the constitutional divide with formal structural bridges. During the final months of Abraham Lincoln's presidency, for example, some members of Congress sought to extend congressional floor privileges to certain members of the president's cabinet as a way to simplify interbranch coordination on pressing matters of public concern—mimicking the question period of the British Parliament. The proposal met with little support by the membership, who saw in this innovation the seeds of executive infiltration into the hallowed halls of the national legislature.[10] Broader efforts to make the American system more parliamentary in design, comingling the executive and legislative branches, were a standard fixture of political science during the last half of the twentieth century. Formal recommendations by the American Political Science Association in 1950, and a highly publicized article by eminent Washington lawyer Lloyd Cutler in *Foreign Affairs* in 1980, were drafted to create a "more responsible" system of executive-legislative interaction.[11] But little came of them. The cultural affinity for the safeguards of division was too deep. Or the guardians of congressional (or, occasionally, presidential) independence were too strong. Or both.

In the absence of such structural reforms, how do Harlow's bridge builders get the job done? Answers to this question, which is at the very core of the functioning of the American political system, are sprinkled throughout the pages that follow.[12]

In part, presidents succeed by widely deploying the *formal* powers the Constitution conveys to the office. Foremost among these, as a growing body of scholarship has indicated, is the presidential veto. No bill can become the law of the land without the president's signature (unless a supermajority of both houses overrides the veto), a fact that gives the president remarkable leverage in the legislative process.[13]

Some presidents, because of the political circumstances of their time and the partisan composition of the government, choose to govern almost completely by veto, while others eschew its use, or even its threatened use, entirely. Gerald Ford vetoed more than sixty bills in less than a full term, while George W. Bush vetoed only one in his first six years as president. Ford saw his administration as one of opposition to hyperactivist Democrats in an energized post-Watergate Congress. Bush 43 governed predominantly with a compliant Congress, one that gave him—until the final quarter of his presidency—little reason to exercise a constitutional negative. Bush once claimed that he believed "a veto would actually hurt his ability to win concessions in the future."[14]

But there is more than a bit of gamesmanship in how the veto is used by a president. The mere threat of a veto, if credible, can lead to desirable changes in behavior on Capitol Hill, so bluffing has its rewards. Clinton CL, Lawrence Stein observes in these pages that the topic of veto bargaining "is a wonderful subject of arcane science."

Veto threats are communicated to Congress in what is known as a statement of administration policy (or SAP, pronounced to rhyme with *map*), which is drafted, usually with the input of the legislative affairs staff, by the Office of Management and Budget (OMB). The SAP includes formalized language that communicates the seriousness of a veto threat.[15] Sometimes it might read that the president's *senior advisors recommend* a veto, which, as George H. W. Bush CL, Fred McClure asserts, provides for a "little out." The use of this language typically communicates to the Hill that the bill is open for negotiation. But the most stringent language is *the president will veto,* and in this case the president's reputation is on the line. If that bill comes to the White House, a refusal to veto would be viewed as a loss of face. Accordingly, as Charles Brain observes, this language is considered the equivalent of a legislative "nuclear bomb," only to be used in instances in which the threat will be carried out. The internal politics about which level of threat the White House ought to issue is a complex business, with the final outcome only dimly reflecting the processes that produced it. This suggests that those who would study veto bargaining need also to pay careful attention to what produces the stuff of their theories.

Added to the formal authority of the president, however, are a host of *informal* powers. Much of what appears in this volume relates to the congressional liaison's role in support of what Neustadt famously characterized as the president's "power to persuade."[16]

A large part of persuasion simply involves the effort to muster convincing arguments in favor of presidential legislation and to communicate those merits to Congress. Bill Clinton, for example, expended enormous energies trying to win support for his 1993 budget deal by making the case, with the aid of his economic team coordinated by national economic advisor Robert Rubin, that serious deficit reduction would have an advantageous effect on economic growth because of the reactions of the bond market. This was a featured part of the administration's lobbying efforts with Capitol Hill. A similar effort followed in relation to the North American Free Trade Agreement (NAFTA), with substantive arguments presented to wavering members of Congress about the impact the agreement would have on such things as employment and immigration. These kinds of substantive interchanges are a commonplace of every president's job. In typically direct language, Harry Truman once said, "I sit here all day trying to persuade people to do the things they ought to have sense enough to do without my persuading them." The power of the president's argument has to rest on its own bottom, because the Constitution does not mandate that Congress adopt the president's logic.[17]

But the world of Washington politics is not all cerebral. And thus the work of the congressional liaison involves a great deal more than channeling substantive arguments to those who will weigh their costs and benefits on an impartial scale. It also involves making important people happy. As Charles Brain notes, members of Congress "want good laws written, obviously. But they also want tickets to the Kennedy Center. They also want [presidential] cuff links. They want White House tours, and they want to speak to the president." Brain terms this a "customer service role." And perhaps the most valuable talent in a White House CL is an aptitude for knowing what kinds of inducements are likely to be most effective with each customer. The range of incentives deployed to encourage cooperation with the president is vast and encompasses everything from trade-offs on complex policy to simple creature comforts. These are what scholar Nigel Bowles has called "small favours."[18]

Take transportation—on ponies, boats, planes, and limousines. An invitation to travel with the president, for distances great and small, has long been valued in Washington as a sign of stature and thus something to be used by the White House to win friends and influence people. As recently as Ronald Reagan, horseback rides with the president have been a privileged excursion. William Howard Taft's military aide described the equestrian minuet this way:

> I am often much amused by the President's methods of securing some bit of legislation which he wants and which he does not like to ask for too pointedly. It is becoming the custom for

> statesmen to ride on the Speedway [in Rock Creek Park] and at about the same hour, too, as when the President usually appears. Some of them use odd means to join him, but I notice that when he asks any one of them he has some purpose in view. Before the ride is over they manage to get in some little request, but usually before they part, he has obtained their voluntary promise to push through certain little plans of his own. I notice that he never makes any promise himself.[19]

Before Jimmy Carter, in a bout of budget cutting, sold off the presidential yacht *Sequoia,* one of the most coveted invitations in the nation's capital was a Potomac River cruise. Kennedy aide Lawrence O'Brien later claimed that this boat was "the most effective lobbying device I ever found," combining singing, dining, and polite goading. (Indeed, Carter's liquidation of the *Sequoia* still is sometimes used as a metaphor for his ineptness in dealing with members of Congress.) Today, rides on *Air Force One* are a signal of standing in Washington, and thus, for strategic purposes, the congressional liaison staff is typically allotted seats on the plane during presidential trips. The fact that Speaker Newt Gingrich decided, in one highly publicized instance, to complain about the indignity of being asked by Clinton aides to exit the rear of the plane was largely perceived in Washington as an act of unparalleled petulance. Not even Washington's most coveted perquisite was enough for Gingrich's ego.[20]

The customer service role can also occasionally lead into the realms of the bizarre. Carter CL Frank Moore explains that nothing was more important to one Kentucky senator than making sure that President Carter had his picture taken with a piece of artwork crafted by a constituent—a portrait of Carter rendered, by spatula, in peanut butter. Carter was famously impatient with this kind of low-brow constituent service. "Well, I gave you the time, and I see you're going to waste it," he complained. But the picture was taken, and the result was a happy member of the U.S. Senate, who presumably viewed the transaction as a relationship builder. Reagan CL William Ball III notes that Moore encountered such a sharp rebuke from Carter because "your greatest asset as a member of the [White House] staff is the president's time."[21]

Accordingly, one of the CL's most important tasks is competing successfully with other members of the staff for a piece of that time and then making good use of it with members of Congress. The mere fact of an audience with the president is a powerful lobbying tool. In many cases members want merely to be able to report to their constituents that they've spoken directly to the president about their concerns, regardless of whether they have, in the end, won the fight over a particular policy issue. Indeed, the Oval Office is often a wonderfully effective muter of congressional opposition. Many a member has charged down from Capitol Hill to the other end of Pennsylvania Avenue to straighten out a wayward president only to be awed into acquiescence by the power and charms of the place.[22]

In some political systems the executive's majority party is the ultimate institutional implement for forging unity among divergent interests and institutions. There, the party *is* the bridge. Cohesive parties arise easily in political cultures in which deference to the leader's preferences is expected and in which the party leadership is empowered with the ultimate tool of enforcement: excommunication from the party, meaning effective banishment from the halls of power.[23]

But this is not the American way. Our instruments of persuasion, however vast and creative (think peanut-butter artwork), are pale imitations of the power within parliamentary systems to ensure majority support for the leader's policies. Indeed, most presidents find that unity within their own party can sometimes be a fleeting commodity. Aside from times of war or other crisis, such as the United States experienced once again for a time after the attacks of 9/11, deference has seldom thrived in a system wherein those judged too close to the president are mocked (in words from Jefferson's time) as "toads that live upon the vapor of the palace."[24]

Lawrence Stein asserts, in a point echoed by many others: "It's extremely difficult to marshal any kind of [party] discipline" on Capitol Hill. Indeed, shows of congressional independence from party ties have sometimes won for those defiant members *improved* standing among their home constituencies. Texan Phil Gramm rose to the Senate through such renegade behavior, spying on fellow House Democrats for Reagan and then shrugging off Speaker Tip O'Neill's punishment by switching parties and still getting reelected. Stein recounts a similar tale about Alabama senator Richard Shelby, who defied the Clinton administration very publicly on a core tax proposal. The White House decided to get back at Shelby by killing jobs at the Huntsville Aerospace Center, a blunt act that sent Shelby into the Republican Party. Stein ruefully concludes that Shelby "is now, I think, the most popular politician in the state of Alabama and is utterly unassailable." Fred McClure reached the same conclusion about partisan unity from the Republican side: "Basically we were powerless in our roles—and

I really think the president may be powerless in his role—to exercise party discipline." Harlow's bridge builders are thus left with a relatively meager array of tools to improvise a span across the constitutional chasm—unless they get a helping hand from the other (congressional) side. As George C. Edwards III has concluded, "The president is in a weak position with regards to Congress. His burdens are great and his assets are few."[25]

The second major challenge for the president that clearly emerges from these discussions derives from a simple *organizational* reality: The job of the president is too big to be handled entirely by any single individual. Accordingly, the president has to rely on a corps of (usually) accomplished and ambitious aides. We see in the pages that follow the extraordinary advantages to presidents of empowering a professional cadre of staffers to do their bidding on Capitol Hill. They expand the president's reach, enhance his ability to know what is happening on their beat, and enrich his understanding of the complexities of the legislative process. But, as is true with virtually every White House staff position, the priorities, perceptions, and preferences of a staff member charged with only one piece of the action are bound to differ at times from those of other staffers responsible for other pieces. These differences generate competition for the president's own attention and agenda. And that becomes a problem to manage. "Nothing in the Constitution," wrote Neustadt, "keeps a well-placed aide from converting status into power of his own, usable in some degree even against the President." But the more common manifestation of this problem is the exercise by aides of derivative power intended to *benefit* the president—benefit as they see fit from their own, perhaps biased, perspective.[26]

Charles Brain notes that the congressional liaison's perspective is inevitably shaped by the fact that the CL is "really an actor and a participant in both branches simultaneously." "The job is positioned about Eighth Street," one presidential aide reported to Kenneth E. Collier, "one-half way between the two great institutions." Each has its own norms and reward structures and accordingly independent definitions of success.[27] For a CL to survive very long, then, he or she must succeed in both environments. This presents a very complex sociological problem of coping and creates the prospect that the president's chief congressional staffer will perceive the virtues of White House initiatives differently from those not so immersed in that alternative universe, including the president.

It is tempting to claim that what the CL actually confronts is the age-old problem of serving two masters. But this overstates the case. Indeed, Brain asserts directly that the president is the CL's "one client." From the president's perspective, the job involves making sure that his preferences are reflected in the important policy decisions that emanate from the ornate chambers of the House and Senate as well as the cubbyholes of leadership hideaway offices. It is very clear that any liaison giving equal weight to the needs of the Hill and of the White House would be fired in an instant.

But the CL's problem is a more subtle one of living at once in two competing organizational cultures. From the perspective of Capitol Hill, the CL's job is the reverse of the one just depicted. There, one Republican CL claims, "'brilliant' Congressional relations was doing everything *Congress* wanted"—that is, seeing to it that the president and a host of presidential proxies in the White House proper, the Old Executive Office Building, and an almost infinite array of executive departments and agencies all understand that their work needs to be undertaken with due deference to congressional needs and intent.[28] This conflicted environment, perhaps as much as anything else, may explain why the life span of the CL is usually so brief. The metaphors the CLs employ to describe their work are revealingly drawn from images of great peril. Clinton aide John Hilley reports that the liaison is "the person standing in the street where the traffic's coming both ways." And Fred McClure was once recognized by Britain's Prince Philip as the executive "spear catcher."

The fact is that in order to do the job well, the president's congressional liaison has to "pass" in both worlds. For most CLs there is a natural affinity for the congressional way of life, because that's the world most of them lived in before moving into the White House. (Frank Moore and Will Ball are conspicuous exceptions, and it is worth noting that both paid for their unfamiliarity by having their know-how questioned by some in Congress as a result.) Typically, CLs move easily on the Hill because they know the language and land as their own. They have the circadian rhythms of Congress in their blood. But because their principal mission is a distinctly presidential one, they must be *on* the Hill, not *of* it. This requires an enormously complicated balancing act.[29]

There was unanimity among those attending this symposium that one of the most important things a CL must do is to spend time on the Hill. (Charles Brain makes a point of noting that his car is parked at the

White House. But the fact is that his vehicle spends vastly more time there than its owner does.) Yet the CL cannot in any way afford to show signs of "going native" or his or her credibility in the White House suffers. In reality the actual threat of a CL going over to the other side is minuscule, but the core problem is one of perceptions. There are forever those with interests in the president's program who for reasons of politics or policy find it useful to encourage the president to take an unyielding position on matters receiving congressional attention. That is seldom, however, a strategy conducive to winning a majority of votes in the House and Senate. The CL's necessary involvement in the hard process of peddling concessions opens the way for outsiders to challenge the CL's basic sympathies. It is for this reason that the president must have an enormous reserve of trust in the legislative affairs operation.[30] This is not easy to maintain when the CL is spending so much of his time in the enemy's camp and when intermittent carping from other senior people in the administration is a given.

The liaison staff members are also needed on the Hill as a conduit. In part they are a channel for the presidential favors already discussed above: access to plane rides, Kennedy Center tickets, cuff links, and the occasional dam or bridge. But they also serve as a channel back into the White House, in good times for information and in bad times for the occasional, often memorable, congressional tirade. One of the virtues of the position for the president is that it is an institutional lightning rod, giving members of Congress a permanent place to vent their angers and frustrations. Indeed, one of the little-known honors within the congressional liaison community is the esteemed, if not coveted, Yellow Sock Award, conferred on those who have weathered a particularly severe verbal beating from a member of Congress.

Moreover, the successful congressional liaison recognizes ultimately that in order to pass the president's programs, the White House must have committed friends on Capitol Hill, and such friendships require occasional sacrifices, sometimes trading off short-term gains for the long run. It requires a delicate sense of balance to achieve this without seeming to others in the White House to be engaged in acts of betrayal. Charles Brain recalls an illuminating case in which he coached a friendly member of the House about how to shake down a cabinet working group from within his own administration to save a jobs project in that member's home district. Brain's intent was to protect someone who had been crucial to him during the impeachment debate, "much to his own political endangerment back home." This is an unusual case, but it illustrates how the CL's sense of mission can be at odds with the perceptions of others within the White House.

It is also important to note here that, because of the centrality of congressional action to Washington's affairs, lobbying the Hill is forever an attractive hobby for White House volunteers. Thus, another piece of the liaison job is to try to keep unwanted intruders off their turf.

"Each morning," observes Lawrence Stein of his time as Bill Clinton's legislative director, "I'd realize that everyone [in the White House] was doing my job. In some respects, the job is extraordinarily difficult and daunting because it is the entire job of the administration. I don't say that hubristically, but it's true. And it used to be extremely . . . irritating that people were always up there doing what, at least from a superficial point of view, fell into the province of legislative affairs." Ideally, the delicate business of managing the president's program with Congress will be handled through a single office, responsible for setting an informed course of action, directing communications back and forth with the Hill (or at least closely monitoring all such communications), and enforcing discipline among those who do not work through the established channels. This seldom happens. "You get a lot of help," says Frank Moore, who found himself having to monitor social connections that promised to encroach on his territory. If "senators . . . can get something from a deputy chief of staff, or if they can get something from an old friend, they're going to do it—because then they don't owe you anything. They've gotten five favors and owe not one in return." The lesson here is that political commerce with Capitol Hill is a complex business that has to be managed by a single bookkeeper. Off-the-books transactions usually end up costing the White House more than is gained.

The fact is, however, that it is impossible for the Office of Legislative Affairs to control entirely the flow of communications between even the White House and Congress. Every White House attempts to police contacts with the Hill, but such efforts are doomed to fail, given the vast numbers of people conducting executive business on the Hill and the existence of 535 separate congressional fiefdoms. That's too many channels to monitor. With a hint of exasperation Lawrence Stein confides that "at any given moment I was always sure that someone was up on the Hill doing something that somehow competed with what we [in legislative affairs] were trying to do—someone from our administration."

In part this is a problem of White House discipline, which is more the province of the chief of staff than of the congressional affairs shop. Able chiefs of staff (including Reagan's James Baker) do seem to be relatively more successful than their weaker counterparts in cutting off some of the more egregious examples of freelancing on Capitol Hill. Further, some chiefs with their own significant Hill experience, including Reagan's Howard Baker and Clinton's Leon Panetta, are seasoned negotiators with Congress themselves and thus have managed to work quite well with CLs who do not feel threatened by accomplished help. Other chiefs have made the job eminently more difficult. Donald Regan, according to Friedersdorf's testimony, was not above lecturing members of the Senate, a practice that did not endear him to the Hill.[31]

But the problem of freelancing is not limited to White House aides. Even a highly disciplined White House staff will remedy only half the problem. The other common area of concern—which brings us to our third presidential challenge, the *diversity* of the executive branch—is unauthorized initiatives from the vast network of executive branch agencies and departments of which the president is titular head. And the routine challenge for the congressional liaison office is the attempt to speak with one voice on Capitol Hill for the entire, multifaceted executive branch.[32] Indeed, the move to develop a more structured White House congressional liaison operation in the first instance was an important step in a series of broader trends intended to help the president assert greater control over relatively independent bureaucratic channels to Capitol Hill.

Although department heads are designated by the president and serve at his pleasure (after Senate confirmation), their ongoing connections to the president after being named are typically quite slender. There is forever a tug on their allegiance, pressure for them to become advocates for the departments they run. Moreover, members of the cabinet often rise to their positions because of personal success in business or politics quite independent of the president they serve. Their biographies tend, then, to make them less reliant psychologically on the favor of the White House. All of this can contribute to some degree of independence as they set their departmental agendas—making for complications in the life of the CL.[33]

Every executive branch agency includes in some form or fashion a congressional relations shop; indeed, these often antedated historically the White House office.[34] An astute White House will work to institute some measure of control over those operations. Some CLs, including Fred McClure during the George H. W. Bush years, are involved in determining who will fill the position of assistant secretary for legislative affairs in the executive departments. The placement of presidential loyalists in those slots has the effect of providing at least an early warning system for the White House in cases in which the department is considering unauthorized approaches to the Hill.

However, occasionally when there are strong people in the departments, their activity can actually advantage the White House. The presence of competent team players in the smaller agencies can relieve the White House of responsibility for taking care of secondary issues, preserving the time of the president's staff for larger problems. Also, cooperative partners in the bigger departments—such as Health and Human Services, Treasury, and Defense—can be enormously helpful to the White House as reservoirs of refined professional expertise. Moreover, these offices sometimes have enduring relationships with key members on the Hill that can also be exploited to the advantage of the White House.

But that expertise, and those long-standing relationships, can also be a source of enduring headaches in the inevitable instances when the president's priorities differ from those of the department. In these cases the executive branch plainly does not speak with one voice, and the most imposing of the multiple voices is often the department's. Friedersdorf explains that "it's difficult to maintain discipline . . . if the basic loyalty of the congressional relations people in the department and agencies is not to the president but instead to the cabinet secretary."

Some agencies are famously problematic freelancers. One is the Army Corps of Engineers. During the Carter administration Frank Moore asked one of his deputies to go to the House to sustain a veto of a water projects bill. "When I got up there," the deputy reported back to Moore, "there were four people with stars on their shoulders from the Corps of Engineers. . . . They were up there lobbying against us, and they had more to give away [to win votes] than we did!" Some CLs claim the entire Pentagon is equally guilty of going its own way—with the Marines being famously independent within that already autonomous realm. These comments hearken back to Franklin Roosevelt's reported frustration with the military bureaucracy. Having bemoaned the difficulties of imposing presidential will on the Treasury and the State Departments, FDR claimed that they "put together are nothing compared with the Na-a-vy. The admirals are really something to cope with—and I should know. To change anything in the Na-a-vy is like punching a feather bed. You punch it with your left until you are finally exhausted, and then you find the damn bed just as it was before you started punching."[35] It is thus a longstanding reality that the divisions bedeviling the president within his own branch will ultimately show up on Capitol Hill, too.

In addition to providing us with an opportunity to view the White House from over the president's shoulder, these symposium discussions afford us one further advantage: a chance to see up close the faces of those who have been entrusted with the presidency. These aides offer us an unimpaired glimpse into the character of the individuals who have served as president—and under conditions that reveal the essential fiber of their temperaments. There is accordingly much that can be learned about the humanity of those in the Oval Office by consulting these observations.

Max Friedersdorf paints a portrait of a Gerald Ford who never wholly left the Hill—managing an Oval Office consultation like a House subcommittee briefing. Frank Moore draws a picture of the quintessential Jimmy Carter—on his hands and knees with Republican Senator Ted Stevens of Alaska, using Stevens's own topographical map to prove to him that a creek he wanted excluded from a federal wilderness area belonged in one watershed region rather than another. Ronald Reagan's ambivalence about Washington makes an appearance in Friedersdorf's account of a president who would rather join the grounds staff trimming the Rose Garden "instead of going to this damn meeting." And John Hilley shows us once again a Bill Clinton adept at seeing every side of an issue—and sometimes more practiced at understanding competing views than sticking firmly to one conclusion. Clinton, asked by staff to call Republican Senator Trent Lott of Mississippi to congratulate him on a completed budget bill, nearly sabotaged his own CL's work by empathizing with Lott over the phone. This was a president who often left his aides worried that in private negotiations with the congressional leadership he'd "give away the store."[36]

We also have valuable character sketches here of some of Washington's other important actors from this period. The Clinton team found it very useful to provoke its Republican opposition into overreacting to some of its core commitments, such as the environment, by occasionally dispatching Vice President Al Gore to the Hill to stir things up. Hilley reports of Gore that "one of his great uses was to send him up there and just [have him] throw gasoline around the place." And Friedersdorf found himself posted outside Ronald Reagan's hospital room after Reagan survived a would-be assassin's bullet to keep senior members of Congress, who were seeking a final photo op, away from the wounded president.[37] This type of portraiture is a strong suit of oral history. These are the kinds of observations that are seldom committed to paper anymore.

Finally, a brief word about institutional history is in order before moving on. Congressional relations has of course been a central feature of the American presidency since the founding. For most of the nation's past, however, the relationship with Congress has taken place at a very personal level, with the president himself interacting directly with the members, usually the leadership. When a more pronounced staff presence in the White House developed in the early twentieth century, a modest piece of their activities also included legislative affairs. But this remained a small portion of a small staff's job until the New Deal. With the explosion in government activity associated with Franklin Roosevelt's activism, presidentially directed congressional relations became a much more prominent component of the White House portfolio. Yet FDR preferred to manage relations with Congress personally rather than institutionally, dispatching select individuals with very specific jobs to perform on Capitol Hill.[38]

It is also important to note, however, that much of the interaction that took place between the executive branch and Congress well into the twentieth century was not presidential—and indeed was not even directed by the president's people. As Abraham Holtzman has reported, "The distinguishing characteristic of traditional executive-legislative relations [into the mid-twentieth century] was the pivotal role of the bureaucracy rather than that of the political leaders who were responsible for the executive departments. . . . The department head . . . was not traditionally the official and controlling point of contact between the legislative and administrative units. Consequently, his authority tended to be undermined and reduced by the direct relationship between bureau chiefs and congressional committees."[39] Accordingly, the overall situation was one in which the typical executive-branch channels to Capitol Hill were highly insulated from presidential influence.

It was during Eisenhower's presidency, however, that a formal congressional relations shop was established in the White House and subsequently institutionalized, partly in response to these realities. The creation of the White House Office of Legislative Affairs was a natural outgrowth of two further strains of Eisenhower's own experience. First, as a military officer he had learned to value organization and order over improvisation and so was not inclined to let informal precedents overwhelm his good judgment about how institutions worked best. "The structure of the Eisenhower White House," observes Stephen J. Wayne, "reflected the president's desire for ordered relationships and systematized processes. He did not desire fluid patterns of interaction." FDR's freelancing was not to be replicated. Second, Eisenhower's military experience had included plenty of interaction with the legislative branch, so he came to the presidency with an appreciation for the legislative role in American politics. The formal creation of the office was in part, then, an acknowledgment of the realities of separate power centers in the post World War II world.[40]

What Eisenhower established has remained a fixture of the White House organization ever since, so presidents must have found it useful. Still, the office remains a relatively recent newcomer to the landscape of institutions in D.C. The formal shop existed for only three presidencies before Max Friedersdorf began working for Richard Nixon. It is fair to say, then, that much of the real history of this operation exists in the heads of those gathered for this symposium. Few eyewitness accounts are likely, then, to be as illuminating, or authoritative, about the condition today of our heterogeneous phantom.

2

THE JOB DESCRIPTION

The Scope of the Congressional Liaison's Responsibilities

The main topics discussed during this session include the primary components of the congressional relations job; the challenges of bringing the president's influence to bear on Capitol Hill; the problems of dealing with multiple channels to the Hill from the White House and the rest of the executive branch; the CL's customer service role; the business of representing Capitol Hill to the White House and the risks of being perceived as "going native"; how historical developments in Congress have affected the president's ability to govern; the CL's role as a lightning rod for congressional anger; the politics of appointments and judicial nominations; and the role of the chief of staff in congressional relations. This session was moderated by James Sterling Young of the University of Virginia.

Young: Thank you all for being here. Those of us who are professors are here to learn, and the people who have been in the White House are here to teach us.

The subject of the first session of the symposium is the job description, the scope of the congressional liaison's responsibilities. I think the entire two days could be spent discussing or arguing about that question, but we'll get somewhere with the particulars in the session this afternoon. Let me begin with a little anecdote of my own. My first interview project was in the 1960s. Lyndon Johnson was president. It was the first time I interviewed anybody in Washington, and my subject was the legislative liaison staff under [Dwight D.] Eisenhower and under [John F.] Kennedy—and what I could get under Lyndon Johnson, who was still in the White House.

Dick Neustadt was instrumental in scrounging funds to keep me in food and lodging and shelter, and I started off, more or less on my own. I began that project *not* by talking with the people in the White House but moving around the periphery. I remember I started with Sam Hughes and Elmer Staats in the Bureau of the Budget of the time and with others who were not in the West Wing.[1] I got what I thought was a very rational, logical explanation of why the legislative liaison staff was established under Eisenhower in 1953 and what its job was.

Then I started interviewing the members and former members of the liaison staff themselves, and my greatest teachers were Bryce Harlow, Jerry [Wilton B.] Persons, and Jerry Morgan, whom Bryce calls the three founding fathers of the congressional liaison office.[2] And I began to see that that job was not at all what I had thought it was based on learning from people who were not involved in it. [The insiders painted a very different picture for me.]

There's still a big question about what the job really is and about what changes and what does not change over time, and why. That's basically the subject we're going to discuss this afternoon. Chuck?

Brain: As the first one of the "formers" to speak, I have to thank you, on behalf of all of us, for this invitation. All of us—having performed this job and spent the time we did in the White House—think it's an important job and plays an important role. We appreciate your studying it and preserving it and having us here.

You mentioned Bryce Harlow. Just coincidentally, before coming down here, I happened to pull out of my file a speech by Bryce Harlow. Larry Harlow, his son, whom a lot of us know, is in Washington and helps preserve a bit of the history of legislative affairs.[3] Bryce Harlow, who did have the job back in the Eisenhower administration and was instrumental in founding the office, describes it more eloquently than I would ever be able to do. I'll just read it, and again, it's a bit of primary history.

He describes his job as "building bridges across the yawning Constitutional chasm, a chasm fashioned by our power-fearing fathers to keep Congress and the president at a safe distance from one another in the interest of human liberty." They don't write it that way anymore. Maybe he got a little more colloquial when he said that his job was to "uncheck the checks and balance the balances so that the whole government might smoothly articulate toward agreed-upon goals." Very well said.[4]

When I think of a general description, for purposes of discussion, of the job of director of legislative affairs, it's really being a vital link between two branches of government.[5] And in linking the two branches, it's a relatively unique role, one that is not replicated elsewhere in government. But it's not just a conduit of information; it's almost like a two-way highway. You're really an actor and a participant in both branches simultaneously. You have a role on the Hill if you're doing your job as you're supposed to. You're up there as often as possible. You're talking to everyone. You know the place just as well as the participants up there. And you're moving them, you're affecting them, you're getting them to do things, quite often, that they don't want to do, to advance your boss's goal.

In that part of the job, I would say, you're a lobbyist. I kept reminding the people who worked for me at the White House, both when I was House liaison and then took over the whole office: "You're lobbyists, you're in sales. Go at it, get up there! Don't do another meeting over at OMB [Office of Management and Budget]! Get to the Hill, talk to someone."

But obviously, you're in the White House, you're in the executive branch. That's where you pull your car in early in the morning and leave from late at night. And there, inside the White House, it's a much more complicated role. To me, that's the tougher part of the job. A lot of us who did it spent time on the Hill [before coming to the White House]. Several of us here didn't, and did the job well. But several of us spent twelve, fifteen years on the Hill and are more Hill types—and we were occasionally suspect within the administration because of that. So in the White House the job is more complicated. You have to reflect in policy deliberations—internally within the White House—what's happening on the Hill, what's likely to happen, what the reaction is likely to be to certain ideas. You sit around at a meeting and say, "Hmm, just not going to happen, won't work, they won't do it. Why? We could go through it, but no, it's not going to happen. Let's move on."

So that's another role—the internal role within the White House—reflecting what's going on in the Hill and what the Hill's likely to do.

Managing resources within the administration—not only within the White House but also across the agencies in the branches with the goal of enacting the president's legislative priorities—that's also a tough role, because you've got power centers across the government and power centers within the White House. Frequently they're going one direction, and you try to pull them another way. You get assistant secretaries on the phone and tell them, "No, don't go to the Hill. Don't let your people go to the Hill." Or, "You're going to go to the Hill. You're going to do this."

Another is a customer service role. To some extent, your constituency is the folks on the Hill. They want things. They want good laws written, obviously. But they also want tickets to the Kennedy Center. They also want cuff links. They want White House tours, and they want to speak to the president. Other parts of the White House don't see the importance of even something like this—of getting Senator So-and-so the Kennedy Center box because he has the mayor in. "It's already been promised to the assistant secretary for whatever and whatever." "Well, we're going to change that!"

As I said, at least from my perspective, I found the internal role more complicated and more challenging. The Hill part, the sales part—that's straightforward and replicated in other organizations. You've got one client. You work for the president. You've got the greatest assets in the world. You try to lobby for your client in terms of access, but it's straightforward. It's the internal role—policy coordination, and customer satisfaction and customer service, too—that I think makes it a difficult and challenging job.

McClure: I agree with everything Chuck said. I remember when I had the opportunity to meet Queen Elizabeth when she came over to visit President Bush. Mrs. [Barbara] Bush was introducing me to Prince Philip and explaining to him in the receiving line what I did for the president. She said, "Prince Philip, this is Fred McClure. He's in charge of congressional relations for my husband." Prince Philip looked at me and said, "Ah, the spear catcher." I think it was a rather apt description of what we engaged in on a daily basis in terms of representing our client, the president, in the Congress.

The other point I'd add would be to emphasize the customer service part of the job that Chuck mentioned—how it affected our ability to sell on behalf of the president, to get that first or that second vote we needed to get across the line, and how important the seat on the airplane or at the Kennedy Center—or the telephone conversation—was in those really close votes. These customer services oftentimes are not seen, or even understood, by those who might study the presidency and study the operation of congressional affairs.

Another challenge that came with the job was ensuring that you had the necessary loyalty to the president extending vertically within the organization. Our job is making sure that we supported the people who worked for us, as special assistants or as deputy assistants to the president, in terms of the battles they often faced. Sometimes they were on the firing line more frequently than we were because they were up there on the Hill standing in halls or standing outside committee rooms or in the offices of members on behalf of the president.

Oftentimes this game came into play: "Okay, we're going to say 'no' five times, and when we finally get the matter up to the chief of staff, we're going to say 'yes.' You just have to be willing to take the heat for saying 'No.' It comes with the job. Yes, you're going to go up to the Hill and they're going to hate you when this is over, and they may not speak to you for another couple of weeks. But until we get what we want out of this negotiation process, we'll just make these guys and gals step into line." It's an interesting scenario, driven, indeed, by the characteristics of the president involved as well as those people who happen to work for him or on his behalf.

I used to describe the process publicly as "crystal ball gazing," which is what we're called upon often to do, as Chuck indicated. You'd sit in a room with your colleagues around the table, and the president would even call and say, "Hey, what's the vote going to be on so-and-so?" You were afraid to say something that wouldn't turn out to be the way he expected the next day, [but you had to give it a shot]. So, counting votes and crystal ball gazing are a part of the job. Unlike in the private sector, you don't have political action committees and all those kinds of things to add to this process. You have to use what resources you have at your disposal, working for arguably the most powerful person in the world from a political standpoint.

Moore: I've got a comment on Chuck's talk, which I agree with, and with you as well, Fred. As all of you know, the Carter White House got off to a rocky start in January and February [of 1977].[6] It got organized and did very well after that—congressional relations did, anyway. I don't know what time it was, sometime about the first month. And as the professor has said, the most important resource you have is the president's time, and therefore the schedule is important. So we decided to revamp the whole schedule. I already had five seats on *Air Force One,* I had the Kennedy Center boxes because my wife was volunteering for the First Lady and she did that. But we needed the time. I said, "I'll just take a block each week of the president's time."

Most all of you here know Dan Tate. Dan sent in a schedule request: He said he wanted Senator Wendell Ford from Kentucky to come in.[7] He had a peanut butter painting that the Women's Club in Louisville had auctioned off and got the high dollar for. It was done with a spatula, a painting of President Carter in peanut butter. I looked at Dan and said, "Dan, I'm not going to send this in. I'm not going to approve it." He said, "Well, we've got to get Senator Ford in. This is all he wants. He gets everything he wants from the Hill. He doesn't want anything from us. We have to ask *him* for stuff."

I said, "Well, I'll explain this one in person." So I went in to see President Carter. I said, "I want to brief you on this. Senator Ford's coming in later today." He said, "Where's the briefing paper? Is it a vote?" Ford was always kind of in the middle, so he swings back and forth in his support, you know. I said, "No, he wants to have your photograph and his photograph made with a painting made of peanut butter."

Carter said, "Well, I gave you the time, and I see you're going to waste it." But we had the photograph made, and Senator Ford was very happy. That's what he wanted. He didn't want Kennedy Center box seats, he didn't want a ride on *Air Force One*. He wanted that photo taken because he had a very good friend back in Louisville who was a fundraiser for him, and she'd made this portrait, and that's what she wanted. If any of the political scientists were ever reading a president's schedule and saw "photograph made with peanut butter," you'd wonder, is that a good use of the president's time? Well, it was a good use. It's better than meeting with the president of Bongo Bongo, whom I displaced. We'd already met with him once and didn't need to meet with him again.[8]

Stein: I don't have any immediate anecdote to match that. At the highest level of definitional generality, I agree totally with what Fred and Chuck have said. I used to be struck every morning when I would go to the chief of staff's meeting. We'd sit down, and there'd be all the highest level people from the administration, and each morning I'd realize that everyone was doing my job. In some respects, the job is extraordinarily difficult and daunting because it is the entire job of the administration. I don't say that hubristically, but it's true. And it used to be extremely irritating that people were always up there doing what, at least from a superficial point of view, fell into the province of legislative affairs.

But it also required a talent that I really think is crucial to this job. That is, imposing some strategic definition on it. There are 535 members of Congress. Well more than half, at any given moment, think that they ought to be in the White House. They certainly believe that every one of their concerns deserves presidential attention. You could spend more time than is available to most of the people in the state of Virginia trying to cater to those 535 members. At the same time, there is a vast—let's call it "bureaucracy" for want of a better word—that is the executive branch.

And most of those people at any given time have interests with the 535 members of Congress. In short, it's almost infinite.

It's funny, because I haven't done that much reflection on all this until right now. But to me, much of the task is trying to take what is really a limitless set of responsibilities and to figure out what you can do on behalf of the president that will truly advance the agenda. Typically, there are a lot of different people who have a lot of different views on that. You've got to take the president's views and try to achieve his objectives.

That, boiling it down, is central to this job. You're advancing the president's agenda on the Hill, and you're trying to communicate the views of the Hill back at the other end of the street. It's two jobs in that regard. But, ultimately, you're shaped by the terms of the time. Your work is shaped by the opportunities that are there, by the character of the president, and by the character of the leadership in the Congress—all of which define the achievable. I think we'll get into more of that, but that's the way I view it.

Hilley: Again, clearly this idea of being a liaison, and being the person standing in that street where the traffic's coming both ways—between the Hill and the White House—is the central ingredient to the job. Just to emphasize a bit of what Larry is saying, each of our terms in the office is defined in large part by the circumstances that are served up to us. I was there, with Clinton, in '96 and '97. Ninety-six was the election, and that colored a lot of what we did agendawise and the input that the political and the message side had into the legislative process. Ninety-seven—for a lot of reasons we'll get into later in the subsequent sessions—was the year that we balanced the budget, and that was the overriding thing that fashioned what we walked into.

Again, you say the goal is to advance the president's legislative agenda, which is true, but I think we all have to recognize that often that's set by the larger political forces outside us that have been brewing, perhaps, over a multiyear period. That was the case when we walked into '96 in the aftermath of the government shutdowns.[9]

The other point I would make is that certainly the infrastructure is a critical component of this as well. You have to deal with the myriad competing interests on the Hill and within the administration. And the personalities that drive that infrastructure are critical, too. I was extremely fortunate to serve under two incredibly capable chiefs of staff—the first, Leon Panetta, and the second, Erskine Bowles.[10] It all started for us—to emphasize the two-way street aspect of this—at seven o'clock in the morning. Around the table would sit the chief of staff—and his deputy, of course—as well as me (the legislative head), and also the heads of substance, the policy committees in the Economic Council, the secretary of the treasury, the head of the OMB, plus one or two top senior political advisers, the top communications adviser, etc.

There would be the context at the beginning of each day. You would be talking about, "Okay, what's the agenda? How do we adjust it? What are we hearing from the Hill?" and all the things that Chuck and Fred and the others have talked about. From that, it would branch out through your own staff into the various agencies, their own legislative people—which would be critical to anything getting done—and on and on, as well as all the Hill relations. Those are just two of the opening points I would add. The large events formed a lot of what we were able to do. And the infrastructure within that context of how you delivered was critical to whether you succeeded on a particular issue.

Friedersdorf: Unlike most jobs, I don't think there's one of us at the table who was handed a job description the day we went over there. But if you asked each one of us, Jim, to sit down and write a job description today, I bet we could write five or six pages of the things we did during our tenures as congressional relations directors.[11]

If I could reduce it to just one sentence, the most simple explanation or definition that I can think of is, "Pass the president's programs." I learned that the first day. I was hired on April 1, 1971, by President Nixon—which was April Fools Day, by the way. I was hired to go on the House staff. Tom Korologos was hired for the Senate staff. We both had Hill experience, and we thought we were pretty hot shots. He came from the Senate side, and I came from the House side.[12]

We went over to the West Wing, and Clark McGregor swore us in.[13] My dear wife and family were there and witnessed the swearing in, and I became a member of the White House staff, special assistant to the president. Later in the day, Clark said, "Tom, I want you and Max to meet the president, your boss." I thought that was a pretty good idea. Clark took us in at the close of the day and introduced us to the president. The White House photographer came in and took our picture with the president, and that was a pretty good thing.

President Nixon said to Clark something like, "Do these boys know what they're doing? Do these boys know what they're here for?" And Clark McGregor said, "Oh yes, Mr. President, Tom here came down from Senator [Wallace F.] Bennett's office, and Max worked on the House side and also worked with [Donald] Rumsfeld over at OEO [Office of Economic Opportunity]. They're good men."[14]

President Nixon said, "Well, get up on the Hill then, and pass my program." Then he turned around and walked away [laughter].[15] I thought from then on I'd never have any trouble knowing what my job was. And all these other things flow from that—the millions of things you do every day, in your eighteen-hour days. Keep your eye on that: Pass the president's program.

I have one other addendum, and that is: Defeat programs he doesn't want.

Ball: Max makes a great point. I was at the Reagan White House at the time when the Senate went from Republican control after the '86 election to Democratic control, and so halting things that were not a part of the president's agenda was very important. Max also mentioned Don Rumsfeld. Donald Rumsfeld, when he was chief of staff in the Ford White House, issued a set of guidelines, I guess. He calls them "Rumsfeld's Rules." And when I got to the White House, I got a nice note from him and attached was the list of "Rumsfeld's Rules." The one that stuck in my mind is that your greatest asset as a member of the staff is the president's time, the same sort of admonition Frank Moore received when he took away the appointment from a foreign leader and gave it to a peanut butter princess.[16]

If anything, since Max was there in the Reagan White House in his last tour, that has become evermore the dynamic. Presidents have a lot less time, and so the responsibility shouldered by this office and this job, as Larry Stein says, encompasses everything. There's less time and fewer resources and fewer ways in which to accomplish this objective of getting the president's agenda through the Congress.

I suspect that most of you have listened to the Lyndon Johnson tapes. It's just astounding to me to listen to the tapes of President Johnson talking to Senator [Richard B.] Russell, talking to Senator Everett Dirksen, talking to other congressional leaders—putting in hours and hours on the phone.[17] Of course, that doesn't happen anymore. That's not a function of the fact that presidents now more and more seem to be former governors and not former senators. That's a function of the time pressures upon the officeholder. So the congressional affairs position, I think, over time assumes even greater importance and is exactly central to getting the president's agenda through. And it's difficult getting others in the executive branch to understand that.

Before I came to the White House, I did a tour at the State Department in legislative affairs for George Shultz.[18] I was called up short one day by some distinguished senior foreign service officer who said there was to be a meeting on a certain key foreign policy issue. I believe it was the START [Strategic Arms Reduction] talks with the Russians. But it would just involve the policy people, I was told, and I didn't need to participate. After the policy people arrived, we would be brought in to give the legislative perspective. [Our role was secondary.] That mindset exists throughout the executive branch, not just among senior members of the foreign service, and in all White House staffs that's a difficult issue to deal with. We can talk about that more later.

Moore: You get a lot of help. I've really had this happen to me when were having trouble with something on the Hill. Somebody would see you at the White House and say, "By the way, I was at a party last night in Georgetown, and I saw Senator So-and-so and had a drink with him. I think, you know, we could really work something out. [laughter] I got along very well with him. Is it okay if I go up and—?" "No, it's not okay. Don't even think about it."

But, of course, the senators, if they can get something from a deputy chief of staff, or if they can get something from an old friend, they're going to do it, because then they don't owe you anything. They've gotten five favors and owe not one in return.

Friedersdorf: Jim Baker would have everybody, if members called in, sent to our office.[19] He issued instructions, "You don't take the call. Refer them to congressional relations." So we got a lot of crank calls and a lot of nutcases, but we also made sure that all of that was coming into the right office. There wasn't everybody freelancing out there.

Question: Were you able to enforce that?

Various voices: No!

Stein: In our administration there was literally no way that could have been enforced. I don't know whether that's because of the massive proliferation of government affairs people in the different agencies—which I suspect has grown over the years—or whether it's something to do with the character of our particular administration, which may be a part of it, too. But at any given moment I was always sure that someone was up on the Hill—someone from our administration—doing something that somehow competed with what we were trying to do.

Brain: I think that if we could commission a study by the Miller Center about the structure of Democratic White Houses (we've had eight years, and can't really speak for others) versus Republican, I think it's much more structured in the Republican years, in their ability to control things and to keep things running on time.

Stein: I wonder if others agree with that. I certainly felt that way, and feel that way now, looking at the way [George W.] Bush is running things.

Hilley: I think it goes back to the question of time, which Will mentioned—not only the president's, but cabinet people. There's only so much that bubbles up to the highest level of political importance and national press attention, and those are the key drivers of the political process. That's what the senior staff, at the chief of staff level down, tackle—that's what they get focused on.

Think of yourself running the Small Business Administration. You're worrying about getting your appropriation and making sure something's not cut off by someone else. So although it's true that in the White House you do try—through coordination meetings and a little bit of the whip—to keep your arms around everybody, the other side of it is that on some of those less political issues, the bread and butter of these agencies, they'd be almost derelict in their duty if they weren't up there taking care of something that, frankly, I don't have time to take care of myself from the White House. Although some agencies are fabulous about sharing information.

It really matters if you've got a good legislative liaison person at HHS [Health and Human Services] or at the Treasury—someone who works with you, who you know what they're doing, and they know what you're doing. Then it works. It doesn't work so well when you have a little bit of the freelancer issue out there. A lot of it comes just with the fact that some issues are really important, and with limited time—the president's on down—that's where the attention goes. Other people have to take care of their business on some of these lesser issues.[20]

Young: Let's hear from some of the Republicans. We have on the table a suggestion that the Republicans have less of a problem with everybody else trying to do their job.

McClure: I don't know that I would agree with that statement. Remember, I had John Sununu and Dick Darman [laughter], so just taking those two alone is enough to give one pause.[21] One of the deals I made going into this job was to at least have semiveto power on who was going to be the assistant secretary for legislative affairs at each of the cabinet agencies. I certainly didn't have any control over who the cabinet secretaries were. But I had some say in who the assistant secretaries were, whom we tried to spend a great deal of time with, and, frankly, who we used, because there were just too many issues—all of which fall into the definition of the president's agenda, or getting the president's program passed—where we needed those bodies. In many instances we needed their technical expertise.

If you're up there doing something on a tax bill, or you're doing something on some weapons system that they're trying to do over at DoD [Department of Defense], those relationships were very helpful. The big issue was just trying to make sure you were able to communicate with them. Needless to say, you'd also have some secretaries within the president's cabinet who had their own agenda that may be different from the agenda of the president, in which case you not only had to worry about that secretary but you also had to worry about the assistant for legislative affairs in that particular department. That's when I made Sununu do some work, because we did have a few errant ones every now and then.

Discipline is a very difficult thing to handle. But those legs are very important. I'd love to get these: You'd be sitting at the senior staff meeting at the beginning of each day, and you'd have someone who had talked to somebody. Everybody had their friend in the Congress who had their hand on the pulse of the Congress: "I talked to him last night, and he says the vote in the committee is going to be 10–8 our way." And you knew good and well you were going to lose your butt. Those are the issues that constantly plague the process and challenge the process as we tried to do our jobs.

Ball: There may be a correlation among second terms. Larry [Stein] was in a second term, and I was in a second term, and I think discipline across the executive branch deteriorates in the second term.

Riley: Why's that?

Friedersdorf: Because it's a lame duck, right?

Ball: Well, I guess that's a good way to put it. I was going to say that the subcommittee chairmen on the Hill, the members who are paying attention to specific issues and specific departments, know their way around the bureaucracy and are skilled at getting the right opinion out of the right person.

Stein: Maybe some of their staff people have gone to work in the administration.

Ball: I know I always look back at those successes that Reagan achieved on Max's watch in the '81–'82 timeframe, and I, in '87 and '88, wondered how in the world he did it. We had lost control of the Senate, as I said, but I think further that discipline and teamwork across the administration are lessened by turnover, an approaching election, and a lot of other factors.

McClure: And it influences, perhaps, the body of the Congress itself, too, in the way they begin to act. Today, for example, you have eight or nine members running for president, and you're holding votes so that people can be in and out of town for whatever purpose. That affects how many messengers they send back in, particularly when you're in the minority.

Brain: It also could be that the president's agenda has changed dramatically. The agenda in year eight for me was very different than the one Howard [Paster] faced in year one—the first budget bill in '93, the beginnings of healthcare reform.[22] We got a few things done in year eight that were important, but you knew the future of the western world wasn't in the balance.

Friedersdorf: It's difficult to maintain discipline and loyalty if the basic loyalty of the congressional relations people in the department and agencies is not to the president but to the cabinet secretary. When Reagan was elected, he came in with a big mandate, and I was told to get the congressional relations staff hired as quickly as possible. Jim Baker and the president said, "Go out and try to find the best people you can and staff up," and I was given the number of slots.

Well, we started hiring, and immediately what happens is you get calls from the Hill. They want to put *their* person in congressional relations. I talked to Jim right away, and he said, "If they call in, tell them to call either me or the president." They backed me up on all the hiring, so we got people with strong Hill—Senate and House—backgrounds. But before they could be hired, they had to be cleared by the White House—had to have my name on it. Then they knew they were working for President Reagan, not for the secretary of defense or the secretary of HHS.

Moore: Did you also fire them? Could you?

Friedersdorf: Yes, and we did.

Young: Could you, Larry?

Stein: Technically, we had that power. I don't think anyone ever exercised it, and I think it would have been a question on a case-by-case basis whether you could actually pull it off, depending on who they were, who their friends were, etc.

McClure: It's kind of like the president's nominee for a Senate-confirmed position. If you had enough faith to hire him, you hoped like hell you didn't have to fire him.

Stein: But getting back to this whole discipline thing, which I find important, John's point is right. There's a vast amount of fundamental legislative work for the executive branch of the government that cannot be either guided or instituted out of the West Wing. To that degree, it *has* to be done by the people in the agencies. The coordination out of the West Wing is the crucial thing, and it focuses the attention of the president's top guys on his agenda. Frequently, I think there's a problem going both ways with the agencies.

Sometimes they're out there representing the interests of the secretary of blank, either for their own personal reasons as they advance their careers or for reasons of personal loyalty or whatever. But frequently, in my own experience, they just didn't know what was going on in the meetings, in the chief of staff meeting we had at 7:00 A.M. Or at least they didn't know it in sufficient detail to be able to contribute to it. So, there's that side of it, too, to be a little bit protective of those people. Sometimes they might have done better up on the Hill had they known what the real agenda was.

But I do think that the crucial thing here for this job is: Given the opportunities of the moment, given the president's needs of the moment—sometimes needs that he didn't shape himself—you have to be able to distill an infinite range down to a few fundamental things and go out and do 'em. That is more important than trying to define it in its broadest abstract terms.

Moore: It's easier to do it yourself than to try to coordinate it. Every White House is organized differently. One of my deputies ran a deputies' meeting at seven o'clock, and then we'd distill that into the senior staff meeting at eight. I'm wondering, did you all have the White House schedulers sit in?

Hilley: There was a seven o'clock and then a subsequent broader meeting with the schedulers included. That was a follow-up to the closed meeting.

Moore: Yes, we had the presidential schedulers sit in, and frequently we'd make decisions right there because things were changing—"Take this one off" or "Squeeze some time there." And we did it a week out, two weeks out.

I had a meeting every Friday with the agency CL [congressional liaison] people. And what I found was that they'd salute and say "yes," but oftentimes they weren't doing CL. Because I'd turned down somebody to do CL, the secretary had hired that [preferred] candidate for another job—a chief of staff, a counselor, assistant, whatever—and *they* were actually doing CL. You had to have a joint decision who the person was going to be. You couldn't say, "This person's going there." It had to be somebody they wanted and liked and felt comfortable with. But we used them. I'd pass out assignments and say, "You're Treasury, you work Ways and Means. You've got good relations with these people. We'll get votes for you. We'll back you up." But it was all different then. Now it's budget, budget, budget.

Brain: Sometimes as the head, rather than coordinating everyone and getting everybody on message and sending teams up, it's just so important that you do it yourself. I've frequently felt that the most important issues you were doing, and largely yourself, with a few folks around you who are needed to put your team together. But on other issues—John has said it well.

Moore: Just do it, and tell 'em about it when you're through.[23]

Brain: Other people on the White House staff, on your team, could be worrying about things that are important, and that's good—"So you keep me informed." And others, the agencies, they're off doing their thing, and that's great, and you hope they're successful. But is everything critical to the success of the presidency? No. And at some point, that's what you're worried about. So you're doing the important things.

Moore: Did you find also if they had a program at HUD [Housing and Urban Development] that the secretary wanted, they were constantly trying to pull the White House in behind it?

Chorus: Sure, yes.

Stein: All the time.

Moore: Then you say, "No, this is yours, you do it." "Well, you know, maybe the president could make a speech on it." "No."

McClure: Another structural issue is the question of whether our colleagues who had different senior-level positions in the White House helped play the coordinating role. For example, a cabinet affairs person, or somebody who was over at OMB in the subject matter area, or somebody in the policy shop—whether they would be conduits of information—so you'd find out what other people on the Hill were doing that you did not know about. I don't know how successful we were, but we tried hard to enlist our colleagues to help us keep control of what was happening at the departments, as best we could with those limited resources.[24]

Young: It was an earlier day, but I'd like to report what Bryce Harlow had to say about his problem. It's something he probably taught many of you, so you're learning nothing new. He was referring to how he dealt with the departmental people. Now bear in mind that the departmental people were already in place when the congressional operation was set up in '53 in the Eisenhower White House, so the option of helping to place people in the departments did not exist in the first Eisenhower term. Also remember that Bryce and all of them had been in the departments themselves. Bryce previously had been a lobbyist for the War Department, as it was then called.

When I asked him about that, he said, "Here's how we handled that problem. Every Saturday morning—*Saturday* morning—we would have a meeting of all the departmental liaisons in the White House. Oh how they hated those meetings, getting them in off the golf course where they wanted to be."[25] He said the purpose of those meetings essentially—besides finding out what each was doing and what was going on—was to reiterate the message to them: "*We* do the president's business, and *you* do the secretary's business, and don't you meddle in ours, and we won't meddle in yours—unless, of course, you ask for some help." Of course, that was not quite true in practice, because it's also the job to stop things the president doesn't want, which is the other side of the congressional relations job.

That was a simpler day, and I'm wondering if that's become virtually impossible today. Larry's point is there are just so many people in the act that it's beyond management. So you have to do it yourself, do what you can, and concentrate on the important things.

Stein: I think it's extremely difficult to manage. We've talked primarily about when the president has a clear set of objectives and you're out there trying to achieve them, and maybe things aren't quite well coordinated because there are so many people. There's another kind of circumstance, which is when there *is* an agenda, or an agenda item, about which cabinet secretaries differ. It may be an agenda item that the president doesn't want to take too frontal a position on. I can think of an example that drives me crazy to this day, and that's the needle exchange program.[26]

We had Barry McCaffrey, who was violently opposed to any kind of liberalization of needle exchange, and we had Donna Shalala, who had a body of medical evidence demonstrating that it was the right thing to do.[27] All of our political judgment—and the political judgment of anyone you could drag in off the street—would be, *stay away from that issue!* Well, guess what? The president wasn't allowed to stay away from that issue, partly because his people, who *are* his people, named by him, couldn't bring themselves to stay away from the issue.

It isn't entirely their fault. Each of them had to deal with that question, but I think it ended up with a less than optimum result on the president's behalf. I don't know that it could have been managed any differently than we ultimately managed it. We did end up with a compromise of sorts. I think it was a compromise that pleased virtually no one, but nonetheless. You remember this one, Chuck.

I think that's the kind of thing you have to think about in this job as well, and it goes back to the fact that a lot of times circumstance controls these sorts of things and you don't have absolute control. So where you can exercise it, you'd better do it, because it's not going to be that often that you really are able to determine your own outcomes.

Hilley: Another reason that I didn't worry much about the underbrush of the day-to-day work is, first, there's only so much that can rise to the political agenda that can capture senior staff's time. But the other trend over the last decade—and it continues to this day—is really centralization. Remember, the other side of our jobs is the Hill. And in the decade of the '90s there was a marked centralization of authority into the leadership, because it all turned into budget and tax issues. And at the end of the day, Congress would sort of melt down—there was a stand-off, in the sense that you had Democrat against Republican, and it could only be mediated through the leadership and through the White House.

Then the Congress would do its work—and I don't mean this facetiously—and then there would be the bills all wrapped into one huge CR [continuing resolution], one huge reconciliation bill, and we'd say, "Okay boys, what are we going to do now?" It's time to say, "Where's the deal on actually getting this thing done?" That was mediated through the leadership.

So in a sense, the big issues were driven not only by outside events and the amount of time, but by the nature of what this last decade's been like, and continues to be to this day. Because the bills get so big, they don't get passed one by one anymore, whether it be a tax bill or an appropriations bill. It all gets glommed up at the end, and then everything comes to a head—the big-money items as well as the smallest rider that some congressman from somewhere put on that has to be stripped out. So what you'd find is that you basically got the last whack at it anyway as it came through on the final budget bills.

Stein: I think the point about the localization of power and leadership on those particular vehicles is crucial. That's really what's been happening over the last ten years, and it's happening more. I think you're seeing more concentration of power. I was just back on the Hill for a year last year. My sense is more concentration of power in the leadership offices in both bodies.

Moore: It's going both ways. I told people at the lunch table earlier today that when I learned I was going to have the liaison job, I went up to New York and met with Larry O'Brien, who was head of the NBA [National Basketball Association] at that time.[28] He said, "Well, it's changed since I was there. I only had to talk to five or six people. I had to talk to the Speaker, the chairman of Ways and Means, the chairman of the Rules Committee, whoever they were. That was it."

Well, when I got there with President Carter, Tip [Thomas P.] O'Neill was in his first year as Speaker and not real secure, for reasons I'm going to describe. In '74 he had the Watergate babies. In '74 he had what, seventy-four new freshmen? He had almost that many come in two years later, so he had 150 new members who got elected not because they came up through the ranks and had any party loyalty, but they were sort of free-wheeling people. They were meeting as a freshman caucus and not telling the Speaker what they were doing.[29]

You had two or three committee chairmen deposed. Mr. [William] Poage at Ag. Tom Foley was the new chairman there.[30] I've forgotten where the others were—

Several: [F. Edward] Hébert?

Moore: Hébert. And then the guys who were the chairmen had delegated power to the subcommittees in order to hold onto their seat. You had Jim Wright, who was majority leader by one vote over Phil Burton, a very bitter personal contest. Senator [Robert] Byrd was brand new in his leadership post. So, when you talk about the other side, the Hill, we had to deal with the fact that the power had dispersed from the five or six people Larry said he dealt with. And I think it dispersed more and more until the Republicans took over the House and centralized it back again after 1994.[31]

So I've seen it go both ways. A freshman member asked me to come and speak with them, freshmen and sophomores, and I scheduled it. I then got a call from Tip O'Neill, and he said, "You don't meet with the freshmen. You meet with the Speaker. Then I'll meet with the freshmen." What he was saying was he really wasn't quite sure he could control those freshmen. He sure didn't want somebody else stirring around there.

I'll make another point about people working for you and against you. Some guy from the *Washington Post* is writing a book about the Corps of Engineers and the Everglades. Maybe he's interviewed some of you all? He had lunch with Jim Free last week. You all know Jim, who said, "We got on the water projects and getting the necessary votes to sustain a veto" [talking through laughter], which is easier now. Jim told this guy, he said, "Frank Moore told me that President Carter wanted me to go up on the Hill and work to sustain the veto on the water projects. When I got up there to Tom Bevill's office, there were four people with stars on their shoulders from the Corps of Engineers. I went over to somebody else's office. They were up there lobbying against us, and they had more to give away than we did!" We were trying to take stuff away from them, and they were giving things away.[32]

We've all had that happen, right? The Corps runs their own legislative shop. They're going to do what they're going to do. You'd call the secretary of defense and say, "Can't you control them?" And he'd say, "No." Did you ever have that?

Friedersdorf: The Corps, working behind you? They're an entity unto their own. They do whatever they want to do.

Moore: Yes, I discovered that the hard way.

Friedersdorf: And the congressmen are all behind them.

McClure: And those projects were always multiyear. I left the Senate staff of John Tower—eleven years I was gone—and there were still water projects that I had been working on five years before, and they were still getting annual funding of some sort to build. Members love the Corps.[33]

Riley: Which other departments or agencies fit in the same category with the Corps as being special?

Stein: The entire Pentagon. In my experience, they had negotiated their appropriations number by February of every year, and it was as big a number as they could achieve, and they didn't give a damn whether it ate into anything else or not.

Friedersdorf: They'd go out and spend all their money at the end of the fiscal year and say they're broke.

Stein: Yeah, and then get a supplemental.

Moore: And a subgroup within them is the Marines. They have their own bill separate from the secretary. [laughter]

Ball: The Constitution says that Congress shall "provide and maintain a navy." [laughter] Well, thankfully, there are some who still take that seriously![34]

Moore: My point is that within the Pentagon, they complain about the Marines.

Ball: Well, they have a special constituency. As someone has reminded me many times, there's no constituency not to spend money. I was on the staff when the first Budget Impoundment Act was enacted, and I was on the Armed Services staff a few years later when Senator [John] Stennis took an authorization bill to the floor and Senator [Edmund] Muskie raised a point of order against the bill. That was the first real test of enforcing the budget process against the Defense Department, against the Defense Authorization Bill.[35]

I remember that well. Of course, at the time there was still a dispute—from the Nixon administration on—that applying those kinds of controls to national security may not have been the right thing to do. But Muskie prevailed, and he carried the day, and the Senate stood behind the budget resolution. Senator Stennis had to rewrite his bill. That was a very significant event.

McClure: Yes, but that was authorization—

Stein: Bring a point of order against the Defense *Appropriations* Bill and see what happens.

Brain: Thinking about projects and working with the Army Corps—They're all still members of Congress, so I can't mention the particulars, but we had a member of the House of Representatives who was particularly helpful to the president [Clinton] during the whole impeachment process, much to his own political endangerment back home. He had a particular project back home, a facility that this department wanted to move out of his district to somewhere else. He kept talking to me about it: "I need some help. If we lose these jobs, I'm going to lose my job."

I kept banging on the agency, banging on the department, praising him to the highest levels. And they'd say all the right things, but because the chair and ranking member of the committee, their authorizers, wanted the move, our good loyal soldier was going to be screwed in the process. They had their own little thing going. So I was working on one of the big trade votes. Talking to this member, a loyalist, I said, "What are you going to be doing on this vote?" "Oh," he said, "I'm with you, you've got me"—again, probably loyal at some peril to himself. I said to him, "No. You're not with us." He said, "What?" "No. No! You're *profoundly* undecided." I said, "Not only that, we've got a little cabinet group that gets together every week and makes calls. Secretary of state, secretary of agriculture, USTR [U.S. trade representative]. You're going to be getting a call from a cabinet member asking you where you are on this issue, and you're *undecided.* Not only that, you've got this problem with jobs."

So, lo and behold, the next time we had this meeting in the Cabinet Room, we're sitting around, getting reports. Charlene Barshefsky,[36] the USTR, said, "Uh, we have this problem with this member." She turned to the other cabinet member and says, "You'll have to fix that jobs project, can't you get it done?" And he said, "Oh, I guess we'll have to."

Young: So it works both ways.

Brain: This guy had been so loyal, so much a friend of the president at his own risk, we couldn't screw him, in spite of the fact that the department wanted to. I've always enjoyed that one.

Neustadt: A couple of stories from an earlier era occur to me that maybe I should put on the record and let them show the change of scale. In the first place, I was raised in Washington by Jim Rowe,[37] who was in the [Franklin] Roosevelt administration, and he told me that in 1935 and '36 the favorite slogan around the White House was, "Never hit a man unless he's down." [laughter]

Roosevelt forgot that in 1938, but anyway, Fred Lawton, who ultimately became budget director in Truman's time, told me that the last big piece of New Deal Legislation was the Fair Labor Standards Act.[38] In the middle of action on that act up on the Hill, the president called him over from Budget—he was a middle-level civil servant—and gave him instruction. The instruction was, "Go find a room with a telephone in the old State Building, the Executive Office Building, Fred, and call my secretary and say what the number is of the room where the telephone is. From time to time, congressmen sent by me will knock on your door. Now take a copy of the budget with you, Fred, and when they come in and ask you for something, give it to them." That was the president. He was negotiating when there was negotiation to be done. Oh, it was a long time ago.

Mr. Truman wouldn't have a legislative staff, although a couple of people tried to persuade him otherwise, partly because he remembered Tommy Corcoran when he, Truman, was first in Congress, being a young squirt representing the White House and kicking him, Truman, around.[39] Partly because I heard Truman say he was afraid that if he had a staff with a specific function, it would attract too much business.[40] I've heard business mentioned, and I'd like to hear what you think about it—too much business with which the departments were now stuck. Truman didn't want it—partly because it was up to the leaders of the two houses to do the vote counting. He relied on them for the counting, even if their counting was often awful. But if he had a legislative staff, it would have become their responsibility to do the count instead, and he didn't want that. So, no legislative staff.

Now, obviously, there *has* been one. Successive presidents have found it useful, and Congress has found it useful. It's one of those institutions that lasts because everybody has good reason for it. So Truman was fighting against the trend. But what about that? There are some negatives here, and I'd like to hear a little more about them.

Stein: I think he's got a point. I mean, localizing it certainly makes it an attractive nuisance in the sense that you get a hell of a lot of calls. But one of the functions that I don't think we've discussed here is being able and good at sitting there getting screamed at by a member. We've talked about some of the projects that people got. For every one that people get, there's at least one that people don't, maybe more. Chuck, you're better at counting those than I am. Don't you think? So to the degree that in creating such an office you provide members a sort of one-stop shop for their wishes and objections, yes.

On the other hand, look, it's one of those things that seems to me for that very reason was inevitable. So whether it's a good or a bad thing is perhaps not the point. It's one of those things that if it weren't there, God would have had to create it.

Brain: The most I was ever yelled at—the worst badgering—was a member of the House of Representatives, a friend of mine, over his personal treatment by the White House Visitors Office.[41] He'd been down there, he had constituents in tow, and the head of the White House Visitors Office looked at him—it was 7:30 in the morning—and said to him, "Congressman, I'm sorry. You're over your allotted visits for the month."

Moore: That's hard to believe.

Brain: I got into the office maybe forty-five minutes later, and he just yelled and screamed and said, "Chuck, the reason I'm picking on you is that if I talked to anybody else, I'd probably kill him." And the most that I ever returned fire and yelled at a member of Congress was over a zip code. He wanted a special zip code for a portion of his district, which—as I found out—we talked about Larry O'Brien and the Postal Service—the White House doesn't do zip codes.[42]

Riley: It's the postmaster?

Brain: We don't have postmasters any more, and that used to be *the* job. Again, as an anecdote, a big vote, bringing members of Congress down and we're going to take them upstairs to the Oval Office. I'm briefing

President Clinton on the way over, "Congressman So-and-so is going to be there, and he's likely to bring up a zip code with you. He wants it." And the President said, "Do we do zip codes?"

I said, "No sir, we don't. It's the Postal Service who does zip codes. So we've referred it to them. It's really up to the postal commissioner." Talk about change—the president looked at me and said, "Who's the head of the Postal Service?" And I said, "I don't know." [loud laughter]

Friedersdorf: But it used to be *the* job—a political job.[43]

Brain: That was it. And one time this member approached me, in the Roosevelt Room, just lurked: "And where's my zip?" I just went off, "We don't do zip codes!" So, it gets back to you. If the office is there, members feed on it. Talk about the two-way flow of communication—they're bringing the communication back from the Hill.

Riley: Max, what was the worst encounter you had?

Friedersdorf: The worst I was ever yelled at was over some stolen silverware in the White House. [laughter]

Stein: Ooh, that's bad.

Friedersdorf: I was called up to Bill Timmons's and Clark MacGregor's office one morning during the Nixon administration.[44] I could tell it was serious. They all had frowns on their faces, and Bill said, "Max, we got a job for you." I said, "What's that?" "Well there was a state dinner the president had for a head of state last night, and there's some silverware missing from one of the tables. We think one of the congressmen got it." [laughter]

Brain: It had to be a senator!

Friedersdorf: And he said, "On top of that, he's chairman of a committee." And I said, "What happened?"

They told me—and I never knew any of this—but at the state dinners, each usher is responsible for the silverware at his table, and it's all from a pattern, like the Millard Fillmore, or James Polk. They're so valuable. The Secret Service is in on it. They make sure those ushers turn all that silverware in. It's really something. He said, "What we want you to do is go up to Chairman So-and-so's office and kind of let him know that we think he's got that silverware and that we want it back."

And I said, "Well, I'm going up there and accuse him of a felony, of stealing federal property?" Bill said, "We've got to get it back, Max. That's the only thing we can do. Tell him—if you can get him to admit it—that the White House will make a replica pattern, a set. Woodward & Lothrop will do this for us (it's a big department store that used to be in Washington), and we'll give him that if he'll return the silverware."

I about quit! Anyway, I did go up there and went to the chairman's office and made an appointment. I can't remember exactly how I handled it, but I told him that there had been a state dinner, and we hoped he enjoyed it and everything. "Oh yes, Mrs. So-and-so and I thought it was a great dinner, Max." He had loved it. I said, well, you know there's some knives and forks and spoons missing from one of the tables, and you know, once in a while that happens. People want souvenirs, and they might just accidentally put it in their pocket."

And he said, "Are you accusing me?" And the old boy was a southerner, and he got real hot with me, you know. But he calmed down when I told him about the Woodward & Lothrop deal, and that he could have a set. He said, "You know, my wife *was* kind of admiring that, and we thought that it was pretty." He never did admit it, but he went over to his hmm—well, he had it in the office there. He gave it back to me, and I took it back down to Timmons and McGregor and gave it to them, and they had a set made by Woodward & Lothrop and went out and made a presentation to him. That's the worst experience I had.

Riley: What's the worst you've had, Will, or do you not want to follow this?

Ball: Oh no. I guess the worst experience I've had was when I had to go tell Jack Brooks that he could not subpoena the president's national security adviser. Of course, the issues now, and then, of executive branch testimony, that's all changed enormously. But in 1986, '87, and '88, principal advisers to the president typically did not—national security adviser among them, and the chief of staff—did not go to the Hill to testify before committees. But that has changed a great deal.[45]

Now one of Max's lieutenants, he may not have been aware of that at the time—he went on to serve with distinction in the legislative affairs office—actually named an award that is given to the members of the legislative staff who've endured experiences like Max did. It's presented on occasion, and it's strictly a merit-based selection, but it's framed and hung on the wall of the winner. The award is called the "Yellow Sock Award." Reflect on that a minute and you'll come to understand. [chuckles]

McClure: Some of us around this table have received that award.

Ball: It's quite bipartisan. It's a distinct honor.

Riley: Fred, did you have a story?

McClure: Not as exciting as Max's, by any means. I remember two in particular, though, one having to do with a member of the Senate and one having to do with a member of the House. The House one was very simple, involving someone I had known for a long time prior to my going to the White House. The president was scheduled to go into his congressional district, and we had already made the determination at the White House that this was a political trip. We had signed off on it, RNC [Republican National Committee] guys had signed off on it, everybody was signed off on it. This particular member of Congress was not going to be allowed to ride on *Air Force One* and appear with the president on this particular occasion.[46]

He was just adamant. He'd gone up all through our staff and finally got to me. He was just yelling and screaming at the top of his lungs, which he has a tendency to do still to this day. At which time I took great pleasure—he's saying, "If you don't do so-and-so I'm going to call the president"—and I said, "Well, good, call him," and I just slammed the phone. It was a very special moment for me, because I knew good and well the president would never take the call.

The other one had to do with announcement of a U.S. district judge, and the whole notification process in a state where we had senators from two different political parties. The question was who was going to be able to make the announcement first.[47] We had a regular practice—at least in our shop, which was established by some of my predecessors, at least on the Republican side—that, like awards grants of significant numbers, we'd call "our guys" first. Then at a requisite amount of time later, we'd call the other party senator and let him know.

Brain: Was it days or weeks?

McClure: Generally thirty minutes. C'mon guys, I was pretty good about it. The guys in my office quaked on this, but this particular appointment had been a negotiated deal between these two senators of different political parties. But I still had to give "our guy" the heads-up so that he could make the appropriate press announcements. This guy had fought so hard in the negotiation that resulted in the nomination that I asked my administrative assistant to actually make the phone call through the White House operator so that we would have a time stamp of when this particular phone call took place to the staff member on Capitol Hill whom we were supposed to call. We gave a heads-up that we were going to call, and then fifteen minutes later, another heads-up. Then we made the phone call fifteen minutes later and waited the requisite time and then called the other senator.

Well, needless to say, the other senator, thirty minutes later—because somebody on the Republican senator's side dropped the ball—made the announcement first. I think I took about twenty-five minutes of it that day in one telephone conversation that was laced with terms that I cannot repeat for this public journal and symposium—even by every other word.

The conclusion of that is he finally let me say something, "Look, I did what I promised I was going to do." He actually called me back, after he reamed his staff out, while I listened to that happen on the phone, and apologized. Not many times you get an apology from a member of the United States Senate when they thought that you screwed up and they turned out to be wrong. I actually got an apology, which is the flip side, but I took a little hell getting there. I knew this guy a little too well.

Young: Jim Thurber?

Thurber: Yes, I was thinking about the comments that Frank [Moore] made. He was there during a very interesting time when there was a decentralization of power in the House down to the subcommittees—They defeated three chairs. They took power away from Wilbur Mills and the committees, and they had the subcommittee Bill of Rights where they voted on jurisdiction for the subcommittees so that John Dingell didn't have all the jurisdiction in his subcommittee or his full committee.[48]

But at the same time, a very important reform occurred that centralized things, and that's the Budget Impoundment and Control Act that you also mentioned. Since then we've had Gramm-Rudman-Hollings, and lately the Budget Enforcement Act in 1990 that puts caps (for a while; they're gone now) on expenditures, firewalls, so you couldn't take the money saved and move it over into Byrd's state.[49] And the whole phenomenon has, over the budget, centralized things. Therefore, all of you have had in your experiences, I think, a problem of decentralization and centralization going on at the same time. I'd be interested in how you handled the centralization side of things in the budget. It was mentioned that you've had these big omnibus budget bills that go through that are negotiated on the leadership side. How did you all get involved, or did you get cut out? Were you trusted by the president and others in these negotiations?

Hilley: Well, in terms of the structural issue first, the key mover really is the reconciliation bill, because in the Senate everything, just about, is filibusterable—sixty votes needed for cloture—whereas the reconciliation bill under the Budget Act is fifty votes and cannot be filibustered. So that has become the vehicle of choice for putting everything in. Now, the original conception, of course, was that this was to reduce the deficit [laughter], but it has morphed into this huge omnibus, anything-goes bill.

So the change in the reconciliation bill is it is the train that always leaves the station and has to fund the government and things like that. So that became the vehicle.

In terms of the question, I always felt centralization was good, and I think there were a few reasons for it. First of all, when the Republicans took control in '94 and the Contract on America came out,[50] as I like to call it (just kidding)—

Thurber: Some of us used that in lectures all the time.

Hilley: But the truth is, with this revolution there was a centralization of power in the Republican leadership, and I have to say that Newt Gingrich, like him or not, could really deliver.[51] He had his guys whipped into shape, and if you wanted to get something done, you went through the leadership or else it just fell apart. So I think that was the dynamic coming out of the House, out of their special circumstances.

The key to this is, yes, we were involved always from the get-go, and it really comes down to relationships that you develop over time. Larry [Stein] was both in the Senate leadership and running the Budget Committee at the time that I was filling various roles at the White House, and so our relationship, and the fact that we're both children of the Senate and serving with a string of remarkable leaders—both George Mitchell and Tom Daschle—let us get in at the front door very early.[52] The flip side, of course, was that being children of the Senate, our relationships with the House were always tougher.

McClure: And suspect.

Hilley: Therefore, we had to depend on other people who came out of the House to do that. But in general, the leadership understood that at the end of the day they had to pass a bill. The meltdown was on their watch if they didn't do it. So they always knew that the president had to sign this bill at the end of the day, so at their peril did they let this get so far off track that it didn't work. Again, a lot of it was relationships and personalities, which is really at least half of the game: knowing people and having a relationship with them. But generally, I always felt that centralization, driven by the Budget Act, was a good thing, because it actually let us get our business done. Whereas, if you left it to committees in this day and age, under the constraints of the Budget Act, things simply wouldn't get done.

Stein: I wanted to add, because I think there's both a centripetal and a centrifugal force here—and Frank, you're absolutely right. What John just described is absolutely true and is becoming truer. It's more and more difficult to get anything through the Senate. I don't know what the statistics are on the use of filibuster, but I'm sure it would be pretty decisive about the growth of the use—

Moore: It's incredible.

Stein: It *is* incredible. A mechanism that was, I think, at one point deemed to be something you would use only in extreme circumstances has become almost the standard operating procedure. John's right, reconciliation and the packaging up of the appropriations bills have become the vehicles of choice for a lot of things. On the other hand, Frank, something you were mentioning earlier I think is definitely true, and I trace some of it at least back to television in the Senate, television in the House: You also had a thoroughly democratizing media impetus. That is, almost every member became his own leader, because they could all go to the gallery and get on TV.

This is something I've puzzled over for a long time. You actually have momentum in two different directions, as you rightly said. And I think it makes everything much more difficult and contentious in a lot of ways. Because the leaders are the ones with the power to get something done, but at the same time anyone can get out and go to the gallery and criticize this and criticize that, which frequently they do. It creates a lot more tension in a lot of ways. I'm not sure what the press democratization side means, but it seems to me that the centralization is going even further with term limits on chairmanships—which again, lodges more power in the party leadership. This is something that I'd welcome some thought about because I think it's very interesting. I just don't know what it all means.

McClure: I'd add that Gingrich, before he became Speaker, had the ability to whip his troops in line—for example, our defeat the first go-around on the Budget Enforcement Act of 1990.[53] That was during Newt's back-bench days, but I think leading up to '94. When you're trying to lead the country from the White House, and you have the opposite party in control on both sides by substantial margins, it becomes extremely tough. You talk about filibuster votes now—back then, it was a question of could you get enough votes to sustain a veto. How many would it take? Thirty-four, or whatever the number was in the Senate. A lot of policy debates and decisions were made in the Bush 41 presidency as a result of whether or not you could get thirty-four. So that has also changed the dynamic.

Thurber: Could I have one quick follow-up? It was at the end of my last question, and that was the question of trust. It wasn't trust with the

Hill, it was trust with the president. Did the president ever think you were "going native" when you delivered bad messages from the Hill?[54] In other words, you were too much of the Hill, and did you then get cut out of things sometimes, as a result of that? I've heard that from others in the Clinton White House legislative affairs operation that sometimes they didn't trust you, and so—

McClure and others: Who are "they?" Define "they."

Thurber: The president and a few close advisers.

Stein: I never felt that way. I felt like John. That would have happened prior to our time if it had happened at all. That may go back to the early, early period where there were some serious mistakes. After John's success on the budget, I don't think either of us was doubted.

Hilley: It's very hard to get organized at the start of any administration. Governors, particularly—which is normally what we get now as president—have a tremendously difficult time getting organized and understanding the Hill, in particular. So that's where your main friction goes. Larry and I came in multiple years later, and by that time people had been pretty acclimated.

Stein: President Clinton may have felt he got bad judgment early on, on health and on judicial nominees and on the stimulus package, which was a rather substantial disaster.[55]

Thurber: The health and stimulus thing is what I'm thinking of, and that's why I was asking.

Friedersdorf: Didn't he just turn it over to Senator Byrd?

Moore: I think the better way to phrase it is *it was turned over* to Senator Byrd. Whether anyone actually did it [laughter]—My impulse is to believe that you don't have to do much turning over to Senator Byrd.[56]

Neustadt: There was a story that made the rounds in Washington that Mr. Clinton had been habituated to the Arkansas legislature. And in the Arkansas legislature, any bill introduced had to be voted on, and it was a long time before he understood that wasn't so in Congress. Is there anything in that?

Hilley: No, not during my tenure.

Stein: Mine either.

Hilley: Tomorrow's the day to talk about particular personalities, but he knew policy inside out.

Stein: And procedure, too.

Hilley:—and procedure, and understood what could and could not be done, at least by the time we got there, he—

Stein: I can't believe there's any truth in that story.

McClure: I didn't work there, but it sounds ludicrous to me.

Frank [Moore] and his colleagues took a lot of heat because President Carter brought a lot of his former staffers with him from Georgia. President Clinton had a different sort of challenge, as I viewed it from the outside, because a lot of people from the Hill, or who had been dealing with the Hill, came to his inner circle and seemed to be surrounding him—in different kinds of positions, but still having a great knowledge of how the congressional process worked.[57]

Stein: Well, too, President Clinton had an economic team that was absolutely hungry to understand everything. I was with the Senate Budget Committee then, and John [Hilley] was chief of staff for Senator Mitchell at the time. The Clinton economic team came to us early. We sat down with them and with the people who really knew the procedure. It was Gene [Sperling], it was [Robert] Rubin, it was Larry Summers, the whole crowd—and we went over the whole budget process with great intensity.[58] I can't remember what particular technical problem there was—it was something having to do with scope and reconciliation—and to my surprise, within a couple of weeks Clinton was bringing it up to [Jim] Sasser at a meeting down at the White House and probably understanding it as well as anyone in the room.[59] So that doesn't ring true to me.

Brain: I think there *is* a pattern of governors coming to town and political people—I mean those people who got someone elected who had been completely dismissed—be it the governor of Arkansas, the governor of Georgia—they got him elected president. And so they think, "Who are these guys up on the Hill? What do they know about it? If they were that smart, they'd be here!" [laughter] There is a tension early on: "Who *are* they?"

Moore: Will mentioned Jack Brooks. My first encounter with Jack Brooks—and this was before the convention, in April or May of 1976. We didn't have a nominee yet, but I was up on the Hill meeting people. We knew we were going to do a government reorganization. We did have a plan—people just didn't think we did. You had to go through Senator [Abraham] Ribicoff and Jack Brooks, Government Affairs' respective chairs.[60]

Sitting in was the member from the ninth district of Texas [Brooks], and he said, "When are you going to quit bashing the Congress?" I said, "On June 9th." He said, "Why June 9th?" And I said, "That's the last primary, it's California." [laughter] I think we'll talk about this some tomorrow, how your campaigns follow you to Washington. It was true: We quit bashing Congress just as soon as we won the nomination. But I took a lot of heat.

And, by the way, it's not true that Carter and I had no experience in Washington. When Carter was governor, your energy czar [pointing to Friedersdorf], czar to President Nixon, froze prices on petroleum products but left out propane. Propane's very important in the South because they use it in the chicken houses, and so on. And propane dealers were gouging them. So Carter came up and met with the energy czar and asked him to put a price cap on propane. And I came with him. So I know both of us had been to Washington. [laughter] That's a myth I want to dispel.

But seriously, there was criticism of me because I had worked in the Georgia legislature. But all my staff came from the Hill—and you all know them all. In the Democratic caucus, someone was complaining about me. Jim Wright was majority leader, and he said, "Let me tell you. Would you rather have someone who knows the Hill and doesn't know the president or somebody who knows the president and the president trusts, and we can teach him the Hill?" And that was me. So that was a great defense, not just for me personally, but for anybody who comes into that situation.

Friedersdorf: Do you remember, Frank, you came into my office? I was the head of congressional affairs for Ford, and we were leaving, and you came in to visit me before the inaugural, and we talked about congressional relations?

Moore: Sure, and you made your staff available to me, and we talked about some of the people who worked for you. I said, "How do you get 212 votes? We've been worried about it." And you said, "We vetoed everything. We couldn't get 144." I love those numbers. You said, "We've run it by veto."

Friedersdorf: It was a magic number.

Moore: Was it 144 for that?

Friedersdorf: 144, 145 we'd go for.[61]

Moore: But I remembered that, and when we first started our veto strategy, I went back and studied what President Nixon and President Ford had done. They did very well with it.

Friedersdorf: We never had either a Republican House or Senate. We always were in the minority, so that's the only way we could govern, really, because it was right before the election, and everything that we would send up to the Hill, they would double the price and send it back down, daring us to veto it.

Moore: And you did.

Friedersdorf: And we did. And we sustained them.

Moore: And you got what you wanted.

Friedersdorf: We got beat! [laughter]

Moore: Yes, I always remember that. I learned a lot from you and your staff. It was a good transition—

Friedersdorf: It *was* a good transition.

Moore: It was a wonderful, wonderful transition from President Ford to President Carter. That could be a model. It was a wonderful transition.

Brain: I would like to tell one transition story, and it won't involve *W*s, or anything like that.[62] The White House is up, working and functional right until midnight or so on January 19th–20th, and it's still got papers everywhere. People are cleaning out. Then as the White House staff leaves, the workers come in and, literally, within twenty-four hours the rugs are up, new rugs, new paint, things are put back. And the new group comes in. Everything's there, but no supplies, no telephone books.

You've sensed the camaraderie, I think, amongst legislative affairs folks. So in the office assigned to legislative affairs, which is the same, as we all know, there's a safe. I'm sorry Nick Calio couldn't be here.[63] I'd known him from various functions, lobbied him numerous times. And so I said, "I'm going to do something nice for Nick." I took a ream of paper, scissors, Scotch tape, pencils, and a White House directory—because all the numbers stay the same, if you want to call the press office, even though there's a different press secretary. I couldn't leave them in the desk, because the workers come in and throw out everything. So I put them in the safe, turned the dial, and I left. Monday morning, about nine o'clock, when I figured he'd be there, I called over and said, "Nick, here's the combination." He was the only person who had anything. [laughter] There's a bond between us folks, having done that job.

Moore: Max left me a nice present. The little thing you pull out on your desk had the Nixon and Ford White House directory on it with the telephone numbers. And I did the same thing you did. I just crossed out "press secretary" and wrote in the new one. It had them all in there, and I used it for four years, your telephone directory.

Friedersdorf: It's probably still there, Frank.

Moore: I left it, four years later. I left it.

Knott: We love the stories you were telling about your worst situations, but if you just add up the stories, it sounds like you are dealing with 535 prima donnas, people who have an exaggerated sense of their own importance. Is that really true? And if it is, do you deal with them differently than you deal with normal human beings? [laughter]

Thurber: Spoken as a presidential scholar, not a congressional scholar.

Friedersdorf: I think that Congress is as diverse as the American population. You have people with all kinds of good motivations, venal motivations. You have optimists, pessimists. You have honest people, you have crooks. It runs the whole gamut, but they all have one thing in common. The thing that's most prevalent on their mind is the next election and whether they're going to be reelected.[64] I would say for 99 percent of them that's true, unless they've announced their retirement, or for some reason they're going to leave the Congress. The thing I always tried to keep in mind was that this person is motivated by his desire to stay in Congress, and he does this or he does that to advance his reelection.

Anybody who runs for public office and attains public office successfully has to have an ego. I have known very few members of Congress or Senate who haven't had a massive to monster ego. That's part of the reason they're in Congress or in politics—they crave attention. You have some of them who are motivated by public service, but even those I've known are still tremendous egos. They are a breed apart.

They are people who are usually highly intelligent, although there are exceptions to that, but generally intelligent, above average, probably. They are people who've been successful in their life, and they're people who love being in the public eye. I would find them a little bit different than the average. You can't treat them like you would the average individual, where you talk about your interests and they talk about theirs. With them, it's all about their interests. They're in the situation where they need constant care and feeding and maintenance.

Moore: I've got one exception, and it's only one. I agree with everything Max said. I was at a reception up on the Hill, and I wanted to meet a member very early in my career, maybe two or three weeks in. There was a congressman from Chicago, and he said, "Come over here, I want to tell you something. I can save you some time. Mayor [Richard] Daley sent me here. I have a tavern at home, I was happy serving in Springfield." And he said, "All you have to do is just ask Frank Annunzio how he's going to vote, and that will be the way I vote."[65]

McClure: Sounds fair enough. Two for one.

Moore: He said, "I always vote the way Frank tells me to." That's the only exception. He didn't want to be there. He wanted to be back in his tavern, but Mayor Daley had sent him.

Brain: I reflect after seventeen years on the Hill and three in the White House. The one thing I think that distinguishes presidents and members of Congress is not so much that they have the next election on their mind, but that they've been elected. All of us—the important jobs we have, important decisions, advice to the president—but we were never on the ballot.

Part of this symposium is about telling stories. My boss, another Chicago member (not the one you're talking about, Frank) was chairman of the Ways and Means Committee. At a budget meeting, looking around, he says, "Would staff leave the room." He looked at the president's chief of staff and said, "I said, '*Staff,* leave the room.'" He didn't leave the room, and they laughed and said, "Okay," and he was able to stay. [But the key is] they got elected. We play roles. We can debate whether there should be more of us or fewer of us. It's changed over time, but those elected men and women—without them, there's nothing.

Ball: I do think there could be an interesting study of presidents over time who have relied on personal relationships with key members of Congress. We're over there in the CL position, we wonder where all those fine members are. As for the composition of the Congress, Max is correct. But I do think that in the age of television, the bloody combat of political campaigns today clearly deters a lot of fine people from seeking public office who might otherwise do so—financial disclosure rules and a whole host of other things.

One sees that in the composition of Congress, especially when the divisions are so close between the parties. As for your characterization regarding 535 prima donnas, I don't quite see it that way. The demands on elective office today are just so much greater than they were before, and the costs that those seeking office have to pay are so huge, that those who are willing to have their reputations assaulted—as they are today in campaigns—are getting to be fewer and fewer. That's not a presidential issue, that's just an observation. Frank [Moore] is from Georgia. If Dick Russell had run for the Senate today, I don't know that he could win an election in Georgia. He wasn't very good on TV.[66]

Moore: He wasn't good at shaking hands at the courthouse, either. I don't think Walter George could run.[67] He couldn't win an election.

Gilmour: Chuck [Brain] told an amazing story about a member of Congress who had to be coached on how to shake down the president. I expect that more often goes the other way—that members come naturally to this. One of your jobs must be to discern when it's authentic and when it's not. How do you do that? And also, what happens when you try and stare down a member and refuse to cave in because you think he'll have to vote with you anyhow?

Brain: Part of it is: What can they do if they're mad? What can they do to retaliate? If you're looking at a member of the opposite party who's going to vote against you on everything anyway, probably never going to do anything for you—it gets easy. If it's a powerful member of the opposing party, it depends on when we'll have something in front of him. If it's a friend of the president—again, I'm describing a minority Democrat, a minority member but a friend of the president who stuck by us—we'll take care of him. How is it important to them and what can they do if the answer is no?

Hilley: I'll just say that some of them are really good at it, too.

Ball: It's usually the same ones.

Hilley: Yes, it's the ones who are smart, and you like. But they just know, "Hmm, I need something for my state, so I'm not going to declare early. I'm going to see how this vote goes. I'm going to see." A couple of my favorite senators are the best at this. I love them both, but they just know how to wait it out and how to position themselves so they can ask for a little something. Ultimately the judgment comes down to understanding their interest and their predicament: "Is this BS, or is this a critical thing to their base?"—this is really what it comes down to. And you either can or cannot do it for them, often.

Stein: You have to do an assessment of what it is they want, sometimes. Sometimes you can adapt it a little bit and give it to them. Sometimes it's so over the top that there's just no way in the world you can do it.

Riley: On this point, isn't there some variation depending on whether the person's a chairman of the Appropriations Committee, like Byrd or Stevens,[68] or—

McClure: We don't need to talk to him! He's got the power!

Riley: That's an important point. Isn't it true that people who have power don't need to ask, so they don't ask?

Stein: No, sometimes they need to ask. When those people call, typically they get what they want. That's the fact of the matter. There are occasions, I guess, when they've asked too much.

Brain: On the legislative matter, Byrd doesn't need to talk to us. I remember sitting around one morning in a White House meeting—"Byrd did something last night we object to. It's stuck in an appropriations bill. You tell him he has to drop it." I said "No."

Stein: Do you remember "mountaintop removal"?[69] Sure, we blocked him. We had to block it. I don't know if he subsequently got it. I know it was extremely difficult. We didn't have much choice. What he was asking was almost unachievable.

Milkis: Max [Friedersdorf] rightly pointed out that the leading priority of the job is to pass the president's program. But another important part of legislative liaison work that I'm very interested in is nominations.[70] And judicial nominations, of course, have become extremely controversial. I wonder if any of you guys have anything that you might relate to us about your experiences in those kinds of contests.

McClure: Pray that the Court lives! I'll do the easy one. When I was special assistant, [William] Rehnquist was promoted to chief justice, and I ended up getting [Antonin] Scalia, which was probably one of the easiest confirmations in the modern history of confirmations.[71] I don't think he answered any question that was ever asked of him during the entire process. So he set one standard, which is the Scalia standard, and in future Supreme Court nominations, members of the Senate would say, "Well, we're not going to let him get away with what Scalia got away with." That's where Scalia is.

Also, in my tenure in this job I had both [David H.] Souter and [Clarence] Thomas, both of whom got confirmed, but under totally different circumstances.[72] Then you just pray that they all live forever and never retire, because that can consume a lot of time and divert attention from the president's agenda. Alternatively, it creates an opportunity for members of Congress to promote their agenda in the context of a judicial nomination, which is exactly what we see today, which is not any different from the way it's been since, I would say, at least going back to the '80s. Will [Ball] had a different experience.

Ball: Well, it's difficult to generalize. This goes to the core of a whole broader issue affecting the Senate's ability to act. I think that the confirmation process clearly has become more of a focal point of disagreement between the parties. It's just not working. I was there during the very difficult time when President Reagan nominated Judge [Robert] Bork.[73] The Senate had recently shifted from Republican control to Democratic control, and there were just not enough Republicans. Though Judge Bork got his vote, his nomination did not pass.

The analysis of that vote is not really pertinent to this discussion, but I think that the edges within the Judiciary Committee and within the Senate as a whole on this issue have become much, much sharper since then. There's far less room for a president of either party to maneuver. It's making it much more difficult, of course, again, to recruit men and women of good will to serve on the bench in any capacity and at any level.

Though there's a lot cited in the Bork fight as precedents, Bork faced a Judiciary Committee that was narrowly divided. He was opposed by the one conservative Democrat on the committee, Howell Heflin,[74] and that made it impossible to get the southern Democrats, who had voted in favor of Rehnquist [for chief justice] eighteen months before. The Republicans then being in the minority was the reason for that.

Moore: I think there's another reason you can't get good people, even when a judicial nomination is noncontroversial. The clearance process takes so long with the FBI [Federal Bureau of Investigation] and the IRS [Internal Revenue Service], and they also can get tangled up in package deals [over other appointments or politics]. Everybody agrees that Judge X would go straight through the Judiciary Committee, "Recommend," but they're held hostage to someone else.

I'm not an attorney—many of you are—but I've had these guys tell me, "I want you take my name off your nominations list 'cause it's killing my law practice." You tell the prospect, "You can't tell anybody you're going to be nominated. You can't tell anybody, because it's not done yet." And the FBI comes to town and starts asking around, and it ruins their law practice. I said, "Man, you're going to be a judge." "Yes, but the FBI's going around, talking to my elementary school teacher, and they're asking, 'What have you done?'"

Stein: That's true. Judges are probably the highest-tier problem, but—let's face it—the whole nomination process hits everybody.

Moore: It's not just judges. It hits everybody. And it drags on and on and on.

Stein: Everyone's connected to everyone else. The fight in the Senate doesn't have anything to do, necessarily, with the quality of the individual. You can be nailed for ancillary reasons. You can be nailed by someone you don't even know is nailing you. Someone can do a three-corner billiard shot and ask another senator to nail this guy so that he doesn't have to admit that he's nailing him. It has grown really, really tough.[75]

McClure: And to top it off, it's difficult to find out who's doing the nailing, if you're in our jobs.

Stein: That's true. Votes in the Senate are secret. I've frequently had to call up both cloakrooms and say, "All right, who's doing it?" That's preliminary. Then you try to figure out why, which can take another two weeks.

Ball: Judicial nominations, though—I may be wrong, but I think they're the ones that have attracted organized opposition: television, newspaper ads. That really began with the Bork nomination. It was one of the first exposed to organized effort.[76]

Friedersdorf: It obviously has an awful lot to do with the president's popularity and clout. I was there during the Nixon administration when we were in the midst of Watergate and Vietnam, and you couldn't get anybody confirmed, no matter how well qualified, because the Hill was trying to embarrass the president, defeat him on whatever issue. That was the Haynsworth, Carswell debacle era.[77]

Contrast that with when Reagan came in. He came down to Washington about two weeks after the election, and he had his executive branch nominees named between Thanksgiving and Christmas. He wanted to try and get the cabinet confirmed by the inaugural, and that gave us three weeks. We had every one of them confirmed by the inauguration. That's a monumental task. Congress wasn't around. A lot of them were away on travel. We had to take those nominees all over the country to meet some of the senators. It was just the fact that he came in with a big mandate, and he had some time there to work. But the farther we went into the Reagan years, the more difficult it became as we lost our clout.

Moore: Consultation is so important. I'm not going to mention any names, but we got some people I'd say were marginally qualified appointed to some regulatory commissions. But if you just take them around to meet and talk and talk on background—not just the courtesy visits—they whiz right on through. I'm thinking of one in particular Dan Tate had to handle. He said, "If you give me any more fools like this, I'm going to quit." Dan told this guy, "Look, I'm taking you to see Senator So-and-so. Don't open your mouth. I'll do all the talking."

Brain: Judicial nomination is a hot political issue today. But I would be fascinated to see someone do an analytical study about what nominees were killed at what point in the process. It can be very obvious at the end when somebody is before the committee, and there's no vote, or there's a filibuster on the floor.

But practices of moving a nomination vary by state, the conventions in the state, with the senators and what the White House has agreed to. So you can have someone killed you've never heard about, simply because Senator So-and-so won't return the papers. I almost think that current nominations are getting further through the process before some of them are being stopped. We saw it an awful lot. It varies over time, but at the end of the Clinton administration people were told, "No. It's just not going to happen. He may be well qualified, but no way." So I've got some different views on the current crisis of nominations in the judicial process.

Ball: It might go back to who was editor of the law review in law school and who wasn't.

Hult: I've heard three chiefs of staff named so far in the discussion: Leon Panetta, Erskine Bowles, and John Sununu. What was the relationship between legislative affairs and the chief of staff's office? And to what extent was the chief of staff fairly strongly involved in congressional liaison activities himself? That is, in actually meeting with members of Congress and lobbying members of Congress on particular pieces of legislation?[78]

Hilley: I'll quickly do the first two, since I mentioned both Leon and Erskine. Leon was, of course, a creature of the House, an expert on budget, so he was totally involved and engaged in a lot of the lobbying efforts integral to those. The coordination with the staff was always good. He brought his House Budget Committee and House personal staff down with him, whom we all knew through the years, and so it was a very easy mix to work with him. They were very well integrated.

Erskine was a different kettle of fish. He had served in an administrative position as deputy chief of staff before coming back to be chief of staff. So he tended to delegate more and leave it to the troops. But whenever we needed him to do anything, he actually liked to see the members, liked to go up there. But he was much less hands-on than Leon. In both cases, marvelous bosses, in the sense that they appreciated our function, gave us wide latitude, and were incredibly supportive throughout. Like I say, I couldn't have been luckier.

McClure: I'd say John [Sununu] was very active on Capitol Hill. And probably I knew about it 95 to 98 percent of the time. One of the great privileges of this job—or at least the way I tried to do it—was that you also were able to develop very close relationships with many members of Congress, not just the leadership, but folks throughout Congress. And they would also oftentimes be your friend—in the sense that they'd call up and say, "Fred, you wouldn't believe what So-and-so said when So-and-so called me today."

It was a two-way street in the sense that I could get information which was then useful for me in terms of my ability to serve the president and do my job internally. Chiefs of staff can be very valuable. Briefly, I had a couple of chiefs—but I also experienced others when I worked previously in the Reagan administration. It's like any personal service kind of business. You just hope that the folks don't break so much china that you can't go in and repair it. Rather than members of Congress yelling at me, I let John yell at them. That creates a circumstance where, if their usefulness finally comes to an end—as what happened to John at the end of President Bush's administration—it comes back and roosts.[79] John had to stop doing it, for whatever those reasons might have been. Our big job is just to make sure we can keep the kind of relationship that's necessary to be able to do the job on behalf of the president, and you use whatever resources you can. Chiefs of staff can be extremely valuable in that regard, but sometimes they can be destructive.

Friedersdorf: I worked for six chiefs of staff. The first one was H. R. Haldeman. Haldeman would never go to the Hill, and he was rather disdainful of Congress. In the final days of Watergate, when the ship was sinking, he wanted to go the Hill and meet some congressmen. [laughter] I took him up there. He was apprehensive on the way, but he made a nice presentation. Of course, it was too late then. We were *in extremis*, terminal. I think if he had started out like a Jim Baker or a Dick Cheney it could have been a whole different story, but Haldeman was not a congressional person.[80]

The second chief of staff I worked for was Al Haig. He took over after Haldeman was indicted and resigned. Haig was in a position of being up to his waist in alligators, and, really, his time was just a holding pattern. Haig was swamped by the Watergate and the Vietnam crises that were going on. After Nixon resigned, Ford came in, and our first chief of staff was Rumsfeld.[81] That was like going from night to day. He was a great chief of staff, very knowledgeable. He did a lot of work on the Hill, but he departed rather suddenly for the Defense Department, and Dick Cheney took over. Up until that time, Cheney would be the best chief of staff I worked for. He was thorough, efficient, ran an open shop, open access to the president, very knowledgeable on the Hill and the issues—just a gem of a chief of staff.

After we left office in the Ford administration and came back to the Reagan administration, the first chief of staff I worked for was Jim Baker. I rate him as tops among all of them I ever worked for. He ran a tight ship, good access to the president. He would go to the Hill frequently, and he would always ask me to accompany him. He was just a tremendous lobbyist for the president. He never had an agenda of his own. He would go in and present to the president the options and the sentiment on the Hill, and he would give it to him unvarnished, never with any bias or prejudice.

Succeeding Jim—as you know, he and Don Regan swapped jobs at the start of the second term of Reagan, and I went back to the White House. Don Regan had an entirely different agenda. He thought he was president and Reagan was a semiretired chairman of the board. Don Regan cut off access to the president by the senior staff. We had to do everything through him. He had very poor relations with the Congress. The first time Don and I went to the Hill, he wanted me to set up a meeting with the Senate leadership, Bob Dole and his team and committee chairmen. We went up and Don spent about forty-five minutes lecturing them on what he expected the Senate to do. Senators hardly got a word in edgewise.[82]

When I got back down to the office, I had a call from Bob Dole. The receiver was burning. He said, "Don't ever come back up here with that kind of presentation." Don had some great qualities—he was organized, of course, but he was not a politician. He aggravated the Congress, and he aggravated the people and staff, and it was unfortunate that he and Baker switched jobs. I wasn't there during [Kenneth] Duberstein and Howard Baker.[83] I cannot comment on those.

Ball: It was interesting to have a former Senate majority leader as a chief of staff. Howard Baker, of course, enjoyed the president's complete confidence and was able to deal with the Congress—and especially the Senate—like few chiefs of staff, and yet understood completely the importance of this position we're discussing today and was very careful to make sure that communications were tight and well connected. He was a tremendous asset to the president at a very critical time.

Now I can tell a story. Like many chiefs of staff, Howard didn't like to be the one giving the president bad news. I remember the day when the House had passed a highway bill that was $15 or $20 billion over the budget, by a huge majority. The Senate had passed it overwhelmingly, and Howard said, "It's time for us to talk to the president about the highway bill." I kept putting this off, and it was my distant hope that this would somehow be signed without a whole lot of fanfare despite the strong objections of the budget director.

But the day came and we had to go. We walked into the Oval Office, and Baker said, "Mr. President, Will has some news to give you on the Highway Bill." [laughter] So I cleared my throat and said, "Mr. President, this Highway Bill has passed the House and the Senate substantially over your budget request, which, of course," I tried to say, "happens a lot.

"But, sir, we've informed the leadership that if it's sent to your desk in its current form, your advisors would recommend a veto." There was a long pause. "And, Mr. President, I have to say that we've gone over this very carefully, and, sir, if you choose to veto this bill, I frankly can see no earthly way that we can gain the votes to ensure that your veto is sustained." There was a long pause. It was a real Reagan moment. He looked at me and said, "Well, what on earth does that have to do with it?" The die was cast. He was going to veto that bill no matter what, and did so. So we had to make a stand and didn't even attempt to sustain that in the House, and did so in the Senate. It was a very tough effort. Max had left the scene by then. We lost, but only by two votes.

Friedersdorf: That's pretty good.

Ball: The point is that presidents over time have tended to let Congress have their way on domestic issues, but this was one that stuck in Reagan's craw because it had been, of course, dealt with in the same way with the Corps of Engineers. It was a trademark throughout Reagan's term that if he staked out a principle—His comment to me was that he felt strongly about the budget for domestic spending that year, and he was going to hold the line and attempt to send a signal. I think that did serve his interest later that legislative year when it at least was known that he would put his veto in, and that's a critical part of the office of the presidency, which if not exercised, tends to be overlooked.

Brain: Just one more thing relating to the veto on an issue that's still current, so I won't mention it by name. Toward the end of the Clinton administration there was a bill that had pluses and minuses. I remember sitting with the secretary of the treasury and the chief of staff, saying, "Is this a good bill or a bad bill?" "There's some pluses and some minuses." We didn't know if we would veto it if it came to us. But the folks on the Hill didn't know, either, if we would veto it if it came to us. And they never sent it. They never called our bluff because they didn't know what was going to happen, and to this day I don't think any of us know what we would have done.

EDITOR'S COMMENTARY

Two topics discussed during this initial session of the symposium merit attention as especially illuminating about the broad subject of presidential-congressional relations.

The first is the great prominence in these discussions of what was termed by Charles Brain the "internal role" of the CL. Most casual characterizations of the liaison's job emphasize the external role, or what Brain calls "sales": "Go at it, get up there!" and pass the president's program. These are, after all, the president's lobbyists, and accordingly their primary responsibility is to move Capitol Hill as far as they can in the direction of accepting the president's policy preferences. That external role is the one that dominates most conventional discussions of the CL's job description.

There is, however, as Brain and others suggest here, a buried assumption in this simplified model—that the CL is a mostly passive recipient of some predetermined legislative product with which he or she is entrusted to carry up to the Hill in the presidential valise. By this simplified characterization, the president's program is a widget, and the CL staff is the president's marketing department, there to apply whatever political arts they practice to make a sale on whatever commodity they are handed. But the portraiture that emerges from these discussions indicates how far that conception is from reality, and indeed how much of the CL's time is actually devoted to activities apart from the narrow business of persuading members of Congress to back the president on this or that vote. What we find here is the centrality of two major "internal" chores: *shaping* the president's program (that is, the "product" they are being asked to sell), and *policing* the avenues of communication onto Capitol Hill—from both the White House and the broader executive branch—to make sure that the president's own preferences are not lost among a cacophony of competing voices.

The sales job of the CL can be immensely simplified if the liaison's judgment is solicited while the president's positions on legislation are actually being determined.[84] Yet, as Reagan CL Will Ball reports, there is forever a tendency within the executive branch for policy advocates to reserve for themselves consultations with the president (or senior cabinet officers), bringing in the liaison after crucial decisions about legislation are made. This is completely rational behavior. If the policy professionals can get a presidential imprimatur on their *preferred* legislation, they feel they are in a stronger position to secure those preferences, in their purest form, as a bill moves through Congress. The perspective of the CLs is usually different. As they see it, the policy professionals too often equate their own narrow interests with the president's. What CLs are especially well suited to do for the president, because of their ongoing immersion in the politics of Congress, is to help establish an accurate reading about what is achievable on Capitol Hill and to reckon fully what the cost-benefit ratio is for proceeding with a variety of courses of action.[85] Theirs is truly an exercise in the art of the possible. Accordingly, a major part of the CL's job includes participation in internal policy meetings, attempting to craft presidential positions on legislation that will meet the path of least resistance—or perhaps the most economical path of resistance—in the halls of Congress. As Bryce Harlow once observed, the CL is in such meetings to be sure that the policy professionals don't "come running in here and give us a lead weight and tell us to float it across a pond."[86]

The other internal chore that occupies much of the CL's time is monitoring executive branch personnel who take advantage of their own channels to Capitol Hill. This is at once an important and impossible job. There is no monopoly on communications between members of Congress and the executive branch—and indeed many of the CLs attending this session remark on how important good departmental liaison work can be for helping the president to achieve the White House's goals. But it is equally clear from these discussions that a considerable amount of liaison energy is devoted to keeping unsanctioned approaches to the Hill from undermining the president's own programs. The liaison's job of enacting the president's program is complicated by everything from informal cocktail party chatter to horse-trading of water projects by the Army Corps of Engineers. For the most part, these CLs seemed resigned to accepting the inevitability of such unauthorized contacts. But they also indicated that a crucial part of their responsibilities includes cutting off egregious freelancing while taking advantage of existing legislative-executive relationships when they can be exploited for the president's benefit.

The second area where these discussions were especially illuminating comes in what the participants had to say about the importance of institutional context in shaping their ability to do their jobs. The success or failure of the Office of Legislative Affairs often arises less from the native skills of the CL, or the political talents of the president, than from the structural realities of the Congress they seek to shape.

These CLs (especially those from more recent administrations) describe an environment seemingly drawn from science fiction—a forbidding place withstanding simultaneous centrifugal and centripetal forces, at once showing signs of centralizing and decentralizing tendencies.[87] Yet for those who regularly study Congress, these descriptions will be completely familiar—even if they originate from the other end of Pennsylvania Avenue.

The devolution of power in Congress can be traced at least as far back as the 1970s. Frank Moore, Jimmy Carter's CL, speaks at length in this chapter (and later ones) about the rapidly changing congressional environment Carter confronted beginning in 1976. Before that time, the prevailing leadership and committee systems on the Hill left most of the legislative power in the hands of an oligarchy—meaning, as Moore indicates, that the fate of the president's program was decided by a relatively few, very powerful, men. Back then, the oligarchs could easily exact their pound of flesh, but the system was highly efficient: Once the concerns of the oligarchs were settled, the Congress would, with relative ease, fall into place behind them. This did not last. For a variety of reasons, including the growing influence of television on Washington and the undermining of trust that resulted from Vietnam and Watergate (and a series of other congressional scandals), congressional power scattered to a plethora of media-savvy members skilled in taking advantage of a new leader-unfriendly environment. The faltering of the old order generated a genuinely more democratic condition on Capitol Hill—for better and worse. Younger, fresher, and more diverse influences were brought to bear on the lawmaking process. However, the scattering of power sometimes led to disorder on Capitol Hill. And this atomization severely complicated the ability of every subsequent White House—except in rare circumstances (including the crisis environment after 9/11)—to pass the president's program.

There followed, however, a reaction to these developments. Some members of Congress, as well as a large community of scholars, grew worried about the basic health of the legislative branch.[88] Accordingly, they promoted reforms intended to counter the runaway democracy that they believed was infecting the institution—generating party-friendly ways to reestablish some helpful hierarchies. When the Gingrich-led Republicans retook control of the House of Representatives in 1994, after a forty-year hiatus, their renewed regimentation functionally mimicked the kind of pre-Watergate congressional oligarchy that Frank Moore eulogized. These Republican hierarchies deteriorated somewhat over time and were never fully embraced by Hill Democrats. But the virtues to legislative efficiency of some restored centralization were unmistakable to those on the Hill.

The impact of such structural developments within Congress on the president's ability to sell his program is, on the evidence of these discussions, direct. Decentralization confounds presidential leadership. Promiscuous use of subpoenas, filibusters, and holds on nominations; camera-ready defiance of presidential emissaries by rank-and-file members; bargain-seeking by even the most junior legislators—all these serve to complicate the business of enacting the president's programs. Conversely, centralization, according to our well-placed sources, simplifies presidential leadership. This is not a logical necessity. One might reasonably assert that the presence of a more centralized leadership structure in Congress would actually create a power center to compete with 1600 Pennsylvania Avenue. But that is not the conclusion these insiders would have us reach. From their perspective, having a few levers to work on Capitol Hill is more desirable than having many, even if those few prove difficult, occasionally, to manipulate.

3

THE PARTISAN DIMENSION

Working with Your Party—and the Other

The main topics discussed during this session include the difficulties—and opportunities—of working in an environment of divided party control of the presidency and Congress; how the White House deals with party and issue leaders on Capitol Hill; the challenges of maintaining unity and discipline within the president's own party; the process and techniques of vote counting on the Hill; the role of interest groups in White House lobbying efforts; the politics of committees and conference committees; and veto threats, including statements of administration policy (SAPs). This session was moderated by James Thurber of American University.

Thurber: This morning we're going to focus on the partisan dimension, working with your party, working with the other party.

It's been an interesting situation with respect to partisanship. In the first two years of the Clinton administration you had unified party government. And according to the *Congressional Quarterly Weekly Report*, which calculates presidential support scores in Congress—I know some of you question whether they're a good measure—Clinton had an 83 percent batting average. In his last six years it dropped into the mid-30s, up and down in terms of how they calculate this. So party control makes a difference.[1]

Also, the environment on the Hill has changed significantly since the mid '70s in terms of partisan dimensions. One component of this is the permanent campaign. The permanent campaign is the idea that you use wedge issues on the Hill to help elect just a few more members in order to get just a little bit more of a majority. That's been very important to both parties over the last two administrations, because we had partisan parity basically in the Senate, and almost so in the House on very large votes.[2]

Last night over dinner, a couple of you said, "Sometimes it's easier for the White House to work when the opposition party is in the lead, when they have a majority." I'd like to start out with Chuck on that point. Is it easier to work with unified party government or divided party government, and how do you work with the leadership when the opposition party is in the majority?[3]

Brain: My answer is "It depends." I've got some Hill experience working with the president of the other party, and then some White House experience working with the other party, and I think the most important thing, from the president's perspective, is that you want to work with a *stable* majority. Yours or the other's, it really doesn't matter—but people you can work with who are going to deal with the issues on the basis of public policy and not looking at only the current election and the next election.

John [Hilley], Larry [Stein], and I—I believe *all* of our term was with the Senate and the House being controlled by the Republicans. But if you worked with them to get things done, frequently (and this is more John's watch than mine), you were considered almost a traitor on your own side. "How can you do welfare reform? How can you do a budget proposal?"[4] But those were important issues to the president, and you've got a certain time period to get things done. The clock is ticking, and you all know it. You may not even get the second term.

Now, if you're dealing with a stable majority on the other side, that's important. Before Newt [Gingrich], the Republicans didn't matter: "Okay, we've cut a deal with the Democratic chairman. This is what we're doing. This is what we're going to get done, and maybe it's unfortunate, but we've got to move."

I think that kind of [so-called permanent] minority was more compliant than the minority that's just out of power and wants to get back in: "If we pick up six seats we'll get there—let's pull together." At that point, the [congressional] party's asking you to sacrifice the president's goal of policy accomplishments for their being in power and their being able to contribute down the road.

I'm not an economist, but I can waffle. So I say, "It depends on what *sort* of majority you've got, more so than the partisan composition."

Hilley: I'll add a little bit of context, and also say that it absolutely depends. The Clinton presidency was an interesting one because there were several phases of it.[5] I came in the middle, which is the anomalous piece of it, where you had a Democratic president working in one instance with a Republican majority—in which, in '96, the Democrats were somewhat irrelevant in the Congress. Then you had an era of bipartisanship after the presidential win by Clinton in '97 as we got the balanced budget agreement done. This middle period was, I think, the anomaly. Think about it as bookends. The early part of the Clinton presidency—even though we had the president and Democratic majorities—was bitterly partisan and very difficult in terms of legislation, particularly the two centerpieces of legislation. The first, the large budget act that Clinton brought forward in his first year [1993], passed, as you recall, on a straight-line party vote by one vote, a tie broken by the vice president in the Senate. It was bitterly partisan. And second, of course, the meltdown called healthcare reform, which was bitterly partisan also.

That was the front end. I was fortunate enough to come in the middle, in this anomalous period of working together, but each year had its own characteristics. Larry and Chuck found the other, later bookend of the administration to be largely partisan because of the circumstances surrounding the impeachment and some other issues. I feel fortunate that my two years were the years where the dynamics—nothing to do with me, certainly—were moving in place to actually work together in a fashion that could get some legislation done.[6]

To speak about those very briefly: '96 was a very interesting year. The background of that, let's recall, was '94, when the Republicans took both the House and the Senate, followed by '95, where the House leadership moved with a very aggressive legislative agenda [the Contract with America], which was fairly characterized as somewhat overreaching, leading to the government shutdowns of '95. That was the context in which we came into the '96 election year, one in which the Republicans had the legislative majority but had not used their first chance with that majority in a productive way.[7]

Then the seminal event was the government shutdown in late 1995.[8] Leading into '96, I think it's fair to characterize the Republican congressional majority as very interested in getting something done to show that they could govern, at a time when President Clinton was very interested in getting something done to show that he could govern—and have something to run on. He wanted to move himself more to the mainstream, which was embodied mostly in the Welfare Reform Act.

So we had a very interesting situation in an election year, where we had a

Republican majority in Congress interested in working with a Democratic president, both for their particular goals. An absolutely fascinating sidelight of that was the fact that the Republican presidential candidate, Bob Dole, had, for a period after he won the nomination, thought he could run his presidential campaign out of the United States Senate, which he quickly learned simply could not be done. Manipulated schedules and rather contrived votes that turned embarrassing, which could be put forward at a moment's notice [by the Democrats]—these led Dole to decide it was time for him to get out of the Senate, relinquish his leadership post, and go run for president.

What happened then, of course, was that Trent Lott came in as majority leader.[9] Because he was interested, for his own reasons, in showing that he could govern as a leader of the Senate Republicans, he was very interested in getting some legislation done as well. So you have this dynamic—in an election year, of all things—of a Democratic president interested in working with Republicans in Congress to position himself toward the mainstream in terms of legislation. You have the House Republicans—having stepped on it a little bit in '95 with the government shutdown—interested in doing something legislatively. And you have a new Senate Republican leader also pointed that way.

It's no surprise in that election year—again, entirely anomalous with respect to the other parts of the Clinton years—that you have all these forces coming together to produce the welfare reform bill, the Kennedy-Kassebaum Health Bill,[10] and some small business legislation. Small business does not tend to be a partisan issue anyway. You have the Senate side basically going along, saying, "We understand." The interesting partisan dimension is that the left-out people of '96 were the House Democrats, the party of the president. So it was a very interesting and anomalous year and led to a convolution of the normal party politics that you would expect at first blush.

Then again, just to finish on '97, it was almost serendipitous, because after the major Clinton victory, basically the House Republican leadership—I'll never forget it, Dick Armey and Newt Gingrich came in and said, "There's a time to fight and there's a time to do something together. We're going to bury the axes for this year and see if we can balance the budget."[11] They wanted to validate that. It had been a long-time theme of the Contract with America. Also, the deficit numbers, because of the economy, were improving so radically that it was possible to actually balance the budget without tax increases. That set forth the dynamic of an ability to work together on what I would call a bipartisan basis, where finally, when the bill was done, the Budget Act passed with an 80 percent vote in the Senate and a 75 percent majority in the House, including 75 percent of the Democrats. So that was, again, a very anomalous year, and the last one I can remember of true bipartisanship during the Clinton years. With that context, I'll stop, and Chuck [Brain] and Larry [Stein] can come back to help describe how things went after that.

McClure: I've taken the view, perhaps wrongfully, that individuals campaigning for the presidency or presidents running for reelection should be careful what they ask for, because they might get it. I remember Bush 41 going around the country saying, "Give me a Congress I can work with," meaning "Give me a Republican Congress."

The question is: Are you really sure that's what you want? There were some challenges, I *know*, that Frank [Moore] and the guys with President Carter faced when they came to town and had a Congress of the same political persuasion as they were. This was the same case that you guys faced with President Clinton.

We had to govern by veto in the Bush years, except for those issues where we did engage in some sort of bipartisan effort—on clean air, Americans with Disabilities, those kind of things—after getting the Nicaragua funding off the table, which had been a big issue during the Reagan days.[12] So when you could find areas where you could grasp the excitement level of the opposite party, even when you were dealing with a Congress that was different from the presidency, you could generate some accomplishments. But you were always going to be picked on by somebody. In other words, Republicans were always angry that you went too far with this—on clean air, for example, because you're getting too close to so-and-so on the other side. There's a lot of hand-holding that goes into that process.

I am of the view that probably some of the best years for governing, frankly, occurred during the first couple of years of the Reagan administration, when you had a Senate that was of one political party [Republican]—because it had changed for the first time in twenty-six years—and a House that was getting pretty close to being evenly divided.[13] There were about 190 congressional Republicans, during that time frame, of the 435. And then you had this crew of 60 or 70 or so conservative Democrats, most of them from the South and the Midwest. You could put together voting blocs and coalitions that would allow you to get across party lines. Ergo, Gramm-Rudman-Hollings and those things associated with the early budget activity back in the early '80s.

And even though the House leadership would be pushing in one direction, the president had an opportunity—because he had Republicans in the leadership on the Senate—to actually propose stuff that had a reasonable chance of getting down the road as opposed to something that was going to be immediately bottled up because it was anathema to the other party. Those combinations and dynamics, when you take out election years, either put you in the situation where you're veto governing, as we did for four years, or you have the opportunity to get something done. This is the window you talked about, John, or the window that President Reagan had early on in the 1980s.

Thurber: All of you have worked with the leadership in the House and the Senate in one way or another, and you've mentioned that the president's time is a very valuable thing. I'd like you to comment on how your presidents worked with the leadership. Larry was talking about how, in the [1997] budget agreement, Clinton and the leadership of both sides sat in the White House and went through the bill in some detail and came out with a budget deal that eventually passed. Did that happen very often on major bills with you? Could you share with us some experiences when the leaders from both sides were brought into the White House? How did you work that?

Stein: I should correct one thing. We never let Clinton too close to the actual negotiations. He was extremely well informed about it on his own, and from the reading he did, and we briefed him regularly. But I think it's important to know—and I suspect that this would be the case with most presidents—you don't want them negotiating directly. I would think that Clinton was representative. They'll give away the store.

Brain: I think, Jim, you're referring to a comment from me about the last budget agreement. We were talking about the president as a lame duck, and I asserted that it never really felt like being a lame duck. Having actually gone through impeachment, we thought, *Lame duck—what's that?* Dead duck, maybe. But again on your point, the final appropriations hadn't been passed. I think it was December—let's say 15th—and the bipartisan bicameral leadership from the Hill was down in the Oval Office, had been there two or three times, and finally wrapped it up. We left the negotiation and everyone then changed into their tuxes and we went to the White House Congressional Ball. So they were there, but I think that was really unusual.

Thurber: It's an anomaly.

Friedersdorf: President Ford had been a member of the Appropriations

Committee for twenty-five or thirty years.[14] And when he became president, whenever the budget issues were discussed, he was in the middle of it. I remember him giving briefings to members of the House and Senate, using a blackboard, on the details of the budget.

Riley: The president?

Friedersdorf: The president himself. He knew more about it than anybody at OMB, he knew more about it than anybody on the congressional relations staff, and he knew more about it than the committee chairmen, because he was an expert on it. That made it very easy for us because we had a president who was so involved. When the bill came up, he would personally lobby on it. If anybody disputed any of the items, he was able to debate or converse with them over the details. It was a hands-on situation with him. I never saw that in Nixon or Reagan, of course, unless there was some issue that they were just tremendously interested in. But it was marvelous to see Ford operate in that capacity.

Thurber: Frank, how did President Carter and you work with the leadership?

Moore: Oh, the same as everybody else. We had a Tuesday morning meeting with the leadership that was essentially useless. We would brief the speaker's staff on what they were going to say afterward, and what we were going to say, so it was all sort of scripted.

I should actually not say it was useless. It was useful for the president to reemphasize his priorities: "There are fifteen bills up there. I really want to get this one and this one. Get it out of the House. Senator Byrd or Mr. Leader, can you guys take it up pretty soon?" "Well, I'll check with my guys." You know. The biggest value in those things—I bet you I can see heads nodding around the table when I say this—is standing around drinking coffee before the meeting, the little side conversations after the meeting, the walk back to the Oval Office. "I'd like to have a word with you on the Colonnade." And riding back to the Hill, putting your guys in the cars with the leadership, sort of a debrief, either using the White House cars or their cars. "What'd you think? What do you think about what Jim Wright said?" and so forth. Then you could really figure it out. They were useful in that regard.

As far as negotiation, President Carter used to negotiate—with Stu [Eizenstat] and me and whoever was in OMB—over bills and stuff. On the energy bill, he did some negotiation with the Republicans, on gas, in the Cabinet Room, you know, and really got down to it, and it worked.[15] Another time—this is a funny story, it's not so serious—it's the Alaska lands issue. Jack Ferguson, who was Senator Stevens's AA [administrative assistant], called me and said, "We want one last meeting. Can you get us in?" I said, "We can get you in tomorrow." He said, "God, that's going to be tough." I said, "Why?" and he said, "We're in Alaska."

But they got back for it. They got in, and Senator Stevens came in and said, "All I want you to do is—One little creek that runs into this little river, we want you to leave that out of the Wilderness." President Carter got a map and put it down on the floor of the Oval Office, and got on his hands and knees. And Ted Stevens got on his hands and knees, and the president said, "No, you're wrong. It does not run into that. It's a different watershed, it comes in and divides and goes this way." Jack Ferguson told me they got in the car going back to the Hill, and Jack said to Ted Stevens, "It's no use. He knows more about it than we do. He knows more about Alaska than I do."

That's a funny example. Ask Jack about it next time you see him. The president did know an awful lot of details.[16] Of course, often a bill is right in policy, but it's not going to fly on the Hill. President Carter was always very good in saying, "Please explain to me Politics 101, and why it won't work." And if you said it just won't work, he'd take your word for it. You didn't have to explain up and down and back and forth. He never negotiated except in broad outlines.

Thurber: Will, what was your experience with President Reagan and the leaders in the House and the Senate?

Ball: I'm trying to think of a joint congressional leadership meeting that he might have enjoyed, and there's not one that occurs to me.

McClure: Somebody telling a good joke.

Ball: After the meeting was a good time to tell stories, and he and Alan Simpson would engage in repartee. But I think his Senate Republican leaders—Howard Baker, Bob Dole, and Bob Michel in the House[17]—found it far more important to come down to a leadership meeting, either a Republican leadership meeting or a joint meeting, and then use the words of the president and the emphasis of the president to go back to the conference and say, "Unity is important on this issue, because the president has said. . . ." There's just no substitute for the leadership going back to the Hill, fresh from meeting with the president, and emphasizing what the priorities are and what the issue of the day is. Staff can say it a hundred times, cabinet officers can say it a hundred times, but it's just not the same. Leaders know it's a lot tougher to tell a president, "No, I can't do this," than to tell one another or to tell one of us.

Riley: That leads into a related question about party discipline. You talked a little about your working relationship with the leadership, but I wonder if you could tell us a bit about what you attempted to do, if anything, to enforce some sense of discipline within the president's party on the Hill, whether it's a majority or a minority.[18]

Stein: That follows somewhat from some of the things I did want to get to. Discipline, in my years, was a word we didn't use.

McClure: That sets the standard way too high.

Stein: Way too high. But going back to the starting point of the discussion, it's useful to note that there's an inherent tension between presidents and the legislative side of their own party. It's a fundamental tension. It's obviously built into the Constitution, but it's deeper than that.[19] We hit on pettiness yesterday. It's a theme that I think is important, and we ought to return to it. There's a lot of ego that gets pushed the wrong way when the only people who get on the weekend shows, and the only people who are quoted [in the newspapers], are the cabinet secretaries and the White House chief of staff. And a lot of the [opposition party] congressional leadership actually, during times of divided government, get *more* noticed by the press because the press thinks it's necessary to have both sides presented.

So along with the inherent tension of a president who typically wants his way and a Congress who doesn't always see it that way, you have a kind of sub-tier [of tension] that deals with the basic human facts of politicians. That needs to be understood. Take the current circumstance. George W. Bush probably never did as well as he did in 2002—I think his public approval numbers were 65–67 percent.[20] I know that's for a lot of reasons—but he had the advantage of a divided government and Democrats to blame. He was very fortunate in that regard. I think you can see what happens to him this year. I noted this morning that he's down to 52 percent. His party's in power, and there's no one to blame but his party.

What John [Hilley] described is the other side of that. There are times when all the stars align—very frequently when you have divided government. We even have a word for it: It's called triangulation. It's thrown around now in both parties, but to me, it's a fact of life. The *Washington Post* didn't need to coin the word or put Dickie Morris on the front page, it's there.[21] It's a function of the institutions of our government. But when you talk about discipline within that context, you at least have an understanding of all the different forces that are involved. It's extremely difficult to marshal any kind of discipline.

I'd like to follow up the story John began [with the other bookend on Clinton's time]. After the successes of '96 and '97, we then got impeachment. We had the triangulation charges [among unhappy Democrats] out there. We had Democrats in the House, especially, but some in the Senate as well, who did *not* want accomplishments. Quite the reverse—they *didn't* want things to pass. [Congressional inactivity made the Republican majority look bad.] They felt that Clinton's fate was in their hands. They thought that they had protected him. There were also Republicans who didn't want things to pass because they wanted to bring Clinton down. So that explains the [presidential support score] numbers you began with early on—36 percent or whatever. I'm surprised we were that high.

Very frequently it's extraordinarily difficult to exercise real discipline. My guess is that Reagan could do it in his first few years. I don't know whether President Carter ever felt he was able to do it. Both when I was with the leadership staff in the Senate and when I was at the White House, I certainly never felt that President Clinton had the ability to exercise discipline. He had the ability to cajole, he had the various powers of the White House that he could use, but discipline was a bridge too far.

Friedersdorf: I worked for a number of administrations that were not bashful about employing discipline. I remember cases where we would have [Lee] Atwater or Ed Rollins call on a county chairman or the state chairman in a state where we had a congressman or a senator who wasn't voting the right way and remind them of their responsibility to support the Republican administration.[22]

I think they went across the line a few times, but if it was a situation where you really needed the votes, you could hammer members a little: the president wouldn't show up in that state next year for a fundraiser, or he wouldn't campaign in that state. And if it was an off year, that would make an impression on them, because the president would be limited in the number of states he would be able to get to. You could call the [congressional] campaign committee and threaten to cut off or reduce the amount of funds they might get for their campaign. You could talk to the leadership, Bob Michel or Bob Dole, and have them lean on them a little. I've heard stories about looking up IRS records. You know, that was hardball back there, especially in the Nixon administration. We were a little more gentle in the Ford and Reagan years, I believe.

We also had a political office. I don't know whether President Clinton or President Carter or President Bush now has a political office,[23] but they were very sensitive to the votes on the Hill, and if we had a real problem with a senator or congressman, they weren't reluctant to get in there and use some force.

Moore: I'll show you the other extreme, and it touches on a couple of points. One point is transition. When we came to town, the Democrats had, for all of the Nixon administration and all the Ford administration, [been in the opposition]. Carter was the first Democrat elected since [Lyndon] Johnson. They were accustomed—"they" being the Democrats, the Democratic leadership, rank and file—they were accustomed to getting up every morning and bashing the White House, saying the most horrible things they could. It's true. They'd do anything to get on *Meet the Press*. Les Aspin was cranking out those Sunday releases every night.[24] [They had to learn how to operate with a Democratic White House.]

I've forgotten what the numbers were in the House in 1977. It was overwhelming: 262 or 270, something like that—but I think every Democratic member, with the exception of four (and those were in Georgia) had run ahead of President Carter in the general election.[25] These guys (and women) are saying, "I'm more popular in my district than he is." So it's kind of difficult to impose discipline there. Plus you didn't have a traditional Democratic Party nominee who came up through the ranks. It was very difficult in that regard.

Stein: I think that's the important point. I can't think of a recent president—I guess except the first president Bush—who's a Washingtonian. These guys typically come as governors, and that's a part of the tension, too. There is a little bit of bitterness that follows it, because they've run as outsiders. That's an element of this as well.

Thurber: Fred, do you want to add to this too?

McClure: Congressional leadership meetings make excellent opportunities for press availabilities. They can sometimes come back to haunt you because of what the guys say when they go out under the White House portico once they've been in a congressional meeting. But we regularly tried to do either partisan or bipartisan congressional meetings. In many instances, they were an opportunity for the president to say something before the cameras—depending on what the issue of the day might be—surrounded by the leadership of the Congress. Hopefully, they would go out and say the right things when it was over. But I remember distinctly the [1990] budget deal that got finally negotiated with the expanded congressional leadership that included the Budget Committee, chair and ranking member, and Finance Committee.[26] We had some guys then who refused to go outside [in front of the cameras] when the meeting was over. There were some noticeable absences among the congressional leadership—noticeable absences by folks who were going to have to do some heavy lifting in the 1990 Budget Act. They went out the back door instead of out in the Rose Garden, which was scary. You take your chances.

I was beginning to think now of party discipline in the sense that Larry was thinking about it. Basically, we were powerless in our roles—and I really think the president may be powerless in his role—to exercise any party discipline. But when you get down to nitty-gritty votes, as Max [Friedersdorf] was describing it, using the political party apparatus to get where you needed to be was often done. I presume it's much used today with Karl [Rove] being advisor to the president, in the role he has now with President Bush.[27]

Thurber: I'd like to pursue that last point. The House is becoming as safe as the politburo in Havana these days. Only thirty-nine seats are competitive, thirty-nine seats people won by 55 percent or less. They get their money outside the party. The interest groups are very strong. It brings deadlock frequently, over the Patient's Bill of Rights, the bankruptcy bill, and a variety of other things. How do you maintain party discipline when you have so much individualism going on, especially in the House of Representatives? Is it a problem?[28]

Brain: I want to underscore Larry [Stein's] observations about the last several years, maybe even longer with the Clinton administration. I'm not sure the word *discipline* was ever used in a conversation. You know, *I'll go up there and make them do something.* It would be a convergence of interests, maybe, to get something done.

But to discipline, you have to have the ability to enforce and punish. Frank Moore, you refer to members who ran ahead of the president. They say, "What are you going to do to me back home? I was here before you. I'm going to be here after you." Okay. To get to your question of discipline: If *we* had ever gone to the political apparatus back in the state, we would have been killed. To a person, even our friends, they'd say, "What the hell are you doing? You don't do that."

Thurber: It seems that times have changed compared to when Max was in.

Brain: Maybe for the congressional Republicans right now, things haven't changed.

Stein: An anecdote, because I think it's useful. I think the three of us who worked for Clinton at least will remember this pretty graphically. In Clinton's first year, Richard Shelby, a Democrat, called [Al] Gore and said,

"Come on up and talk to me about the BTU [British thermal unit] tax," which Gore proceeded to do.[29] They talked, and when they came out, the assembled Alabama press was outside the door, and Shelby announced publicly his opposition to the BTU tax. Gore, justifiably angry, goes back to the White House and says, "We can't allow this." The only thing they could think to do was to shut down about seventy jobs. They went after the Huntsville Aerospace Center. Not only did Shelby subsequently change parties, he is now, I think, the most popular politician in the state of Alabama and is utterly unassailable. And you can trace his heroism to that moment.

So when you talk about party discipline, you should remember that incident, and so should virtually every president. If someone chooses to change parties, or to oppose a president, or to oppose party leadership, that's frequently an extraordinarily popular thing. It hasn't hurt Jim Jeffords.[30]

Friedersdorf: When we had people like Ed Rollins and Atwater doing the political office, we were at odds with them a lot of times, because it was self-defeating in congressional relations to have them do all of that stuff. I would remind them that we may not have Congressman So-and-so or Senator So-and-so on this vote, but there's always another vote. And if you alienate them on this vote, you alienate them maybe on the rest of the votes. President Ford, bless his heart, understood that. I recall one instance when Senator [Larry] Pressler, of South Dakota, voted against us on a very important bill, and it was crucial.[31] One of our congressional relations staffers, who was from South Dakota, did an interview with the biggest paper in South Dakota on what a turncoat and scumbag he was—a really bad interview about Senator Pressler. Well, I got a call from Senator Pressler.

Stein: Predictable.

Friedersdorf: And Senator Pressler read me the interview. It was quite over the top—

McClure: Bet that was an exciting conversation.

Friedersdorf: And he said, "I'm going to talk to President Ford about this." I said, "Larry, let me talk to him." I took the story in and explained to President Ford what was going on there. Pressler did go ahead and call him anyway. The end of the story is that President Ford called me and said, "Max, I want you to fire the congressional relations person who gave that interview." And I did have to fire him. That was how that ended up. Pressler was just totally off the wall.

Moore: The discipline worked the other way—back to the White House.

Riley: Max, were you serving when Phil Gramm switched parties?[32] Can you tell us, if you recall, about your relationship with him on budget matters back in 1981?

Friedersdorf: Well, Phil Gramm, of course, was a Democrat. When we started out with the first Reagan administration, the first year, the president said he was going to have only three legislative goals: the tax cut, the budget cut, and restoring the military. He worked on those three things, and everything else was put on the back burner. And as we started getting in to drafting the budget—Dave Stockman had the lead on it for OMB—Phil Gramm emerged as an ally. We were leery at first, because we didn't know where he was coming from. But he began to take up residence at the White House. He was down there constantly with Dave, and he—with some of his colleagues like Kent Hance and Charlie Stenholm—just became great allies and helped write the bill. We couldn't have done it without them. Those Boll Weevils were obviously instrumental in our ability to pass the tax cut and the budget cut that year.[33]

Thurber: You mentioned three agenda items at this point with Reagan. Yes, the president has an agenda. But also the leaders on the Hill have an agenda. How did you work that out when the leadership and the caucus had a slightly different agenda than the president?

Hilley: Just to come back first to how the president was involved with Congress: In our couple of years—which, as I say, were anomalous—there was a lot of communication constantly among the staff, of course, the day-to-day kind of thing, and actual relationships, particularly with the Senate leadership.

President Clinton's role was to be a sounding board. He never negotiated, as Larry said—although I have a funny story I'll tell in a moment about the one time we teed him up to negotiate. We'd get down the leadership to the White House, the bipartisan leadership a lot—more so, of course, the Democratic leadership, House and Senate. But the other thing that was central was to bring in the various affected parties: the chairmen, the extended budget groups, the Hispanic, the Black, the Asian caucus, the women. Clinton was constantly the sounding board, the listening person, the persuader. The meetings would be used for a lot of listening, as the congressional groups would vent their frustrations or their desires.

In my two years, President Clinton was instrumental as a sounding board and a general persuader. He would never engage in the specifics of the negotiation of the legislation, but just set out the broad themes, explain why he wanted to do what he wanted to do—a lot of good listening going on.

But Fred mentioned the photo ops afterwards. Typically, the meetings would be about half listening to the congressional side; the next quarter would be the administration putting forth its views; and the last quarter would be, "Okay, what are we going to do when we go outside? What are we going to say?" That was absolutely critical. "Does anyone want to go through the back door?" Clinton was instrumental in this, although he never participated directly in negotiations.

The one little story: It was August of '97, and we had finished the budget bill completely. It had been agreed to, we had the votes, and everything was going along. So—I think as a matter of whimsy more than anything else—we said, "Mr. President, why don't you call Senator Lott and congratulate him? And by the way, there's this one issue that's still a little bit unresolved, and we'd like you to see if you can get it out of him." He said, "Sure, I'll give that a try."

It's such a small issue I can't remember what it was. He had his talking points, and he gets there, does the whole script, "Congratulations, this is a great thing for America. And, by the way, there's this one little item I have to bring up." And he does, as he always did, brilliantly on his talking points. But then he's sitting there going, "Uh-hum, uh-hum, uh-hum," and he covers the receiver and says, "You know, he's got a lot of good points." We [jumped in at that point and] said, "Okay, Mr. President, we'll take it from here!"

Moore: I would like to revise and extend my remarks. President Carter did negotiate on the Panama Canal treaties—a lot, face-to-face time with members in the Oval Office, line by line. He'd kill me if he ever saw a tape of this and I said he didn't negotiate.[34]

Brain: The question Jim Thurber posed is about the president's agenda versus the leadership agenda. I'm not so sure that I can think of a leadership agenda. You've got their predispositions, their reactions. But really it's the president—through the budget, through policy—who's laying out "Here's what we want to do. We want to raise the minimum wage. We want a patient's bill of rights. We want bang, bang, bang." This gets to the nature of the relationship between the two branches. You've got Congress reacting to that, largely.

Thurber: So the caucus meetings and conference meetings are meetings to react to the president, rather than to establish the—

Multiple Voices: No.

McClure: Maybe the closest thing to a congressional agenda or leadership agenda in recent memory was the Contract with America. Otherwise, there are issues that each side hopes they're going to get to over the course of time, and it's again affected by circumstance: Okay, is this going to be a year for Medicare reform? Is this going to be a year for tort reform? Is this going to be a year for some other issue? But generally the president guides that, particularly in his own political party. They give him the leeway in that regard. I don't remember instances where they've been that much in conflict.

Friedersdorf: After President Carter was elected, I went up to the Senate Policy Committee as the staff director. Senator [John] Tower became the new chairman, and he instructed us to form a Senate domestic and foreign policy position paper on all the issues. We took into consideration the program that President Carter put forth.

Thurber: Of promises?

Friedersdorf: Of promises. We could be more comprehensive because we weren't the administration. We took the full spectrum from liberal, to the center, to the right wing, of our Republicans in the Senate, and put that together. And whenever a bill would come up, we would measure the position of the party on how they should vote—or how we recommended they should vote—as based on that policy. So we did have that agenda. And we had enough support for it from all spectrums of the Republican Party in the Senate to hold pretty much party discipline on how they would vote. Of course, there would be deviations, but we would measure that against the Carter program. It was an agenda. I don't think we ever formally presented it, but when there would be lobbying going on, we would present our side of the story, what we wanted.

Stein: Chuck [Brain] and Fred [McClure] have said different things, but I think they're both really right. Chuck's point is that it has always been, I think—certainly through the years I was there—very difficult for Congress, for the leadership, to have an agenda. You've got so many different personalities, so many different power nodes, etcetera. The truth is that what Gingrich did was seminal in that regard, and that's one of the reasons that everyone remembers it. Now, bad or good, I don't want to say, because I think it has gotten a lot more credit for the '94 elections than it really deserves. There were a lot of elections that year where elements of the Contract were used against Republican members, and pretty effectively. But the point was, "This is what you get if you get a Republican Congress. This is what we're for." It was a point of definition. And in that regard, it was extremely well received, and it became, I think, a standard against which subsequent leaderships tried to measure themselves. I know when working for Daschle afterwards, he always wanted one. [Richard] Gephardt always wanted one. And I think the Republican leaders feel the same way. But that said, the one phrase that's used over and over again [about the president] is, "You've got the bully pulpit." And that's the truth.[35]

Starting with the State of the Union and the budget at the beginning of every year, the president has the ability to set the agenda. He sets it before the American people. I can't remember how many—but it's forty million or something—who watch the state of the union. There's really no way that Congress as an institution can compete with that in defining a clear set of legislative objectives. That just doesn't happen. That doesn't mean that throughout the rest of the year they don't chafe against what he wants, because they do.

Moore: When you say the "party," you have to define the party. Senator [Hubert] Humphrey used to tell me there are four parties in the Senate: the liberal Republicans, the liberal Democrats, the southern Democrats, and so forth. And there are at least six in the House, including the Gypsy Moths and the Boll Weevils.[36] You can slice it and dice it any way you want to. You know, Jim Wright had an agenda on Nicaragua, separate from the administration's or from the Speaker's or anybody else's. Phil Burton always had an agenda on national parks that was separate from anybody else's.

I was moving, and I found a book in a box in my garage about three months ago. It's pretty crude by the standards you all did. I never told anybody on the Hill about this. In fact, this is the first time I've ever told anybody about it. We took all the votes from the last two Congresses [before Carter came to Washington] and analyzed them. Les Francis did it and put the data on a Navy computer in Philadelphia.[37] We didn't want it in the White House. We didn't want it to leak.

We broke out committee chairmen, subcommittee chairmen, freshmen, sophomores, people who had run five points ahead, westerners, southerners. We sliced them and diced them any way we could, and when we were going to have a vote, we would run it. It was a labor-saving device, because what we wanted to do was get the undecideds and work on them early. If you knew someone was going to vote this way or that way, don't waste your time on them.

We then refined it a little bit further. We'd say, "Well, that's about two years old." So we'd get someone to offer an amendment, essentially to get a test vote. We knew it wasn't going to pass. Get it on the floor, go talk to someone on the Rules Committee, and get a modified rule. Then we'd just take that vote count and look, and you'd see if you had twenty people to convince, or forty or whatever, for when you put up your real legislation. I know that's very crude compared to what you guys did. But I think we may have been the first ones to do it.

Thurber: That's very interesting. People in political science do this all the time, but Pat Griffin is on the record, not confidentially, saying the Clinton congressional affairs office never did that sort of thing.[38] I'd like to hear from all of you.

Moore: Jim Wright or Tip O'Neill would have gone through the roof. They'd say, "We count the votes, we know." Had they known we were sitting at the White House running a computer to see how their guys voted on an issue, they'd have just gone through the roof. That's why I've never said anything about it.

Brain: It changed over time. You had to have your own vote count.[39]

Moore: Oh, yes.

Brain: In our case, the whip was very good, and again, post-impeachment, the congressional Democrats and the president became much closer together, especially in the House. So we worked very closely. But you have to have your own vote count. Especially in the last couple of years when we pushed a number of issues—trade-related issues—where the leadership wasn't with us. That's really where you get to the importance of the liaison staff. And again, talk about good, old-fashioned lobbying: People from the White House go up, talk to members, "Where are you? What are you going to do?"

Moore: The leadership is lobbying against you in these cases.

Thurber: Did you have models like that, databases where you were analyzing various factions of votes in a computerized way?

Brain: I kept a couple, but they were largely specific to trade votes, because there had been enough trade votes [to identify a trend]. You could see who was going to go with you.

Thurber. You're generally saying no.

Stein: No, no. What we typically did was do them by thematic cluster. We'd go back a certain number of years. In the Senate, I had done most of the whip checks myself prior to my going down to the White House. And you [John Hilley] did them before me. I didn't [always] have to use a computer. I had memorized the Democrats who were trouble, had them emblazoned in my memory. So that wasn't a problem. In the House, I relied on Chuck [Brain], who was as good as any counter there was, and who also had enough institutional memory. You used to be able to remember the votes for most of these guys. We had available data, but we didn't use it that much.

McClure: When you've got, what, eight abortion votes during the course of one appropriations cycle, you kind of know where the members are.

Moore: This was new stuff we were proposing—civil service reform, consumer protection. We had two new departments; we did Energy and Education.[40] And there are no records on how people are going to vote on new departments, so you had to go back and get something similar.

McClure: We didn't do a computerized deal, but we analyzed where people had been previously on issues. And as Frank said, you make sure your guys are with you, where they are. Then you work on those who truly fall into the category of being undecided. Our view, at least when we were there, was that the only way we could get an accurate answer was for one of us on the legislative staff to talk directly to the members themselves, which is why we spent twelve to fifteen hours a day up on Capitol Hill as opposed to back in the office in the East Wing. I learned that from Max and Will and others.

Friedersdorf: We would take the leadership's whip check first, and we'd comb that, and then we would do our own whip check. If they came in and said he's *Yes* or *No* or *Undecided,* we insisted that they talk to the member himself and not to a staff person. You get a lot of chaff from the staff people. They're going to obfuscate or mislead.

Finally, after you get all the yeses and nos down, and you get the undecided, you finally get a list of "maybe" on any vote—I would say a minimum of ten or twenty and sometimes thirty who are truly undecided. That's when you really go to work on them. You save the final, *final* undecided for the president to call. And you don't give him a list until you're only twenty-four hours or forty-eight hours away from the vote. And when you give it to him, they can't be people you don't have good information on. You have to be exactly accurate.

McClure: That's when you get in the position to see that little newspaper article or that quote where such-and-such a senator says, "The White House has never talked to me on this issue." You can respond with, "No, no, no. We know exactly who it was, and this is who talked to you," because we actually forced the conversations.

Thurber: Will, what would you like to add to this?

Ball: I think it probably is a little easier today to spot patterns than it was when Frank was there and when Max was there in the first Reagan term, given the proliferation of votes today. You have a lot more votes and a lot more issues and a lot of the competitive voting on similar issues. Just the volume is so much greater. As Larry says, you know, after seeing this over and over again, where the alignments are, and you try to spot who you can peel off from an anticipated position. I think this is getting trickier to do. And the party realignments—especially the southern constituencies that would send conservative Democrats to Washington, which now almost completely send Republicans to Washington—alter the business quite a bit. Because we would always know there's going to be in the Senate five Republicans we're not going to have on a fiscal issue or a foreign policy issue, but we're going to get five to eight southern Democrats. And that arithmetic was the key to a lot of these votes, the pluses and minuses. But those trade-offs aren't there so much any more, and that makes the discipline issue a problem.

Friedersdorf: Then after the vote you find out, when you analyze it, who the liars are.

Ball: Occasionally.

Friedersdorf: We had one—

McClure: One!

Friedersdorf: Well, one who sticks in my mind. In the Ford administration we had a close vote, and Jack Marsh and I were working this guy, a Virginia Republican.[41] He had promised us on a stack of Bibles that he was going to be with us. So we put him down as *Yes,* and the son-of-a-gun voted against us. I said, "Let's go up and see him. I just can't have that." So we went in there, and he told us, "You know, the day of the vote, I got my [voting] card in the machine wrong. I made a mistake on the card. I was really going to vote with you, but I just couldn't get the card in right." And that's the worst excuse I've ever heard. [laughter]

Moore: He could have said his dog ate his card.

Friedersdorf: If he'd said, "I changed my mind," I wouldn't have minded it.

Moore: Max, I bet you knew this one from someone like Clifford Case.[42] We always counted on him to vote with us.

Hilley: But the Republicans couldn't do anything. He had labor support in New Jersey. What could they do to someone like that? Or John Chafee?[43] They're going to vote the way they want.

Young: You've been talking about dealing with the members directly and with the leadership. What about the congressional staff? Dealing with those people—for what? Was it good? Was it not? What was the experience? Over the years you've been there, there's been quite a growth in committee and personal staff, and of course we have some veterans here.

Hilley: Well, both bodies are run by committees when it comes down to it, so it's committee staff that is really where the interplay is. And, given the dominance of the money committees—the Ways and Means, obviously, and Senate and House Appropriations and Finance—that's where the communication happens beyond the leadership. Clearly, everything goes through the front door of the leadership, or you're just doing yourself a world of hurt. The relationships on the Senate side, during my tenure with Clinton, were particularly good. But it was critical to work with the committees of jurisdiction, because at the end of the day, these guys have to move the bill through committee. They've got to get it out of committee, they've got to bring it to the floor. That's your first test vote. That's where it all begins—communication with committee staff. Every week we would attend the leadership-sponsored staff directors' meetings. That was a Monday meeting, where you learned a lot. But also it's [their chance to say], "Here, why don't you take this problem?"

Stein: I hated that.

Hilley: That was really critical—communication at the staff director's level.

McClure: And the leadership staff.

Hilley: It starts with leadership, right.

Stein: I think that when you're constructing legislative strategy, you definitely have to work with the staff. The staff directors—those people write the bills. But when you're dealing votes, you have to talk to a member. If you're trying to figure out where a guy or a woman's going to be, you've got to talk to the member, because you very frequently get misdirected by the staff.

Brain: If you had only four spots on your speed dial on the phone, it should be the four leadership aides: the chiefs of staff to the House and Senate D and R.[44] You have to work with other people, and we did an awful lot of briefings, and even the House and Senate deputies would go to other meetings with legislative directors. We did an awful lot of that. But the four key calls you're going to make—those are the four.

Thurber: What about working with interest groups? NAFTA [North American Free Trade Agreement] had a coalition-building effort by Anne Wexler.[45] She was doing it for the president, paid by others. Did you go to heads of interest groups or to interest groups to put pressure on people on the Hill to get your agenda through?

McClure: Big stuff like that went fast-track from NAFTA during my tenure, and there was a huge outside effort. Most of it was conducted by folks in public liaison in conjunction—

Thurber: But not by you?

McClure: No. There were times when we participated in their efforts. For example, "Fred, you need to come talk to these guys because they need to know what you can tell them, the dynamics." Almost a pep rally. We, on the other hand, on the legislative side, got the benefits of their head counts. That fed into our decision making process and was a double check on whether we were moving in the right direction.

Friedersdorf: In the first year of the Reagan administration, when the president announced his program for budget reduction and tax cuts, the business community—led by the Chamber of Commerce, I believe—asked us to come over and inaugurate the first meeting and speak to them. Public liaison carried the ball after that. But they wanted to be in some congressional relations meetings because they didn't want to feel they were on the fringes or the edges. So we included some of their top lobbyists in our deliberations and our meetings. I would say they were very instrumental in passing some of those programs. That was an unusual circumstance. On each of the bills, if there's a group out there who can help you, you're naturally going to gravitate toward them, or they're going to gravitate toward you. So we made as much use of the interest groups as we could.

Thurber: Frank, what about the situation with the National Education Association and Mr. Carter? It is reported that all of the NEA members at the 1976 convention voted for him and that he pushed the creation of the Department of Education with their help. So they were up front working on this. Like the Energy Bill this time [with President Bush 43], people got together before it went to the Hill.[46] I mean, that's what's reported. Is that common? And did you work with that?

Moore: I did a lot of delegate selection [in 1976] in sixteen or seventeen states, and I chose people who had helped us in the primaries. Oftentimes it was the communication workers, because they could work the phones, and teachers, because they could talk on the phones or use their shoe leather [for door-to-door campaigning]. I think we did have a disproportionate number of NEA delegates at the convention, but we also had a lot of communication workers and UAW [United Auto Workers] workers. UAW was very helpful to us in Iowa and Florida and in North Carolina against George Wallace. I don't know if we made any promises to create a Department of Education.[47]

Thurber: That was what was reported generally.

Moore: It may be true, I don't know. I'm not aware of it.

Thurber: The issue here is not the promise, but did you work with them, this interest group?

Moore: Yes, we worked with them, and we worked with others. We worked with some of the international unions and their members on the so-called Chrysler bail-out.[48] It was a loan guarantee. We went into every district where they had a Monroe shock absorber plant and had sixty workers there. We worked it backwards through the numbers. A lot of those were in the South, where people weren't necessarily going to vote for the plan.

The one that impressed me, though—I later worked as a private business lobbyist on NAFTA because my chairman wanted me to. And after I saw what the Business Roundtable and the Chamber did, and the money they were spending and the phones and the polling, it scared me to death. I said, "My gosh. That is a powerful, powerful force." I mean, who did we have? The chairman of Motorola, the chairman of Caterpillar, Amoco—you're talking about the five biggest businesses in Illinois—calling a member and saying, "We want your vote." That's powerful. It's powerful stuff.

Brain: It's a legal line, I think. I don't know when it became implemented, but all administrations follow it, and people in legislative affairs are aware. You can't lobby someone to go lobby the Congress. Public liaison will hold a meeting, and you can come in and talk about the status and how it's looking. But you won't find someone sitting there and saying, "We have a problem with Congressman Smith. You guys go up and get us Smith." The information's available, but that line is observed very diligently.

Neustadt: My impression is that when Anne Wexler took over public liaison in the Carter administration, that was changed. I'd just like to get the story on that.

Hilley: That was changed to where we could lobby people to lobby people, you mean?

Neustadt: It was made much more of a pointed, targeted operation.

Hilley: That's true.

Neustadt: And you lobby to go after the member.

Thurber: That she did grass roots, or top roots, the leaders of these groups, to then go after the members.

Neustadt: Yes, it wasn't veiled at all. Now, for reasons I've never understood, no other administration seems to have followed that Wexler formula.

Stein: No one has needed it as badly.

Brain: I think public liaison as a whole different branch of the White House operation can vary in that. And even the heads of public liaison that I saw, some of them are almost "captives of the interests," you know, the teachers or whomever. Okay, how many White House tours can those get? So public liaison comes to you as an advocate for them. And again, some of the trade votes are where a lot of these coalitions come together. In the last couple of years of the Clinton administration, public liaison was very effective in reaching out, getting those folks, and bringing them to meetings and mobilizing them. Maybe not to the extent that Anne did—she's probably unique. But I think all too frequently public liaison is a captive of the groups.

Thurber: I may want to challenge you a bit and follow up on this. You have all talked about having an influence on where the president goes. The president goes above the heads of Congress sometimes—as George W. Bush did on his first tax cut in Montana and Louisiana—to put pressure on those members through those visits. How involved have you been in structuring where the president goes to put pressure on members who seem to be wavering on an issue?

Ball: I think that's a relatively new phenomenon. I recall in the '86 election that the president's political schedule included a lot of stops in states where there were competitive races. But I don't recall any trips that were based on giving talks, making points in a constituency [about pending legislation]. But that was before the day of the television campaigns that the groups are running now. It's no longer just special interest groups organizing mail or postcards or shutting down congressional switchboards. Now, television stations in Washington are just a regular on-going feature of advocacy advertising from this or that group. So it's changed. The communications environment is quite different.

McClure: We'd sometimes use the president's travel to give him an opportunity to collar somebody in Congress who might have been wavering on an issue. Or we weren't quite sure where they were going to be, so we'd put them on the airplane with the president to give them a chance to talk to him directly. My office participated in regularly scheduled meetings that took place within the White House apparatus for the purpose of deciding where the president was going to go. And ultimately that bubbled back up to the senior staff and ultimately the decisions made by the chief of staff.[49]

I distinctly remember a meeting about a Caribbean Basin Initiative, which was going on in the middle of tax reform in 1986, and the Finance Committee had to stop and deal with CBI for some reason. The senator then from California, [S. I.] Hayakawa, we couldn't figure out where he was on the vote. Normally he sort of followed along whatever Senator [Lloyd]

Bentsen did, and we knew we had something that was a tie. We finally learned that the senator wanted to ride on *Air Force One* and had never had a chance to do that. So we popped him on with President Reagan, they rode to California, and the guy came back and voted right. I don't even know what they talked about on that trip out. But we occasionally used it in that fashion, as opposed to popping in and talking in your territory.[50]

Thurber: Let's move, after Frank, to the end of the table for some questions.

Moore: One quick one. I don't think you can ever do discipline, but you can build up real goodwill. I'm sure everyone around the table ran a midterm election operation. We ran it out of our shop. We used all the surrogates, used all the cabinet, First Family, vice president, so forth. We did the scheduling for the airplanes. I think we did maybe two hundred trips in the midterm: "We don't want the trip for us, Mr. or Mrs. Member. We want it for you. We want to reelect you."

You build up some goodwill there, and it also gives you a chance to talk. We always had a member of my staff going around. It gives you a chance to talk to people. The vice president [Mondale] was a good fund-raiser, and the First Lady [Rosalyn Carter] was a good fund-raiser. The president—we used him for Senate races, but not many House races.

Young: You had the town meetings, so called, when Carter would go around the country. This wasn't ostensibly for public liaison, but there were a lot of issues you would discuss or focus on in those meetings. Did you have something to do with the use of that?

Moore: Well, I had something to do with the fact that we had the first one in Yazoo, Mississippi. It wasn't a coincidence that it was [G. V.] Sonny Montgomery's hometown.[51] But you get the members to ride with you and include them, and frequently the members were impressed by sitting and watching the president taking questions like a talk show host and bouncing them around and talking knowledgeably about issues. That benefited you some. But the thing I'm talking about, Jim, is separate from running a midterm election campaign. At other times, "We're available. We've got people available to go with you, make a speech with you, announce a grant, do whatever."

Wayne: I have two questions. When you become involved in voting, did you get involved in the committee voting to send the bill out, or did you wait until it got to the floor?

McClure: Sometimes.

Stein: Frequently had to, especially if it was tight and important.

Brain: More likely your deputies and the specialists who'd been assigned to a committee would be working that committee. They'd be there. They'd be going to the mark-ups, and only on relatively rare occasions, close votes, big issues where—

McClure: Close votes or nominations, CIA director or Supreme Court nominations.

Friedersdorf: It's always easier to change a bill in committee, to start out right, than waiting to try to change it on the floor, which is pretty hopeless. We would have people in committee meetings, subcommittee meetings, mark-up. It was just routine to do that.

Patashnik: Following up on that question: To what degree were you focused on procedural votes? Sometimes the procedural votes are so critical to structuring the way a bill is going to be considered, but explaining to the public why this rule is really critical is obviously difficult. So how do you handle the tension between using the "bully pulpit" and the resources of the presidency versus trying to influence an arcane matter about the structure of legislation?

Friedersdorf: The Rules Committee was critical to us in the House, because if you don't get the right kind of rule, you can't get the right kind of vote. So we were very deeply involved in the drafting of the rule and trying to lobby for the right kind of rule, so that when it came to the floor, the issue would be presented in a way that we wanted it to be presented. If you just let the Rules Committee go their own way, you might get a rule that you couldn't change or you couldn't defeat or you couldn't deal with on the floor.

Thurber: Max, the LBJ tapes are wonderful to listen to. He was recorded calling the chair, Judge [Howard] Smith, and saying, "Now I realize that So-and-so-and-so are doing this and that."[52] Did your presidents, all of you, get down to that level inside the Rules Committee?

Friedersdorf: Well, Trent Lott got his start as staff director for the House Rules Committee. He was a born politician even when he was a very young man. I can't remember any of the presidents I worked for calling him. Of course, they'd call Judge Smith, but Trent was critical in knowing where the members of the Rules Committee were on both sides of the aisle. We always tried to work through Trent and the Republicans on the committee.

Thurber: Steve, you had a second question?

Wayne: Yes, I wanted to know the extent to which your lobbying extended to scheduling the bills. Did you defer to the leadership on that?

Or did you try to influence when they brought things up and how they moved it along?

Ball: Well, timing is frequently critical. I think most of us were very engaged in the timing and scheduling of major issues, because in the ebb and flow of events, so many other things would affect the outcomes of those votes. Sometimes more time would be needed to give emphasis to the president's position, give an opportunity for a few more public statements and appearances. Sometimes you instinctively knew time was on the side of the opposition, and a quicker vote was in order.

McClure: "Let's get this over with."

Moore: That gets back to Eric Patashnik's question, too, because if you didn't have a rule, that bill wasn't going to the floor. But at least when I was there, you contacted the chairman of the Rules Committee at your own peril, because it's a leadership committee, the speaker put him on there, it's his people. We did contact him, but it oftentimes would be when the speaker says, "I can't do any more with him, you call him. He won't do it for me." It happened to be [Claude] Pepper from Florida, I believe, who was Chairman. [Richard Bolling] first, and then Claude Pepper.[53]

McClure: We did engage in another aspect of the rules process. I'll make this comment first of all about the Senate, since I'm a creature of the Senate: The Senate has no rules, so it doesn't make any difference. This was a different sort of a scheduling issue. When we had to veto a number of bills during the Bush administration, the guys and gals always asked us, "Make sure you give us the clearest signal you can of what you're going to do before we get ready to walk the plank. Don't cut the limb off from under us." So we did a lot of work with the leadership in terms of letting the House do the veto sustaining this time, letting the Senate do it next. If you look back over, you'll notice it went back and forth so the same guys didn't have to walk the plank. That was a part of our effort in terms of trying to coordinate that with the leadership staff. There was a little bit of a scheduling issue there.

Hilley: I want to emphasize that to work through the leadership is the critical thing. And since it's the prerogative of the leader to handle the scheduling, it was always through the leadership office that we would do that. I agree that in the House, the Rules Committee really, through the leader, sets the agenda, and so one would have to defer to that committee. But in the Senate, where there's either changing rules, no rules, or a lot of rules, depending on the day, the leadership staff on both sides is really amazingly adept at exploiting all the procedural aspects of either slowing something down or speeding something up.[54] We would defer to these people who were just unbelievably good at that, to help us structure the timing or create impediments to various pieces of legislation. You turn to the procedural experts on the floor who know how to drive it.

Brain: If we really want to get to the procedural minutiae for the historical record here, you can even get to the point of negotiating when a bill is going to be sent to the president, or when a veto message is going to come down. You say, "He's going out of town. You'd better get it down here tomorrow, or else he's going to be in Africa. We're not going to send a messenger on a plane to Africa to get this signed."

Stein: Oh, but we've done that.

Brain: We've done it, yes.

Stein: Didn't we send Lisa Kountoupes to Asia to sign a continuing resolution, or the government would have shut down?[55] I think she got lost in Europe, too, if I remember correctly. [laughter]

Brain: But "Don't send us a veto message, don't send us a veto bill right now, give us a little bit of time." You get into that really deep stuff.

Moore: The one time the president can control something to do with legislation is *when* he vetoes a bill.

Gilmour: As a bill is working its way through Congress, the White House will often issue veto threats, saying, "If the bill is presented to the president in its current form we will recommend it be vetoed," or "If a certain amendment is adopted, we will recommend that it be vetoed." I'm wondering how much ambiguity there is about a president's position when a veto threat is issued and whether it's possible to use ambiguity or uncertainty about the president's position to move Congress?[56]

Stein: This is a wonderful subject of arcane science, this really is.[57] We would struggle over the degree of veto threat, whether it was at agency level or senior advisor. I can't remember how many gradations we had, but at least four.

Moore: "Would recommend" and "would strongly recommend," absolutely.

Stein: Oh yes, the wording of that one sentence in the SAP [statement of administration policy]. But, I must say, when I was still on the Hill myself, I would scan the SAPs, and if there was a veto threat in there, I'd weigh in my own mind about whether he'd do it. I never paid that much attention to the language of it, but in the White House we would go through enormous intellectual gyrations in trying to figure out what the right phrasing was. I've never been sure myself how closely they look at it on the Hill. But for the most part, I always treated it as crap when I was up there [working for Congress].

McClure: On the receiving end.

Brain: But you do have the hierarchy, and I think all administrations probably use the same rules. To say in a SAP, "The president *will* veto this bill"—at *that* point, our rule was that he has had to have made some public statement beforehand.

McClure: That's the least frequently used terminology.

Moore: You need to be very careful when you use that, because once you've done it, you've given about twenty-five or thirty people a free vote, maybe more. Maybe given forty people a free vote.

Brain: When I worked the House for President Clinton, Dave Bonior took me aside and said—again, this is impeachment or post impeachment, so we're all together.[58] He tells me, "When you say the 'veto' word, we're going to go out and bust our ass to make sure you've got the 145–150 votes. So don't throw that around frivolously, because we take that seriously, and we'll do everything we can." And I think in eight years the Clinton administration lost one vetoed bill.[59] Now, there's an interim process, too. If you're not going to get the votes, then maybe you don't want to veto.

Thurber: And there's also the statement of administration policy, the SAPs. Larry mentioned it, you mentioned it. There are degrees of threat in SAPs. It's not just vetoes, it's also "We want $150 million for this particular program." Were you all involved in writing SAPs?

Stein: Certainly in deciding on the degree of a veto threat, yes. Usually OMB wrote the substance, and then sometimes they would come to us, at least when I was there. We would alter them occasionally, depending on our assessment.[60]

Thurber: Max, before Carter there weren't statements of administration policy, but what did you use? There wasn't that term, SAPs?

Friedersdorf: I think President Ford is a good example. He vetoed sixty-six bills, and we sustained fifty-four of them. I can't ever recall one veto threat that he made that he didn't follow through on. I think the reason was that he came from the Hill, and he was of the old school of Mike Mansfield and Sam Rayburn and Carl Albert, that you did not make veto threats idly.[61] If you sent a veto signal up there, it was going to be vetoed. There was no hanky-panky about degree of veto, and he appreciated that. He was very careful about making a veto threat. Even if it was only $10 million over the budget, and he said he would veto it, and they cut it to

$5 million, he still would veto it. He was not going to be accused by the leadership of crying wolf on vetoes.

McClure: I went second-degree beyond the president himself, saying, "It was *senior advisors* who recommend veto." With this, you always gave yourself a little out, in case the president decided he didn't like what the senior advisor said. It went down by gradation. You might have a couple of cabinet secretaries who would recommend veto, or even a department.

Stein: On the Hill, if you didn't see presidential veto, you know if you got one of those lower ones, you knew those were negotiable.

McClure: Negotiable. That's exactly what it was.

Gilmour: There's a question in political science about the degree of uncertainty over the president's position. I've been puzzled in looking at statements of administration policy and the different grades of veto threats. Now, what Max said about Ford's approach made a lot of sense in that it's sort of either/or: "Yes, we're going to veto it," or "We're not." But the grades of veto threats puzzle me a little bit, because it would seem that a lower-grade threat, such as the cabinet secretary threat, conveys a yellow light to Congress, while a presidential veto threat is a clear red light. Why would you ever want to give a yellow light on a veto threat? It's almost inviting Congress to ignore it.

Hilley: Well, the requests for these often come from our congressional side up on the Hill, wanting some more ammunition to fight a bill out in committee. As Fred and Larry said, anything below the presidential threat is a sign we want to negotiate. So you go back in and say, "Hey, look, if you fix X, Y, and Z. . . ." It's most useful as just a detailed indication—again, OMB does most of the work—of what we'd like to see changed, *like to* at that level of the yellow light, as you say.

But often the various threats are requested from Congress as a way to fix things in committee, which is the first test, but then also on the floor. The other thing you sometimes run into is certain senators saying, "C'mon, we need a veto threat. Oh, c'mon, the president has to stand up on this one." And we're saying, "Okay, well, let's see the votes. Where are we on this?"

Stein: "You're going to work your colleagues to make sure we get the vote."

Hilley: So sometimes you're invited and induced to do this, but since it's the president's name and reputation on the line, we tend to be cautious about this.

Stein: There's one other dimension that I was just talking to Stephen [Wayne] about during the break. On several occasions you're pressured by your own cabinet, who may have a particular interest. There's one example that I was just alluding to. It's a complex one. Pete Domenici and Secretary [William] Richardson were in a New Mexico–based fight over the energy labs in New Mexico.[62] You'll remember this one, Chuck.

Secretary Richardson insisted over and over again that we do a presidential veto on a defense authorization bill, a relatively important defense authorization bill. If I remember, we were at war with Kosovo at the time. He wanted a presidential veto because he did not want Domenici running the New Mexico labs—largely for political reasons, I think, but there were others. Domenici was probably well overreaching whatever congressional power should be exercised over a cabinet department. That was an immense fight, and we ultimately talked Richardson out of it. We refused to do a presidential veto. I think we were right. We would never have been able to sustain it.

Brain: To give you another example: An appropriations bill, not one of the major ones, with a ranking friend in the Senate, a particular environmental issue, and he was not able to keep a rider out of the bill. He came to us and said, "I need you to save me and veto this bill." The bill was otherwise fine, perfectly acceptable. The issue, even from our perspective, was that it could go either way. The senator wanted it, so we said, "The president *will* veto." And everybody on the Hill looked and said, "We understand, yes, that's got to go." He won. We used the nuclear bomb for this member in this instance.

But I think the ambiguity the political scientists are seeing about the threat frequently reflects the ambiguity surrounding the bills. They're very seldom black or white. I just used an example there where it was clear where we were going: some particular riders—Mexico City, abortion, some emotional things.[63] The issue I was referring to yesterday, bankruptcy reform, was ambiguous. We were literally sitting around in the chief of staff's office, "What will we do? Is it a good bill or is it a bad bill? There are pluses and minuses." We closed the administration not knowing what we would do if that bill came to us. There was not any particular indecision—so I think what you see—red lights, or yellow lights inviting negotiation—reflects people sitting around the table saying, "Hmm, what will we do?"

Moore: You try to gather information whether it's a good bill or a bad bill, and oftentimes you'll get different information. You might have OMB do an analysis or Treasury do an analysis, and one of them says it's a good bill, and the other one says it's a bad bill. Right?

Ball: Exactly.

EDITOR'S COMMENTARY

Probably the most unexpected—and most unconventional—turn in this symposium's discussions occurs in this session, on partisanship.

There is no more firmly established rule within the literature on presidential-congressional relations than that party affiliation shapes support for the president. "Year in and year out," writes George C. Edwards III, "members of the president's party provide him with considerably more support than do members of the opposition party." What might seem to the casual observer to be the product of adroit presidential manipulation of the levers of power is, then, more properly understood as a natural consequence of larger structural forces, especially partisan affinity. The effects of partisanship usually swamp anything less consequential, including the transactional talents of the White House. Indeed, some scholars have called into question whether anything so vague and etherial as "presidential skill" can withstand close inspection. Edwards has concluded that "[There] appears to be no relationship between the [congressional] support obtained by presidents and their legislative skills." Rather, the ability to lead Congress is shaped by the president's "strategic position." "Often outcomes that are popularly attributed to presidential leadership . . . are actually the products of other, more powerful forces structuring the environment of executive-legislative relations"—including partisan strength on the Hill.[64]

This being so, we would naturally expect those responsible for selling the president's programs to emphasize the virtues of single-party control of the government. But something very different happens in this session.

These CLs directly refute the notion that unified party control of the government makes it easier for the president to work with Congress. Instead, five of the seven former aides attending the symposium (with Republicans Friedersdorf and Ball remaining silent) make the case here for the nearly heretical notion that the White House might be able to work more effectively with the opposition party in control of Congress. Is it possible to square these evidently competing views—or are we left solely with the option of deciding whether the scholars or the practitioners don't know what they're talking about?

The crucial element for making sense of this apparent schism is perspective. Scholars usually focus on macropolitics, while the CL is a practitioner of micropolitics. Therein originates the differing conclusions about partisanship.

Our scholarship on congressional behavior is generally derived from large quantities of data about such things as roll-call floor votes, which, when examined with the appropriate quantitative tools, yield patterns of behavior often unrecognizable to the naked eye. The trends political scientists detect about the value of single-party control of Congress emerge from just such studies, which are intended to wring idiosyncracies out of individual data points. That scholarship clearly demonstrates that presidents benefit from having their partisans in control of both houses of Congress. Under such conditions, presidents tend to experience greater levels of success in winning congressional support for their proposals.

Yet the view "on the ground"—the view offered in this symposium by the president's chief lobbyists—evidently looks very different. I will suggest here two reasons for this contending viewpoint.

The first, I think, has to do with how the CLs heard the question posed to them: "Is it easier to work with unified party government or divided party government?" In a literal sense that is a different question than: Do presidents do better when party control of the national institutions is unified or divided? "Is it easier?" could be interpreted—and, I think, is here—as a question about economy of effort. And it is clear from these discussions that even though members of a president's party, on balance, can be counted on to support more often the president's program, some wooing of fellow partisans still must be done to seal the deal. The CLs were not asked, as they might have been, "Would you have traded in *x* members of the opposition party to improve your own party's standing by that same number in Congress?" I suspect the reply to that question would have been, unanimously, "Of course!" (Although Fred McClure's assertion that presidents seeking more of their partisans in Congress should "be careful what they ask for" seems to refute even this assertion.)[65]

Scholar George Edwards does concede that "all presidents experience [some] slippage in party cohesion in Congress," and thus one of the core duties confronting every president, as the head of the party in government, is to secure the votes of his own partisans—who may be inclined to adhere to their constituency's interests when those diverge from the president's preferences.[66] So although it remains true that partisan ties are a powerful force in American politics, votes from within a president's own party cannot be taken for granted. Indeed, much of the discussion within this symposium testifies to the pains CLs must take to win *by persuasion* votes that would *by right* be the president's in a strong-party system. Moreover, the tone of these discussions indicates that the business of securing the votes of people who ought, because of shared party label, to back the president anyway can be an especially irksome chore. This reality suggests a variation on Harry Truman's complaint that he spent much of his time trying to convince people to do things they should have the sense to do on their own.

A second, corollary, reason these CLs may have emphasized the virtues of divided government is related to the question of *expectations.* When a single party acquires organizing control of the White House plus both sides of Capitol Hill, popular and scholarly expectations rise dramatically: Unified control means action. If action doesn't happen, there is widespread disappointment. Those on the ground know, however, that legislative productivity is not guaranteed by nominal party control—and indeed that inflated expectations can create headaches for them and for the president. In some ways, then, it is easier for the CL to work within an environment of divided control, wherein a higher level of failure is expected and accepted. Unified control means unified blame when things do not go well. The day-to-day pressure on the congressional liaison operation, then, is greatly reduced when the opposition party can be implicated in failure—within a constitutional system where failure is more nearly the norm than success. Divided control means that blame can be distributed. That opens up opportunities for the president to benefit politically from failure in a way that is virtually impossible when his own party controls the Hill, too.

This dynamic of blame avoidance, then, helps to explain why these very partisan members of the president's staff might find advantages for the president in sharing control of Capitol Hill with the opposition party—notwithstanding what our best studies say about the advantages presidents enjoy when their own party also controls the House and Senate.[67]

4

BICAMERALISM

Working with the House and the Senate

The main topics discussed in this session include the different political cultures in the House and Senate and how those influence the White House's approach to the Hill; the role of the vice president in congressional relations, and more generally, the involvement of the vice president in the policy making process in the White House; the politics of conference committees; summit negotiations; the use of outside interest groups to support the president's program; and structuring the congressional liaison office. This session was moderated by Russell Riley of the University of Virginia.

Riley: Let's move to the question of bicameralism. I'm a product of this government department here at the University of Virginia, and I feel that I got a very good education in Washington politics while I was here. But my true education about the politics of Capitol Hill came as I was leaving this department and began dating a woman—now my wife—who was working at that time on the House side. One of the lessons that I learned when I first moved to Washington after we got married was that there really is a very deep divide between the House side and the Senate side of Capitol Hill.

McClure: Oh no, no!

Riley: Fred's objecting to this. [laughter] There's a sense of a social as well as a professional distance and—at least to a very close observer from the outside—there are two very different worlds on Capitol Hill.[1] So the subject for discussion now is, how does a president deal with these two very different universes at the opposite end of Pennsylvania Avenue? To help me out with this question, I've asked to lead off here Larry Stein, who is a creature of the upper chamber, and Max—

Stein: I like that "upper chamber."

McClure: That's a very good way to do it! You're going in the wrong direction. [laughter]

Ball: You're going in the wrong direction. Stop the tape!

Riley:—and Max Friedersdorf, whose experience is in the United States House.

Stein: But Max has some Senate experience, too.

It's a little daunting, and I'm just going to try and provide a point of access to what I think is a vast area, because you're right: It's literally two different cultures. The rules are the beginning point, and I think a rather rude observation was made that the Senate has none.[2] I think, as John pointed out, you could also say that the Senate has too many.

The Senate is chaos, and the House is absolute order. That's the simplest way to start to think about it. To me, at least at this point, it's more useful to get below the abstract level of the differing rule structures and to look at them a little bit politically. My own experience was—and I'll postulate this for people to ridicule—I used to ignore anywhere from 70 to 90 percent of the things the House did, largely because most of them were on suspension.[3] We had divided government. Most of what passed was stuff that Gingrich was doing for symbolism. He never even expected it to be taken up in the Senate, and in most instances it was not.

And taking that little premise, I'd like to make an observation about what is going on now in the House. It struck me as a paradox. It's curious, because every two-year election cycle there are a very small number of House districts that are contended, up for grabs—and getting less, I think. Chuck, is that your sense?

Brain: Yes.

Stein: And those few districts are almost exclusively swing districts where it's neither urban nor rural. They are districts that require pretty subtle politics, where you're going to be a moderate, and you're going to try to position yourself in the center, and you're going to try to get votes from both sides.

And yet, even though that's the big enchilada in determining who's going to have power, if you look at the way the House has gone recently, it's been extraordinarily to the extremes. That is, each side's rhetoric and its message are aimed at the base, particularly in the Democratic Party.[4]

It was always astonishing when I was in the White House—I always felt that the Democrats were pushing drastically towards their base vote, the very liberal vote. And what really was needed, if they were going to take back the House—which was supposed to be their Holy Grail—was some set of political constructions that would enable their moderates to win swing districts.

I'm not sure I'm getting into it the right way, but that's something that has befuddled me. I have not been able to figure out why that's the case. But I think it has rendered a lot of the House votes moot. Again, Chuck, correct me if I'm wrong, but we used to ignore a lot of them.

Brain: To take it a little further, as we talked about yesterday, we had to ignore a lot of what Congress was doing. But we had to pay attention to the issues that really mattered to the president's agenda, both advancing the agenda or stopping things he opposed. So you're really looking at maybe 10 percent of the volume of things coming through.

Friedersdorf: I was very fortunate. I had ten years when I first came to Washington as an administrative assistant in the House. And when I look back and think about those years, it was like the Senate did not exist. We were totally oblivious to what was going on in the Senate. It was like two worlds. Then I did have experience as a staff director of a committee in the Senate, and I started thinking the House didn't exist, and that the only thing in the world was the Senate. But you have to get back to basics when you start setting up a liaison staff. Obviously, when you set up a staff on the Senate side, you want people who have worked on the Senate side, and on the House you want people who have worked on the House side. And that's what we did.

But from the perspective of the presidents themselves: Nixon had been a member of both the House and Senate, so he was not biased in either direction. He had good friends on the House side and good friends on the Senate side, and he cultivated both bodies. When Ford came in, it was totally House. He was buddy-buddy, first-name basis with 435 members of the House. In fact, many of them still referred to him as "good old Jerry," and it was just like he was still a member of the House. We needed strength on the Senate side, and that was not his forte. We tried to beef up the Senate side with strong people.

When President Reagan came to town, he, of course, had not served in either body, House or Senate, and the first thing he wanted to do was meet the leadership. He was very anxious to become familiar with the House and Senate, and I think the first formal event we had, after he went to the

Hill and met the leadership, was a private dinner in the residence with the Speaker and Mrs. [Mildred] O'Neill. He started a good relationship with the speaker at that time.

He was more willing, actually, than I could have imagined, to meet with congressmen and senators, and willing to make phone calls. And he became—at least during the time I was there, in the first term and then early in the second term—quite familiar with most of the key congressmen and senators, and got to know them on a first-name basis. But there's no question, you've got to deal with each of those senators almost like there's a fiefdom up there. Each one of them has a little country they're running. Their staffs are huge, their committees are loaded with people, and you're dealing with an awful lot of people. Whereas on the House side, when I first went to work there, we had four people. I know it's increased quite a bit since then. We had an AA [administrative assistant], LA [legislative assistant], the receptionist and a secretary, and I think now they probably have five times that many. There's no question they're both different bodies, and you can't treat them the same. You've got to work with the differences.

Riley: Is it possible to say whether the House or the Senate is intrinsically more difficult to lobby, from the White House perspective? Is there something about the nature of the bodies that makes one of them more difficult?

Hilley: I grew up in the Senate, but I found the House members more knowledgeable about the specific subject matter because they were not stretched nearly so thin. You could talk to a House member much more about the substance of a bill. They were more tuned in to the substance of the bill than a Senate member tended to be.[5] The Senate member had to—except in some rare exceptions or exceptional Senators—rely on their staff and their committee to take them through substantive issues.

The second point is echoing what Larry said. The implication of this is—again, this can be discounted, because I did come from the Senate—the Senate has become a much more important place to lobby, by the nature of events of the last decade. That is, we have this split party and no one has a supermajority. So when you walk into the Senate needing sixty votes on bills that can be filibustered, that has a moderating influence. All sorts of stuff comes out of the House, depending on which party's in control, which is off the wings of each party and more at the extremes. So the moderating of extremes and getting a bill ready to be signed—the real working of the bill—can best be done in the Senate. And the members there tend to be less polarized, also, because they have to appeal to a wider constituency in their states. So I think that the more important body, these days, to be lobbied is the Senate. Because as a bill comes over from the House, a leadership-passed bill—that's the opportunity to moderate a little bit on either side.

The final point, as we said yesterday: Where the House really has its impact is through the leadership and the centralization of authority there. As the growth of these omnibus bills has come along, because of the Budget Act, bills tend to be litigated and negotiated at the leadership level. So the real impact of the House comes back at the end, where the leadership steps in and says, with the Senate leadership in the White House, "How can we get a bill that will pass?"

Friedersdorf: One problem with the Senate is that about half of them are always running for president.

Hilley: And the other half think they ought to be president.

McClure: They should be *acclaimed* so.

Ball: I've heard this story, I'm sure Frank has. Senator [Richard] Russell, when freshman senators called on him, would make it clear that senators—unlike members of the "other body"—enjoyed six-year terms. Senators were expected to be statesmen for two years. Occasionally, in their second two years, they could once in a while demagogue an issue a little bit. And then in the last two years, senators would understand they had to run for reelection.[6]

Jim [Thurber] mentioned earlier the "perpetual campaign." So Senator Russell's formula may indicate a dimension of the Senate that is changing and that change makes it sometimes more difficult for a White House to gain the support of senators with conflicting constituencies in that first two years, or the second four years, of a six-year term. But there are going to be some senators who are a lot less loyal to an incumbent president of their party, or more in opposition to a president of the other party, when they are not facing the voters immediately. I think that makes, in some ways, the Senate more challenging in terms of herding those who are on the edges of either party into an important position.

McClure: In the analysis of some of the votes—particularly some of the closer votes in the Senate—where you see a party's folks not toeing the line where the president wants them to be, [the White House has said] "Okay, you can walk on this one" because we were able to make up that vote somewhere else, based on the whip count that we shared. So sometimes a voting record, on its surface, may not reflect the texture of what was going on. "You've got a pass on this one because you've got an issue and you're up for reelection."

Brain: Frequently, not only are you living in your own world, but the only time you're really going to the other body is in conference. Nobody has put it into the record yet, but the old line is that "the Democrats and the Republicans aren't the problem, the problem is the Senate." I'd go off to a conference [from the House side] and cross that point, the midpoint in the Capitol—

Stein: The demarcation line.

Brain:—yes, and say, "Feel it, the air's getting thinner." But looking at it from the perspective of the administration, you can use that chasm, because you're the only one who's talking to everyone. It gives you second and third bites out of the apple. You're looking for people who share your views. "Well, if you haven't won here, maybe you can win there," by bolstering your allies, even in conference. You go back to a few House members—maybe you didn't win in the House, you won in the Senate.

Stein: That's a really good point.

Brain: You're taking care of your House friends. You're trying not to manipulate the process, but you've got your tentacles all over. And if you do it right, you use that lack of communication [between the two bodies to your advantage].

Stein: When you ask "Is one chamber harder than the other to work?" I think the most useful way to think of it is holistically and in terms of a specific case. What Chuck is saying is true: Since the two are separate and you're down at the White House, you have a huge advantage. You know what's going on and you can play them off against each other. Take the way [George W.] Bush probably has to do it right now, and has been doing it. He'll start with the House, where he gets passage for his most extreme desires, and he starts with that as a premise.

Then he tries to figure out how much he can get in the Senate. So it's really not a question of easier or harder. It's a question of understanding where both of them are at any given point, using one against the other, as Chuck's saying, or in combination. I do think the hardest part of it, though, is the political differences between the two. To me, the House is so strident right now, so partisan, so difficult. That's an element that makes the mechanics much more difficult to decide.

Neustadt: Since the leadership has no formal place to meet, except with the president, is this an advantage for the people you represent? And if so, how do you use it?

Brain: I think it *is* an advantage, more in terms of indicating what the agenda is, indicating the priorities, even getting them in the room, saying, "Well, this seems to be okay with them. Do you think you can bring your guys along?" You do use it. When the leadership is running well—and it hasn't always been functional—they *are* meeting together. It hasn't always worked well. I think Denny Hastert, [Nancy] Pelosi, and Gephardt spend a lot more time together than Gingrich and Gephardt ever did.[7]

Young: In my earlier interviews I interviewed some people in the House and Senate. I interviewed Senator Dirksen and spent a while with him, the Republican leader in the House. We were discussing the utility, or the advantage, of the congressional relations staff. Dirksen maintained that it was of good use to him. He said, "They used to set up camp right here, outside of my office. One of the advantages to me was they knew what was going on on the other side," implying that this was a way, for intelligence purposes, to find out what was going on in the other house. I got the same confirmation from some of the leaders on the House side. My question was, "What good are they to you?" And this was among the things that they mentioned.

Stein: It used to work the other way for me when I was in the Senate, because I used to call Chuck Brain [by then at the White House] to find out what was going on in the House. Really, we had no way of knowing, and frequently if we tried to find out, the House guys wouldn't tell us.

Brain: To get back to Professor Neustadt's observation that the leadership has no place to meet: Congressional relations generally has no place on the Hill, either. We camped out outside of Leader Gephardt's office. And at one point, before I was there, it was particularly tough. Supposedly a staffer ripped out all the phones in this little hallway and said we couldn't be there anymore. Other than using the vice president's office—you can use their facilities—there's no place you can go.

McClure: We used the whip's office.

Brain: Yes, I know, but it's all ad hoc. If your relations aren't good, it's "Use the pay phone."

Friedersdorf: During a vote in the Ford administration we were trying to sustain all the vetoes. We used to station ourselves in a lobby between the floor and the men's restroom. You would send in a message that you wanted to see Congressman So-and-so, and of course he would ignore it. But when the debate was long, eventually he would come out to use the restroom, and we would catch him in that little lobby.

One day we sustained a veto by about two votes on a real crucial one—I think it was emergency medical services.[8] We were celebrating out there in the lobby just a minute or two after the vote, and Tip O'Neill came flying through the doors and out there. He didn't grab me, but he went right up against my chest, and he said, "Friedersdorf, if I ever see you in this lobby again, I'll ban you from the Capitol! You will not be in this lobby again." And they banned congressional relations from coming into that lobby for the rest of the time. I don't know if you can go in there now, but he wouldn't let us in there then. So we'd just stand out in the hallway after that and try to catch them.

McClure: On the steps. You get further and further away! [laughter]

Riley: The vice president's position has come up here, and actually was the subject of some conversation over dinner last night. This seems to be an appropriate spot to raise that. Talk a little about the vice president's role in the entire congressional relations operation. I would expect that it would be highlighted on the Senate side. But are there instances where it takes place on the other side?

McClure. We had Vice President [Dan] Quayle in our shop.[9] Vice President Quayle, particularly in the Senate, but also in the House, was a nice link back to the conservative block of the Republican Party in the Congress. I often used him to ferret out what was going on so that we'd know what we were going to be up against as we tried to get enough votes to do something. Quayle was also very useful in terms of the House, some of it stemming primarily from his days as a senator and having been a member of the body and having dealt with the House on issues. We used him an awful lot in our lobbying process. Of course, when Bush was vice president we did the same thing.

Ball: The vice president goes—I think to this day—to the Senate policy lunch the Republicans have, so they're on the Hill at least once a week. It was certainly useful for then Vice President Bush to engage senators at the policy lunch and other informal meetings. I had regular contact with him in terms of issues. During 1987 he had to break a number of tie votes, and, unfortunately, I think two consecutive back-to-back votes that he had to break the tie on were on biological-chemical warfare research.

I remember the morning of a cabinet meeting where we had a DoD [Department of Defense] bill on the floor, and he had just had to go to the Hill to break two successive votes two weeks before that. He had received a phone call from his mother, because she had read in the papers that he had twice broken a tie enabling the research on chemical-biological weapons to proceed. I think this was the Pryor amendment, when David Pryor was trying to curtail research.[10] So it was a complicated issue.

In the middle of the cabinet meeting the steward came in and handed the vice president a note. It was the worst possible news: The Senate was stuck in a 50/50 tie on yet another effort to address funding for this kind of weapons research. He stood up to get the quick car up to the Hill and turned to President Reagan and said, "Mr. President, while I'm up at the Senate, would you mind calling my mother?" He did his job and was glad to do it. He did spend a great deal of time up there, and although he has served in the House and not in the Senate, he engaged his role as president of the Senate very vigorously.

Riley: I'd be interested in your observations about his sense of the House of Representatives. Did he spend much time working on the House side? Had his experience been in such a different era that it really didn't apply so much to—?

Ball: No, he had maintained close relationships with a number of key members. He and Dan Rostenkowski had a close personal relationship—also Sonny Montgomery.[11] I don't think he spent as much time physically on the House side, owing to his Senate duties, but he had ongoing and continuous informal contact with them. This was the second term of the Reagan administration, and he was clearly seeking the nomination and intending to run for the presidency. So he was maintaining those contacts and was an active part of the administration.

Brain: I think he spent a fairly good amount of time over in the House. We could always tell, when the Secret Service was standing outside the House gym, that Vice President Bush was up in the gym working out, and it happened fairly regularly.

Will was talking about breaking tie votes in the Senate. I think logistically it's just pure mechanics. That's one of the toughest things—to know when it's going to be a tight vote and to coordinate where the vice president's going to be and when you need to get him back. It may be one thing if he's at a meeting or in his office. If he's up at the [vice president's] residence, and it's ten o'clock at night, or on the other hand, if he's traveling—do you stop the travel? There's a series of judgment calls that on a personal level are tough to make.

Moore: Vice President [Walter] Mondale was our vice president. He'd been in the Senate for twelve years. He left in the middle, but he was on the Finance Committee, I think, for eleven years.[12] So he had a lot of close ties, but it was with the liberal wing of the party in the Senate. We used him a lot. I think he only had to break one tie vote, and then he had a lot of people mad at him, a lot of his buddies.

Informally, at luncheons in the vice president's office in the Old Executive Office Building—not the one off the Senate floor—or just in a private room, everybody would let their hair down and gripe, and he'd bring the message back. What was particularly helpful was what he called the "Bureau of Naval Affairs," which was the Senate steam room. When he told his secretary he was going to the Bureau of Naval Affairs on an important mission, he was going to the Senate steam room. He knew that Lawton Chiles was always in there, Senator [Charles] Percy from Illinois was always in there at a certain time—four o'clock in the afternoon when there was going to be a vote that night.[13] Predictably, about four senators you just knew would be there. I guess if you go to certain bars, you know somebody is going to be sitting on a certain stool. He would go up and feel them out and talk informally, and of course give us the feedback. It was very helpful. On the House side, he'd go and have lunch with the Minnesota delegation, which by definition is liberal. Then they started expanding that into a sort of ad hoc liberal caucus. It was very helpful to gather information.

Riley: Gore?

Stein: I think there are probably multiple books on Gore's vice presidency as it relates to his colleagues in both the House and Senate, because it's an incredibly complex thing. Going back, both to his extended service in the Senate and his earlier service in the House, he had friends and he had enemies—maybe more the latter than the former, in all honesty. Compounding all that was the fact that—especially during Clinton's second term—Gore was obviously the heir apparent, making him, for Republicans, an absolute target. Anything he was *for* became something they were *against*.

But, in truth, there was resentment inside the Democratic Party as well, among those who thought they should be the heir apparent—which, as we were saying, is always with us. So using Vice President Gore for advancing an agenda was a complex matter, very complex. And also, trying to defend an agenda that he had gone to great lengths to try to lay out as his own, and that the Republicans knew about pretty well—that became part of our job, because it was understood that we in the White House wanted him to be able to succeed. There were a lot of different incidents. The one that strikes me is one we actually won. Chuck was referring to how difficult it is to locate the vice president sometimes. Do you remember the gun show vote? This was right after Columbine, very contentious, very tough—as all gun issues are—but this one particularly after Columbine.[14]

If I remember right, it was either a birthday or an important anniversary, and Gore was having dinner with his wife somewhere. We didn't know where. I was virtually certain the vote was 50/50. And it was—which was an enormous error on Trent Lott's part, an absolutely huge error, because Gore got right in, cast the tie-breaking vote on a gun issue at a time of [public outrage]. They should have thrown that vote, but they didn't. So, a good one for us.

Brain: On Gore, I sensed a changing role internally in the last two-thirds [of my tenure]. The last year, when I was deputy, I think I ran into Gore in the West Wing twice, in his office. If you had people in for lunch, you would always know that you could take them up to the vice president's office and show them the office because he was not going to be there. The stories I hear from friends who were there earlier on was that he was involved in every major policy discussion—and so he was there working. So that's a role that changed over time.

In doing my job in House relations, I remember I was afraid, coming into the '98 election, that afterward we would have two Democratic candidates for president, Al Gore and Dick Gephardt, and my job as house deputy was going to be hell, trying to walk that line. The day after the election, when it turned out the Democrats had picked up seats and we were within four [of a majority], it was clear to me that Dick Gephardt was going to see if he had a better chance of becoming speaker than president. So he would stay where he was, and the next two years were fine, because—as Larry was alluding to—we were all behind Gore.

Hilley: One thing that sticks in my mind is that in my two years Gore was very much involved in all the policy deliberations. He sat in on everything. His staff was involved and really a part of the strategy team from A to Z. Often he would disagree with some of the ways we were moving—particularly in '96 on some of the moves to the center. But I'll tell you, afterward he would stand up and salute every time, completely loyal. We never batted an eye about where he stood when we'd go out of the room. And he'd go out and perform, completely loyal.

On Larry's point: At the end of the cycle, when the appropriations bills, the all-nighters, were going on, you could bet your britches—there's always Mexico City, the last issue. But before we got to the last issue, there were all of Al Gore's projects, his environmental stuff. As Larry said, the Republicans, seeing him as the heir apparent, would kill those programs. And we'd have to stand there and stare each other down until we put them aside. And it got pretty visceral, too. It got pretty ugly. He could inflame the other side. One of his great uses was to send him up there and just throw gasoline around the place.

Stein: He was good at it.

Hilley: He was very good at it. But the main thing from my period was his complete loyalty to the president and performing as asked.

Stein: Which he carried through impeachment in a way that probably hurt him. But he carried it through, and that's something people don't remember well.

Riley: Will, did you have a similar experience with Vice President Bush, given the fact that he was being viewed as the heir apparent? Was there a politically charged situation for him in the years you worked with him?

Ball: I don't think it was so politically charged for him, but it was not always easy in the sense that the Senate majority leader was also seeking the nomination. You can just think about the tension that was inevitable there. This was in '87 as the '88 primaries were drawing near. The president had been very clear in instructing the staff not to engage in political developments. Howard Baker was then the chief of staff, Senator Dole was the leader, and so he would set certain issues.

This was the time when negotiations with the Soviets were at a pretty critical point. There was a vote on the INF [Intermediate-Range Nuclear Forces] Treaty that we were attempting to get scheduled. The Iowa caucuses were looming on the horizon, and Senator Dole had not yet declared whether he would vote for or against the INF Treaty. At the time, there was some debate ongoing about that particular treaty and what Soviet intentions would be. Remember, this is 1987. As it turned out, he called a press conference and announced his support for the treaty. That was not an event the vice president thought was a good one to conduct at the White House. At any rate, the treaty was ratified. [Mikhail] Gorbachev came to Washington, and it was signed in the East Room.[15]

But all through that year was a difficult time, with the president's agenda being subjected to a lot of forces and this political contest. It was some time before Vice President Bush secured the nomination. So it was not quite the same in that environment as it was in the Clinton term.

Thurber: I'd like to follow up on the vice president's involvement in policy deliberation in the Carter administration. From the outside, it looked like Vice President Mondale was more involved than any other previous vice president in terms of working with the president and working certain policy areas. Would you comment on that?

Moore: We *said* that was true. I don't know if it *was* true, but we did move him out of the OEOB and into the West Wing. We negotiated this stuff at the convention—three of us and three of Mondale's staff—what his role would be. We did this not before he was named, but afterwards, the day after: Dick Moe, Mike Berman, and Jim Johnson [for Mondale]; and Jody [Powell] and Hamilton [Jordan], and me.[16] The vice president wanted to see all the papers that came across the president's desk, not to be excluded from any of those. I have to say that Mondale had very strong feelings about it because of Hubert Humphrey's experience with President Johnson. He'd heard all this stuff from Senator Humphrey: "Don't take the job unless. . . ."

They had a weekly lunch, private; nobody knew what they talked about. Vice President Mondale never said anything, President Carter never said anything. He was totally loyal. You have to remember that one of President Carter's objectives was to balance the budget, and we got within $4 billion of it. The last budget was within $50 billion, and that was with a huge increase in defense. I don't think Mondale was elected from Minnesota—or thought he was—to come to Washington to balance the budget. But he was loyal in doing that, very loyal. And then he had Bert Carp, a deputy in domestic policy, and Eliot Cutler, one of his guys over in OMB, and so he had them kind of salted around.[17] He was involved in all policy, sat in on all the meetings. He didn't have to come, but he was invited to come, and he came to most of them. If he couldn't be there I don't think anybody came in his place. Toward the end, Dick Moe or someone would sit in on some of his stuff. But he was involved in everything.

Brain: He did have one of the great lines, back in '76, regarding office space—on being in the West Wing. He said, "If you're not in the West Wing, you might as well be in Baltimore." And it's true.

McClure: The vice president has more offices than anybody else in town, when you add his Senate offices to those at the White House.

Neustadt: This raises the question I was going to ask before. Mondale told me once, while he was vice president, that Humphrey had told him—and it was based not only on Humphrey's experience but what he'd understood from President Johnson about his vice presidential experience. There was a rule you always had to follow: "Never, ever be seen by a third party differing with the president, unless it had been arranged in advance." I believe that was a rule that the elder George Bush followed also. But you're saying that for at least six years Gore did not have to. What changed?

Hilley: He didn't have to follow the president's lead?

Neustadt: No, obviously from what was said here, he felt himself free to differ with the president when a third party could see.

Stein: Oh I see, an internal—

Hilley: Okay, third parties, meaning even inside the White House?

Stein:—meaning inside deliberations.

Neustadt: Oh yes, absolutely.

Hilley: I think it was, appropriately, a very inclusive group that was involved in policy, and obviously he was, too. We all considered ourselves part of the same team, and that was part of it. He would have his views, as would the treasury secretary and the OMB director and all of us. Then at the end of the day the president would decide, and we'd go out there and salute.

Stein: But Gore never diverged publicly.

Neustadt: No, I understand that. But that was not what Mondale was talking about. Mondale was saying you didn't—

Stein: Even in policy deliberations inside in the Oval Office?

Neustadt: Yes, yes—

Stein: Hmm.

Neustadt: Mondale said anything he wanted to at their private lunch because nobody else was present.

Moore: Maybe on big things, but he sure would join in and say, "That's the craziest thing I ever heard of, you guys talking about doing that. Here's what's going to happen to you if you say that." But then if we did it, he'd say, "Okay."

Brain: I think it gets to the involvement of the vice president in policy discussions. If you're called in, saying, "Here's what we've decided to do," well, the vice president then salutes and goes out. But to the extent that Gore, at least, was involved in the discussions—why be in the policy discussion if you can't have a view? I think it's part of the changing role of the vice president that internally you've got your view just like he does, and I do, and you will.

Neustadt: Okay, it changed somewhere along in this process that you all know about, and you're saying it changed earlier—that the late Mondale felt free to differ.

Moore: I remember early discussions where he would express his opinion. But if it didn't carry—like mine didn't, usually—we'd all salute and say, "This is the president's position." He might have disagreed privately or sitting around in the Roosevelt Room,[18] but he never told anybody that outside the White House.

Riley: Do you think that was true also on the Hill? Are there instances where they had such close connections on the Hill that behind closed doors they might go on and say—?

Moore: We would have heard. We would have known.

Stein: You would have known in six hours.

McClure: In six minutes.

Hilley: You'd have known in six minutes.

Riley: Well, I guess I got the definitive answer to that question. Let me go back to the question of conference. Is there any kind of internal delicacy on the Hill about being involved in a conference? Were the members of the conference committees particularly protective of their role, or was there a sense that that was an appropriate place for the White House to bring its presence to bear?

Moore: We were invited to a lot of them. Starting off, I wasn't invited to sit at the table. I was in a chair back here, but as the session got going and if you made any sense, they'd say, "Scoot over, come on in here." But oftentimes you were being used by one side or the other, and you knew it. Everybody in the room knew it.

Brain: I think it really varies—even the White House attitude towards the conference. Do you want to be in the room?

McClure: Please don't drag me in!

Brain: I can remember where we were going to have a bill, it had the right title, it was going to do some percentage of things we wanted, but it wasn't going to be 100 percent. We had a guy who was in there fighting for as much as he could. But when he came out and said, "We've got the bill, here's as much as I could get," we would all say, "Fine, that's great." But had I been in there—or somebody else for us—we would have been party to that direct compromise, and we would have gotten killed. So it's ad hoc.[19]

McClure: We ran into that.

Moore: I'll tell you who always wanted someone from the White House in conference: Rostenkowski's predecessor, [Al] Ullman, from Oregon. He always wanted as many people in there with him as he could get when he was going up against Russell Long.[20] He really did. Sometimes we didn't want to go, but he'd say, "Come on, what's your position?" You'd have a Treasury guy standing outside the door handling papers.

McClure: We were disadvantaged in some measure during the Andrews [Air Force Base] excursion that Chuck's boss [Rostenkowski] and others were participating in. We were glad to participate, to know what was going on, but I think we were disadvantaged in terms of the dynamics of that situation.

Riley: Strategically, then, there were reasons for you to want to avoid being in that place.

Ball: But it's changing. I think this energy bill pending now is a good example. Increasingly, just to get a bill done, the House will send something over. The White House will wink at it just to move the process along—as was the case with the tax bill.[21] Then the Senate will do whatever it takes to get its version, and the real work is done in conference. It's quite different. Ten, twenty years ago it was not the same kind of process.

Stein: I think in a lot of cases, conference is the crucial place.

Ball: Right.

Stein: I think you may not want to be there for a lot of reasons, but you pretty much have to be there sometimes. You get beat up. You get beat up a lot by both sides. But either it can be a very high priority for the president, or you can have a veto threat out, as we were discussing before, and your credibility's on the line, and you've got to get the bill at least to a point where you can put a signature on it and not be too embarrassed. In some cases you're almost better off losing some of the ancillary issues when you're going to lose the big one, because then you have four reasons to veto rather than one. There have been numerous occasions when I've just rolled over on a couple of them.

Brain: I remember Larry getting yelled at in a very small room with stone walls in the Capitol. Senator [John] McCain ripped him up one side and down the other.[22] I just sat there and said, "Thank God he's got the top job."

Stein: That was Y2K and Y2K liability.[23] That's true. We just sat there and said, "We're going to veto it. We said we would veto it." We didn't veto it. This was when one of those late-night calls to the president screwed the thing up.

Brain: Larry referred to the House sending extreme bills over with the Senate doing its thing and then we're in conference. The issue for this President [Bush 43]—but all of them face it—is, "Okay, do we want a bill, and can I sell the compromises necessary to get a bill to my base? Or do we want an issue? Will they take my leadership when I say, 'Energy: We're not going to get ANWR [Arctic National Wildlife Refuge].[24] Guys, we're going to live another day, we're going to get an energy bill, and that's important.'"

Does the base salute and say, "Sorry, Mr. President, that's nice, but we want ANWR"? That's a critical judgment that the White House has to make in conference, a test of leadership—can they bring folks along?

Hilley: Conference is enormously important. It's one of the last stops.

But I think the thing that all of us appreciate, having been in the legislature, is that you never lose sight of the fact that it's the Congress that legislates. At the end of the day, you've only got so many bullets, so many vetoes, so many times when you can annoy a chairman by telling him what you'd like him to do and not do. It reemphasizes the point about getting started early in the process, depending on your chairman, depending on the leadership. Because at the end of the day, when all is said and done—and we've all been on that side—that really is 90 percent of the lifting. You have to put it off on the chairman and the leadership to help you out and get it done. If you try to do it all yourself, there's just no way. So that's a part of getting in the process early. And you pray you have a good leader you can work with, who's loyal to the president, who'll do a ton of that lifting for you. And you need a good committee chairman as well.

Riley: My assumption is that on procedural questions of the two bodies you steer completely clear of that. Maybe I'm wrong. But let me throw that out as a hypothesis.

McClure: In what sense?

Riley: In the sense of staying out of leadership elections, votes on internal rules, or things of that nature. Is that a false assumption on my part?

McClure: Up until recently. [laughter] Up until recently we stayed out of leadership fights. We didn't get involved in the Jim Wright deal.

Riley: My question is, are there other areas that the president's involvement, or your involvement, is taboo? Are there places where clearly the general signals from the Hill are "Butt out. This is our business and not yours"?

Brain: They want it to be taboo on the question of pay raises, in legislative provisions providing pay raises. But frequently that's an area where you can exercise some influence.

Friedersdorf: You don't want to talk to them about committee assignments or chairman assignments or rotation and that type of thing.

Moore: Or two chairmen fighting over something, jurisdiction.

Friedersdorf: You'd better stay out of that.

Thurber: I'd like to follow up with Fred, just a quick one on the summit out at Andrews Air Force Base in 1990, the Budget Enforcement Act, and ask about the involvement of legislative affairs out there compared to Darman.[25] The picture was that—

McClure: Darman was leading it.

Thurber: Yes, it might have gone a little bit further than people wanted him to go on the tax.

McClure: It depends on whether you're talking about round one or round two.

Thurber: Round two.

McClure: Round two probably, most assuredly, was when we finally go to the point of "Read my lips. No new taxes" and tried to artfully define it as "revenue enhancement" as opposed to a tax increase, which is what it was.

Stein: A Sununu phrase?

McClure: No, I think that was a Darman phrase. I don't know where it came from. Darman was leading that effort in both rounds of those negotiations with the very strong involvement of Sununu. In the first round, we got child care tax credits and all sorts of other things that were wrapped up in the package. That was the one that we lost on the House floor when Gingrich and his colleagues decided to not toe the line.

Then we came back with round two, thinking we were disadvantaged from a negotiation standpoint because it was pretty clear that those on the other side could say, "Look, you can't bring your own people to the table on this deal." So it gave them an advantage from a negotiating standpoint, and we ended up giving up more than we wanted to. We couldn't hold our folks. The numbers were what they were, and we ended up having a different package. Now when you look back in retrospect, you get the other piece of it, because that's when we started doing the floors and the ceilings and all those other things that added some discipline to the budget process at a point when all we had hanging out there was Gramm-Rudman-Hollings–related types of things.

In fact, if I remember correctly, you guys [nodding to Hilley and Stein], when President Clinton first became president, actually ended up using our floor/ceiling thing on something that was right out of the box—something to do with Veterans' Affairs, or something to that effect. So in hindsight it had some usefulness, and you can make the argument that it had usefulness in terms of the economy beginning to turn around at the end of 1992. It just didn't happen soon enough from a political standpoint.

Gilmour: [Dan] Rostenkowski is well known for not liking summit negotiations because he preferred bringing out his bill and then negotiating from there. Does that mean that the White House is advantaged in summit negotiations? I think a lot of you were involved in one of them or more. I'm just curious what your feeling is about the bargaining power of the White House in summit negotiations as opposed to the normal legislative sequence.

Stein: It depends on the negotiations. I think in '90 the president was disadvantaged from the start, very significantly. That was a huge—the '90 bill was in magnitude a massive thing. But I actually agree with Fred [McClure]: On balance, there was a lot of good policy in that. But no good deed goes unpunished.

At the end of every appropriations year, it's been demonstrated overwhelmingly that the president has the cards. At least that's been my experience. I did two or three of them. I don't know what the others think. We always felt that we were in a much stronger position than the Republican leadership to get our priorities, and I think the record will show that we proved that true.

Brain: From a constitutional perspective—and as I would frequently remind people in the White House when I was on the Hill—the constitution gives the president one role in the legislative process: deciding whether to affix his name to it. Of course, that's a vast overstatement. You've heard stories here, "Send it to us, we'll veto it." But once you let the White House in the room, they've got something—power. Whether or not it's a good negotiation, if you're in the room, you're a player. And, in fact, you've turned it into a three-party negotiation—House, Senate, and White House—when it's meant to be a two-party.

Hilley: One thing I will never forget. Newt figured out very early that we had all the cards at the end of the day on these big bills. We had the power to say, "Okay, guys, do you want to be here in December, or do you want to go out and run for reelection?"

Stein: Exactly. That's true.

Hilley: Newt came over and said, "Okay, what's the price for getting the ticket punched? What do I have to do?" And we'd say, "Okay, here's the list." He understood that these appropriations matter, but also that we'll all be back next year. It wasn't live or die. And he'd rather have the card punched and get his guys out campaigning than sit there and fight with us.

Stein: He got punished for that. His understanding of that was entirely right, but his right wing just never accepted it.

Ball: President Reagan did not, either. The omnibus appropriation bill was something he had great distaste for, and he invested a lot of time and energy in advocating what the governor of California had—the line item veto.[26] It was frequently cited in his Saturday radio address and frequently in his speeches. But he liked the regular order in the budget and the regular order of thirteen separate appropriations bills and the right to review each on its so-called merits. It was objectionable to him to have this huge bill.

I remember the state of the union address in '87. Up came the draft text, and it was passed around for review, and it was just a flat statement: "I have asked the Congress not to send me a continuing resolution or omnibus spending bill. And if you do, I will not sign it." Well, there ensued this vigorous internal debate. I felt pretty strongly that that was waving a red flag at the appropriators, and I thought that was not the right thing for the president to say in the state of the union at the beginning of the session.

The speech was all but done, but the president, typically two or three days before the state of the union, would sit down and rewrite passages himself. I went in and made an appeal: "Mr. President, this is not a sentence you need to use. I think it will be provocative, and I think it undercuts the appropriators." He listened and said, "I can tell you don't think I can pull this off." [laughter]

To make a long story short, it stayed in the speech. We go up to the Hill that night, and we're sitting there. He gets to that part of the speech, and he has last year's CR [continuing resolution] sitting there. And he put that grimace on his face and said, "And I would ask that the Congress not send me—" and he picked it up and plopped it on the desk with a big thud "—not send me one of these. I will not sign it." Both sides jumped out of their seats. I'll never forget Howard Metzenbaum cheering.[27] And I thought, *Well, so much for my counsel about what works in the state of the union!*

Stein: Yes, but how many of those [omnibus bills] have we had subsequently?

McClure: You were right on the substance.

Stein: Yes, you were absolutely right.

Brain: We had the opposite problem. We didn't want the Congress to go out. We wanted to keep them in town. So we threatened to veto adjournment resolutions. And it got to the point that they figured out that they could do a week at a time—maybe come in one day, let's say on the first, do three recesses that would follow, and they wouldn't have to come back until the end. We said, "If you do that in that form, we'll veto them. It has to be done and sent to us." And they bought it. We did it. They stayed around.

Hilley: Would you have vetoed it?

Brain: Yes.

Patashnik: I'm curious about the presidential management of the two chambers and how the office uses lobbies. When I was a committee staffer on the House side, the only way we often thought we could find out what was going on on the Senate side was talking to lobbies. We felt we couldn't call our counterparts in the other chamber, so we'd ask the interest groups, "What the hell's going on over there?" How does the president use lobbyists as a resource for gathering information or trying to influence the two chambers in the process?

Hilley: Highly overrated.

Ball: Highly overrated.

Stein: I can't remember ever doing it.

Hilley: Fred's example of NAFTA and those bills—they stand out because there are so few instances where you can mobilize the lobbying forces. But for the day in and day out [business], our intelligence was so much superior to any outsider's. Most of the time we had to keep the groups at bay as opposed to enlisting their support. Eighty percent of the work was trying to keep them from undermining what you were trying to do as opposed to helping you.[28]

McClure: Sometimes, too, you end up going on wild goose chases because they'd be giving you intelligence that perhaps was not that accurate. I remember that from the [Clarence] Thomas nomination, because we had all these groups involved in the Thomas nomination. Everybody had their view about where a particular member of the Senate was on this issue. "You have to have the vice president call him, because I just saw him last night and he's off the reservation, and oh my God." You start buying bridges by the time the process is over. It's a lot easier to just take the information under advisement.

Stein: The fundamental fact is interest groups have an agenda that's virtually never exactly coincident with your own, and the information they're going to give you is going to be filtered through the lens of their interest. You can listen to it. But if you listen to it without discounting it to the degree that it's slanted, you're making a huge mistake.

Hult: When you talk about dealing with the House and Senate from legislative affairs, how did you structure your offices to do that? What, if any, difference was there between the House side and the Senate side in White House congressional liaison? Different strategies and different things that they focused on. In some of our literature, there's a discussion that the House side focused more on committees, but the Senate side didn't specialize to that extent. Are those things accurate?

McClure: Probably not.

Stein: No.

McClure: Our design in the Bush administration was just like it was in the Reagan administration, which was just like it was in the Ford administration that Max had been involved in.

Stein: I think it has been the same for years.

McClure: There may be some difference in terms of the level of participation of special or deputy assistants to the president in the policy process and apparatus, but the reaching out and touching is virtually the same thing. At least it was over the twelve years that I referred to.

Stein: I think it's equally divided, House and Senate, with the staff. I don't recollect any difference in the way we tried to assign responsibilities. It was typically by cluster of committees. There was no real difference in philosophy, how you went at it. I think that the individuals who did it adapted to the differences in the institutions.

Hilley: You must be cognizant of personal relationships, of course, which are important. But the split was House, Senate, and by substance in committee. That seemed to work best. Of course, when you wanted to count votes, you have to identify this guy.

Brain: I have noted a stylistic difference—I'd be interested to test the proposition here—between some of the Republican White House affairs operations and some of the Clinton ones. My friends who worked in the Reagan/Bush White House said the instruction to House deputies was that you always called a member by his first name. It was Jim, Bob, Pete, whatever—the theory being you're as close as they're going to get to the president that day. You're not a staffer. It's not "Congressman Smith," it's not "Congressman Whatever." And when I came into legislative affairs, I had to tell people, "You're not staffers." It's Bill, Bob, Mary, whatever. And while it's minor, it does indicate a little bit of the relative relationship between you and the member and the two branches. Did you tell people to call them by their first name?

Ball: Well, I didn't call John Dingell "John." [laughter]

Brain: If you did, it was "Dear John."

Ball: But you didn't know him.

Moore: We didn't call Senator Byrd "Bobby."

Friedersdorf: We did just the opposite. I told them to call them "Congressman" and "Senator." This is not bragging, but I literally did know every member of the House by their first name. But I would never ever call them by their first name. I would also call them "Congressman." I learned that very early as a House staffer. I had a friend who was in congressional relations, and he always referred to the members as "Congressman." One day I said to him, "Why do you always call him 'Congressman'? You know him so well." He said, "They've earned that title. They were elected by 500,000 people. It's the most important job in the country, and it's a sign of respect." I never forgot that, and we really emphasized that. The lowest member, the freshman member, was "Congressman." He was never called by first name.

Ball: Or "Mr. Chairman."

McClure: I did it a little bit differently. I didn't direct myself one way or the other in terms of how to refer to members. Always in a public environment it was "Senator," "Mr. Chairman," or "Congressman." But I did develop relationships with members of Congress and was on a first-name basis with them. And if you're with eight members upstairs [in the White House residence], hanging out with the president, having a little cocktail to try to talk about an issue, they felt comfortable, and we did it privately like that.

Riley: Was the Senate as easy to crack in that regard as the House was? Was there a greater reluctance?

McClure: I saw none. I didn't have any problem with it.

Riley: No lesser sense of approachability?

McClure: I didn't run around calling Bob Byrd "Bob." It really depended upon the individual. There were just some guys you could get close enough to that you could have that kind of relationship, but you never took advantage of it in a public setting, which showed that your pants were too big or something.

Friedersdorf: Titles seem like such a small thing, but it's very important. I remember when President Ford took office and so many of the members would call him "Jerry," not "Mr. President." Over the years, President Ford has had an annual dinner at the Capitol Hill Club in June for all the former White House staff and Cabinet. Priscilla [Friedersdorf] and I always sit with the Michigan delegation. The [William] Broomfields of this world, the [Al] Cederbergs, the Chuck Chamberlains, the old guys.[29] President Ford always comes around to each table and makes a little chit-chat, and they all say, "Hi Jerry, how you doing, Jerry?"

Senator Bob Griffin always resented that.[30] Every time, he'd say to me, "Why do they call him Jerry? Damn it, he's the President." He would tell Cederberg about it, tell Broomfield about it. Do you think they'd listen to him? It's "Jerry" all the time. Of course, it didn't make any difference to President Ford, but Griffin thought, when he was in the office, that the familiarity of calling him "Jerry" diminished his respect and political clout with the other members. But you're never going to change those guys. They're going to call him "Jerry" until the day he dies.[31]

EDITOR'S COMMENTARY

The trinity of the United States' political order is a key part of every schoolchild's civic catechism: "legislative, executive, and judicial." Yet in this chapter we see that there is something fundamentally flawed in speaking about the nation's legislative branch in the singular: "Congress *is*." The fact of two discrete legislative chambers is, of course, as well known as the basic constitutional trinity. However, the profound *distinctiveness* of the two can easily be understated. These proceedings indicate how significant the practical differences are.

In his classic work *The Washington Community, 1800–1828,* James Sterling Young found that those populating the early capital were so infused with the virtues of constitutional propriety that they settled themselves physically according to the Constitution's own design: that is, into separate legislative and executive villages. The community's plan and residential map thus provided a representational portrait of their governing charter.[32] Although Washington today displays a more chaotic residential arrangement—in part because members spend so much of their time in their home districts—the matured landscape of the seat of government unmistakably reveals at least one new pattern: the presence of two separate *legislative* villages, one each for the House of Representatives and the Senate.

The heart of each village is the meeting chamber, one on either side of the Capitol's central dome. But from there a vast complex of office buildings spans out from the center, giving rise to parallel universes of activity—separate cafeterias, coiffeurs, and employment offices, and even completely independent banking systems. And as anyone who has spent much time in Washington will know, one's professional and social identity there is largely a function of which side of the Hill he or she inhabits. The folkways and social networks of the Hill tend to respect and reinforce these bicameral divisions. The choice of bars or restaurants frequented is often a function of which side of the Hill they are on. And the choice of residence is often made because of where an apartment is in relation to a grid of subway lines, which, tellingly, does not connect directly these separate congressional villages.

More to the point, the conclusions suggested by this evidence from social anthropology are thoroughly confirmed by the oral testimony offered at this symposium: Political behavior in today's Washington community replicates—perhaps even amplifies—the bicameral divisions of the parchment Constitution.

Something as simple as intelligence about the other chamber's activities and intentions seems to be in remarkably short supply. Larry Stein noted that, from his staff post in the Senate, "we had no way of knowing [what was happening in the House], and frequently if we tried to find out, the House guys wouldn't tell us." One of the symposium's academic participants, Professor Eric Patashnik, reported that in a previous position as a Hill staffer he often found it necessary to rely on lobbyists to find out "what the hell's going on over" on the other side. And Charles Brain observed here (with a hint of good-humored sarcasm) that he could actually feel the air getting thinner as he left his home turf in the House and entered the Senate's domain. We accordingly have a portrait of enduring folkways of congressional rivalry, reinforced by one chamber's legitimate claim to being more democratic, the other's to being more elite.

The fact of this bicameral divide obviously makes for complications in the business of getting enacted the president's programs. There are twice as many shoals to navigate than would presumably be the case in a unicameral congress. And the distinctiveness of the two chambers means that their idiosyncrasies have to be well known and accounted for by the president and his liaison team in order to succeed. Sophisticated quantitative studies—for example, those conducted by George C. Edwards III revealing major differences in presidential success in the House and the Senate on close votes—provide solid evidence over time of important differentials in receptivity to presidential leadership between the two chambers.[33] Yet even in cases in which the president's percentage of support on a given bill turns out practically identical in the House and Senate, it is fair to say that different kinds of lobbying efforts had to be waged across the chambers to achieve that equivalent outcome. The persistence of this reality is reflected in the fact that the basic organizing rule for the CL's operation has always been separate teams for separate chambers.

This being true, one of the most striking observations to emerge in this session is that the depth of the bicameral division in some ways works to the president's advantage. Several participants noted that the two chambers' extraordinary jealousy of their own prerogatives—to the point of closing off avenues of information about strategy or tactics to the other chamber—actually had the effect of benefiting the executive. In this institutional environment the White House can find itself serving as the conduit for such communications or, more consequentially, as a mediator for the resolution of interchamber disputes. As Charles Brain reports, "From the perspective of the administration, you can use that [bicameral] chasm, because you're the only one who's talking to everyone." Larry Stein seconds Brain's point: "Since the two [chambers] are separate and you're down at the White House, you have a huge advantage. You know what's going on and you can play them off against each other."

Even simple logistical protocols can work to the president's advantage. With no truly neutral common space on Capitol Hill for the congressional leadership to meet, the physical space of the White House provides the president a venue for bringing together competing legislative interests. And it is a site with decided "home field" advantages.

Moreover, given the plural nature of congressional interests, there will be in virtually every political dispute somebody who finds it in his or her interest to appeal to the White House for intervention—perhaps to change the balance of competing interests or to firm up wavering commitments to a delicately crafted compromise.[34] This, ironically, can give the president leverage, although it is also clear from these discussions that the White House has to be judicious about when and how it intervenes. Participation by the president is typically sought by those who wish to advance their own interests on the Hill, which may or may not coincide with the president's interests or priorities. And, as was said in several of these sessions, one of the biggest responsibilities of the CL is to determine which of an almost infinite set of demands on the president's attention will be accepted. The observations recorded in this session, however, indicate that we ought to treat seriously the proposition that the divisions of the two chambers can actually work to the president's advantage.

5

WORKING WITH AND FOR THE PRESIDENT

The President's Style, Political Circumstances, and Priorities

The main topics discussed in this session include how the congressional liaison job has changed or remained the same over the last fifty years; differences between the first and second terms; using the president's time; presidential anger; White House involvement in congressional elections; the congressional relations dimension of executive orders; civility in Washington; communications strategies; and the press and congressional relations. This session was moderated by Richard E. Neustadt, Douglas Dillon Professor Emeritus, Harvard University.

Riley: Professor Neustadt, you'll be leading us off this afternoon.

Neustadt: Let me remind you what this session is about. Our agenda says, "Working for and with the president: the president's own style, political circumstances, and priorities." One introductory matter before we get to that. We haven't put on the record something that's quite striking about the operation in which you were all involved. It's recognizably of about the same size and character as it was in the middle '50s when it started. And so far as I know—and you all will correct me if I'm wrong, I'm sure—if Bryce Harlow came back today, or Larry O'Brien, they wouldn't find it all that different. They might find Congress different, but they wouldn't find the White House operation all that different.

So there's this striking uniformity, relative uniformity, if I have it right.

You have the same number of people divided between deputies in the House, deputies in the Senate. And you have that duality representing Congress to the president, the president to Congress, including the mix of White House pressures on the president. All that's the same. But think about the personalities, political situations, and motivations of the following named people: If you want to go back to me, you start with Harry Truman, Dwight Eisenhower, Jack Kennedy, Lyndon Johnson, Richard Nixon, Gerald Ford, Jimmy Carter, Ronald Reagan, the elder George Bush, Bill Clinton, and the younger George Bush. Now that's about as diverse a set of people, of human beings, and about as diverse a set of political circumstances as we've ever had in this office. So you've got this relative uniformity serving this great diversity, and that's the subject for today. Now I'm going to let Messrs. Moore and Ball answer, in either order.

Ball: [Pointing to Moore] He's our senior. [laughter]

Moore: I get a discount.

Neustadt: I'm going to turn it over to them to get started.

Moore: I agree with you, but there's one constant in all that. It's the constant that Max [Friedersdorf] mentioned the first day. What is your job? Pass the president's program, regardless of who the president is, what his style is. I would disagree with you in one regard. I had a lot less staff. I had two guys at the Senate and three or four in the House. I know in the Clinton White House you had four people working the Senate and nine in the House at one time. I gradually increased it. I started off with just one person in the Senate and three in the House. But overall I think you're right. The function is constant, [but the situation in which you govern does matter, and that often changes]. I've talked about it a lot. I came in under new leadership, new president, new speaker, new so-and-so. The Democrats had to learn, then, not to get up every day and bite the White House, because it now belonged to their own party. Now *I'm* going to name some names: Birch Bayh, Frank Church, [Henry] Scoop Jackson, Lloyd Bentsen. They all had run against Jimmy Carter in the primaries and all been defeated. Add [Morris] Mo Udall in the House. Mo Udall came very close to winning the nomination. People forget that. The Wisconsin primary—a couple thousand more votes. Also, two people walked up to the wire and decided not to run: Hubert Humphrey and Ted Kennedy.[1]

Now you say 535 people look in the mirror every morning and think they should be president. Here were some who thought they should be president enough that they actually ran. Scoop Jackson *still* thought he should be president. But Bentsen was very good. I told somebody this story the other night. Bentsen said, "I ran, I lost, Carter won, I'm a senator, he's the president. Let's go to work. Tell me what you want to do." I didn't get that from other people. If you take a Senate that has all those people in it, it's tough. Going right in there was resentment. That's the situation we came in to.[2]

I'll tell you how we were organized and also cover the president's time. I had a block of time every morning. I can't remember if [Zbigniew] Brzezinski followed me or I followed him, but oftentimes I would take time from him or he would take it from me if I didn't need that much. I think it was a fifteen-minute block, and I could go thirty minutes or whatever. On Wednesdays, the CIA guy came in, Stan Turner, and briefed the president. He came right after me, so oftentimes I'd just sit in and listen. If Brzezinski came before me, I'd say, "Who's in there?" And the secretary would say, "Brzezinski, but go on in. His time's elapsed." I'd open the door and the president would say, "Come on in and sit down. You ought to hear this."[3]

I could use that time with my deputies or get a little committee together if we were working on something special like the Department of Education or civil service reform. I'd use that time to make a briefing for the president. I was afforded great access. Anytime I wanted, I could walk into the Oval Office or the study, and anytime I wanted I could walk into the residence. Of course, you don't abuse that, you guard it.

Of the president's own style, a lot of people have written that Carter was a terrible politician: he couldn't get along with members of Congress and so on. But I never saw that. He was absolutely wonderful one-on-one, or one-on-three, or one-on-five, or one-on-thirty. I've often seen votes change just by a presentation. They'd say, "Well, now I've changed my mind. I'm going to vote with you."

Again, as Max [Friedersdorf] said, you want to limit the president's time in making calls. President Carter was so efficient. You'd give him ten calls and you'd think it would take him two days, but he'd call you back in an hour and say, "Give me some more, I've done all these. And these two guys you said were undecided, they're not undecided anymore. They're for us." He really wanted to do more than we wanted him to do in that regard. We wanted to limit him for this reason: If you do that too often, why the hell are the members going to talk to you and me? They'd say, "I'm waiting for the president to call." You have to limit that. At least I think so. Maybe you all disagree with me.

Friedersdorf: Oh, I agree with that.

Moore: On *Air Force One,* I always had, I think, five seats. It was the old plane. I think I had five seats we could use any way we wanted. We had ten seats at each state dinner, five for each house. You'd usually get the Foreign Relations guy and the leaders, so it really gave you two or three that were discretionary to invite people on. It's not true that we invited Leon Panetta to the Japanese state dinner, thinking he was Japanese, as they reported. [laughter]

McClure: It's not true.

Moore: Or that we invited [Norman Y.] Mineta to the Italian. It's not true. We did know the difference. But those are just examples. We had a lot of tools we could use, considering that we didn't have the *Sequoia.*[4] We had the cheapest cufflinks ever made from the Democratic National Committee and tried to give those out. We did have all this stuff. But the most important thing we had was the president's time. And never, ever in four years do I recall asking him—or any of my staff asking, through me—to do something that he didn't do. He'd make a call, a special effort.

Ball: Professor Neustadt, the size, the structure may not have changed since Bryce Harlow was in this position, but clearly the demands on the president's time in the modern presidency have changed dramatically. Over time, that has put more responsibility—dramatically more responsibility—on this operation we're talking about in terms of the legislative trains that run whether the president is overseas or traveling in the country or preoccupied at a summit. There seems to be a lot more engagement over time, even today, on those issues and those kinds of trips than there was in '86 and '88.

You look back at the day-to-day routine in the Oval Office of Lyndon Johnson. It's inconceivable to me that a modern president today could devote that kind of time to discussions with leaders.[5] More and more it's the job of the assistant to the president and the chief of staff to know what the top congressional leaders intend to do, want to do, feel like they need to do. President Reagan was one who set a tone of delegating responsibility. He told people what he wanted accomplished but certainly not how to accomplish it. In some respects, representing his agenda before Congress was simplified by the fact that you knew what those principles were that he had stuck with over a long period of time.

So, addressing legislative issues that would arise from time to time, it was not that complicated to ascertain which ones fit within his agenda and which ones did not. He had a disdain for bureaucratic processes, and when he left Washington he spoke of the difficulty of any president moving the bureaucracy. He talked about how difficult it is today for any president to address the alliance between the bureaucracy and the press and the embedded interests before the Congress and to change the ways of government.

The force of his personality—the strength of his ability to deal individually in informal settings—was a great asset in the way he dealt with Congress. He did not follow the Lyndon Johnson way of speaking to leaders about detailed issues and schedules. Rather, he used his personal relationships in informal ways over informal suppers at the White House and occasional meetings, which he much preferred to the formal settings of leadership meetings. He felt like he got a lot more accomplished that way. That was certainly an effective way for him to address the issues.

I think, looking back, we perhaps spent too much time worrying about particular developments before Congress that perhaps were not central to his agenda. That's one of the dangers of this kind of operation, where you're addressing yourself every day, day in and day out, to activity in this dynamic process. It becomes easy to be distracted from the objective. Ronald Reagan was in office during the Cold War, and it was understood that U.S.–Soviet relations were right at the top of his agenda—and the arms control talks and other developments. And that gave a lot of clarity to what we did in that arena. But on the domestic agenda, it was then, and is now, a lot more complicated, as government is more complicated today.

In sum, while I think the structure, size, and the way the office is arranged are pretty much the same, the level of responsibility, I suspect, is much greater. The complexity of government is much greater. Presidents today, of both parties, depend a great deal more on the legislative affairs operation because of the demands on their own time and the fact that they are away from the Oval Office more and more as the years go by.

Hilley: One comment about what changes and what stays the same. I agree that it's been so much fun to listen to folks who have held this same position over time and to realize a lot of the similarities—and to see that we all had a tough job. I think one thing that's changed quite a bit going back over the last thirty years is the integration of the communications and media aspect into every other aspect of the White House. I credit the Reagan administration for raising the bar to a new level of "When's the news cycle? When do we want to do something? What are we doing?"

In our [Clinton] operation, our media outreach—communications, press operation—was integrated into the policy discussions, the legislative discussions, in a way that I think the modern presidency just has to do these days, because the news cycle and the shaping of events on that side are critical. The CL's basic function hasn't changed, but I think there's an overlay of media communications that has changed over the last several decades and that's integral to everything we do now.

McClure It's twenty-four hours a day. It's nonstop. Think back. It was during President Carter's time that we first saw *Nightline*,[6] and now all of these things have burgeoned from it and everybody can find a talk show they can get on to try to influence the public discourse on the issues with which we've had to deal. *That's* what's changed dramatically—in terms of the environment—from the earlier days.

Moore: I told you I had a set time every day with the president. But oftentimes I didn't need it because of just what you're talking about: legislative pace and the rhythm of the Congress. At six or seven o'clock at night you'd do a memo and walk it over to the residence, or put it on his desk in the Oval Office, saying, "This is what happened today. This is what's going to happen tomorrow." And by the next morning, things had changed. You couldn't go in to a nine o'clock meeting and say, "I think this is what's going to happen today," because you really didn't know what was going to happen today. You had better be up on the Hill trying to find out what was going to happen rather than getting your picture made with the president.

Friedersdorf: I recall following the Clinton impeachment with great interest because I found my mind dwelling on what was going on in the congressional relations office. I knew what hell they must be going through. It occurred to me at that time, and it's been reinforced this week, that each administration probably thinks what they're going through is the worst thing that's ever happened in the history of the United States—

Stein: I feel like that.

Friedersdorf: When we went into the White House with Nixon, if you recall, the Vietnam War was going on. I can recall tanks being parked on East Executive Avenue. When I went in the West Gate in the morning, I remember having my car beat on by protestors. If you think you have trouble, that was big-time trouble. Then Watergate happened, and before long we were counting impeachment votes. And then, of course, the president resigned. Going through that—

McClure: You win, Max. [laughter]

Friedersdorf: Let me continue. Then Ford steps in, and it's like going to "Hello, sunshine America. Things are sunshiny again—"

Neustadt: For a month.

Friedersdorf:—and within one month, he pardons Nixon, and again the clouds roll in. The campaign's already under way, a certain governor in California decides to try and knock us off, which he came within a few votes in the state of Louisiana of doing.[7] And then you get defeated, and there's nothing worse—maybe death is, but defeat is pretty close—as I'm sure you recall, Frank.

Then I think about the Reagan administration. We hadn't been in office two months until the president was shot in the chest by a [would-be] assassin. I'd like to tell you just a quick story about that. The president was shot that day, and I was told to come down to the Situation Room. There was chaos there, to say the least. Cap Weinberger and General [Alexander] Haig were trying to decide who was in charge, while we didn't know whether the president was dead or alive—and of course, Jim Brady.[8] But the second day I got a call from [chief of staff] Jim Baker over at the hospital, and he said, "Come right away to George Washington Hospital." I got in the car and went over there and went up to the room. The Secret Service were standing outside President Reagan's room, and I said, "What's the matter?"

Jim said, "Listen, Mrs. [Nancy] Reagan is very upset. Strom Thurmond came over here and flashed his credentials and talked his way into the president's room.[9] And there the president was lying there with all of these tubes running in and out of his nose, his throat, and his arms. Mrs. Reagan is very upset that here he is in critical condition, shot, and a member of the Congress is here standing by his bed. I want you to stay over here and make sure that the Secret Service—I don't care if they've got credentials from the pope, don't let them in here." So for about three days I stayed over there and kept congressmen and senators from coming up there. They wanted to get their pictures taken with him by the death bed, you know.

So that happened, and then after that, you think about the Cold War. In retrospect, the Cold War is all over, and we won and everything. But at that time we were trying to get cruise missiles into Europe. Thank God for Mrs. [Margaret] Thatcher, she went along with it.[10] You know, if we hadn't outspent the Russians, we might still be in the Cold War. And then the Berlin Wall fell.

I read the other day where one of Bush's aides—I think it was a military person—said that the United States has not had as bad a time since the Civil War. Well, where was he during World War I and World War II? And Korea and Vietnam? We're talking almost thirty years' difference here in this group, ranging from the '60s to what John, Chuck, and Larry have been through in the '90s. It's a lot of change and a lot of trauma, but each president has to confront it. So I don't think we ought to say that this was the worst of all times, or this is the best of all times. Each generation has its own problems.

Neustadt: It reminds me—and this will astonish some of you—that through the Truman and early Eisenhower period the custom prevailed that any congressman or senator or person in the executive branch with a commission from the president—which meant assistant secretary and up—was entitled to a fifteen-minute interview with the president within twenty-four hours of asking.

Stein: I'm astonished.

McClure: They didn't have much to do then.

Moore: Was nothing going on then?

Neustadt: When Jack Kennedy was first elected and thinking about his incumbency, Clark Clifford told him this, and he was appalled.[11] It was the inevitable boredom more than anything else that I think he was appalled by. But it turned out not to be true, because, after Eisenhower's heart attack, that custom had departed from the White House and never was resumed. I think it's fair to say that over time presidents have shucked a lot of crappy responsibilities that, if you carry our conversations back a little farther, presidents used to have to take as a matter of course.

I remember going through old Budget Bureau files and discovering that every letter from the budget director to an agency head—whether it had declared a program in accord with the president's program or not—was reviewed by Herbert Hoover. So these guys have always had too much to do, but the job does change from time to time.[12] I think it's very important to get on the record any changes, such as the twenty-four-hour news cycle, that not only alter processes and calculations but actually change the workload that the president has to be involved in. I think this business of going abroad *is* more frequent than it used to be. There may be some others that have been happening that we haven't really noticed, that substitute for old-style busywork. But there's always been plenty of busywork.

Brain: Well, presidents certainly have their own styles in terms of use of the Oval Office. The press reports of the current president have him showing up at the Oval Office at seven o'clock. At eight o'clock, the chief of staff comes in, and things are running like clockwork through the day. President Clinton seldom showed—In fact, when we were scheduling events, we'd say, "We don't want to do anything with him before ten." He would stroll over at some point late in the morning. He really used, increasingly, his office over in the residence, and that would be his office where he would get reading and things done.

You could always tell when the president was in the Oval Office: the door was shut. As you were walking through the West Wing, you'd notice that that wouldn't be until noontime or the afternoon. But then you'd hear stories from members of Congress that he was calling them at 1:30 in the morning to talk about this or that.

Neustadt: That must have been popular.

Brain: Well, I've had more than one congressional wife tell me that the phone rings in the middle of the night and, handing it to her husband, she grumps, "Yes, it's him again."

Riley: One aspect of this also is personality. I have a question about anger management. Tell us about how you deal with presidential anger, especially as it relates to issues directed towards members of Congress. Will [Ball], you sort of flinched when I said that. I don't know if you have anything in particular in mind.

Ball: No. Presidents are human, and so you see the full range of emotions in official and unofficial duties. President Reagan, as Max mentioned, and Tip O'Neill—while they had ideological differences that were obvious—had a fairly close personal relationship. But that's not to say there weren't some very tense meetings. There were some. I think the president felt that, owing to their personal rapport, Tip should have understood certain things where they disagreed. I remember one meeting where he clenched his jaw, and I ended up receiving the brunt of a lecture after the meeting, a sort of "Doesn't he understand?" type of lecture. I think the speaker understood it, but there was a pretty fundamental disagreement there.

I never saw him allow his anger to surface in a meeting. He was measured in his tone and, as I said, didn't relish the formal leadership meetings as much as he did the private discussions afterward. I never witnessed what I would call a temper tantrum, but rather impatience with the inability of a member or two to come around on an important issue, most of which were foreign policy–related.

Riley: Fred, did President Bush have a temper?

McClure: He's a pretty even-tempered kind of an individual. When you first started talking about anger, the biggest challenge in life is to make sure the anger is never directed at *you* for something you should have done or did not do.

Probably the times where I found him to be most stern—which is a precursor, maybe, to being very upset—was when *ad hominem* types of approaches were used and you got beyond the policy stuff and started getting down to the individuals and taking personal potshots at folks. That was something he just didn't think was the right way to govern, or for public servants to serve. He would get very frustrated with that. That's probably where I saw him come closest to getting really angry. This president [Bush 41] also had a tendency to get something in the back of his mind that he wanted to get resolved, and he would be impatient until that matter was resolved. You might get more phone calls from him than you desired because you hadn't gotten the answer back to him yet—an impatience element there.

Ball: I've omitted something important that I want to add to the record. I wasn't involved in the 1980 campaign, but I guess the most famous evidence of Ronald Reagan's temper was in the New Hampshire primary, when he seized the microphone and said, "I paid for this microphone." And those who knew him from way back made the reference that that was the old Dutch Reagan. He banged the table and you saw a flash of anger in his impatience. I remember that scene that may have manifested itself again later in a policy decision with the air traffic controllers' strike. I wasn't there at the time, but he clearly lost patience and acted decisively in that.[13]

Riley: Max, how about the presidents you worked with?

Friedersdorf: Going along with what Will said about President Reagan—there was one time when he was calling during an AWACS [Airborne Early Warning and Control Systems] vote. We were up in the residence, and he got the senator from North Dakota on the phone, Mark Andrews. Mrs. Reagan was in the residence, and she still had her housecoat on. She hadn't gotten dressed. And the president had had that trouble with his colon, and he was doing the phoning from the residence because he'd been ill. We were down to a couple, two or three votes. [Robert] Packwood was working the other side against us, and Mark Andrews was on the fence. The president had Mark Andrews on the phone, and he was begging him for his vote. I don't think he was making much progress.[14]

Mrs. Reagan said [whispering] "Ronnie, Ronnie, do you remember when we went up there in that snowstorm and campaigned for him?" And the president turned around and said, "That's right." Then he said, "Mark, do you remember when we went up there and campaigned for you?" We got his vote. He wasn't mad, but he was on the verge of it.

The only other time I saw a burst of anger was not from him but from President Ford. President Ford had a pretty good temper. I'd hate to play across the line from him in a football game. One day, when he was minority leader—this was during the Vietnam War, and they had a troop-cut amendment on the House floor. The State Department lobbyist was Hal Eberle, remember him, Will? Hal had given him some language that the State Department had worked up on what we would take. He was out there trying to sell this language. And in the meantime, Ford got a call in the cloakroom from the White House—I don't know who it was back there, probably [Henry] Kissinger, saying, "No, we can't take that language."[15]

He'd been out there arguing for it. His fuse just went off, and he came charging through the double doors out to the lobby. He came flying through there with his coattails flying. Hal was standing there, and he took Eberle by the lapels and just put him right up against that marble wall. He said, "What kind of language are you giving me? The White House says they can't take this language." And he chewed Eberle up with about fifty people standing around. You could have lit a match on Ford's forehead.

I never saw Nixon lose his temper. I think he was mad all the time. [laughter]

Riley: Did Bill Clinton have a temper?

Stein: Mythically he had a temper. It's been reported numerous times. I can't say I've ever been the object of it. I have seen him go off numerous times, but it always seemed to me almost theatrical in that no one really took it personally. I'm not sure it was intended that way. There may have been a kind of therapeutic element to it. They all get frustrated.

I should put in the record right now—especially given Max's description—that I started to work at the White House the very weekend the Monica Lewinsky story broke, so my entire tenure was essentially impeachment related.[16] At least that's the way I think of it. It certainly had profound effects on him. As has been reported, he became, I believe the term is "compartmentalized." He became quite isolated in a lot of ways. I'd be delighted to share stories with Max, too, to hear how President Nixon dealt with this.

To a large degree we had to be careful how we used him in legislative affairs because of this. I think he was acutely conscious of the debility it created and therefore disciplined himself remarkably in how he engaged Congress and how he engaged congressmen. He was extremely sensitive to the pressure he was imposing on Democrats and extremely sensitive to what Republicans were trying to do to him. I think he does have a temper.

It's a very real one. [George] Stephanopoulos has told me it's a very real one.[17] Again, it never hit me, but—judging from the degree of control and discipline I saw in him when he was under extreme duress—my sense is that the visible anger was probably mostly staged, or close to that.

Hilley: I was with Clinton in two really good years, so I never saw an outburst of any kind toward anybody. He was always just honestly, "What's the right thing to do? How should we do this?" and very much engaged. I think it's the tenor of the times. It would be interesting to get Howard [Paster] and Pat [Griffin] in here, because that [1993–94] was the period of healthcare reform, the loss of the House and the Senate, his low poll numbers.[18] So that was the pressure period, on the front end, where the stories come from. But I agree, anything he'd say like, "Goddamn" or whatever was sort of off into the sky, like, "Why are these guys doing this?" It was just sort of a way of verbalizing, trying to figure it out, or some frustration about something in the process.

One attribute of Clinton's, a side of his personality that I found remarkable: This guy was subject to a lot of *ad hominem* attacks throughout his presidency. But his capacity to not let it get to him and to be unbelievably forgiving, and have somebody who had just said the vilest thing about him two weeks before down to the White House and try to deal with him on an issue as if nothing had been said—that would have been beyond me to be able to do, to be honest with you. But that capacity to be forgiving about some very personal attacks—which are the ones that do sting deepest, of course—was just a remarkable attribute, and potentially a weakness, as well.

Stein: I think it was his wife [Hillary Rodham Clinton] who said, "Every day's a new day for him." It sounds like a trite phrase, but think about it a little bit. It's absolutely true of him. He did not look back. He moved forward, and I consider it incredible, actually, given what was thrown at him.

Neustadt: Is this the Clinton you knew?

Brain: Yes, and I agree with John. The stories of the anger really come from the first couple of years, which we didn't see. Larry and I both started at the same time, and in fact we spent the first couple of months looking at each other in his office, saying to each other, "Well, well, Gore will keep us, won't he?" [laughter]

I was going to lament my situation—nothing compared to yours, Max. Having a good Democratic member of Congress, a friend of the president, a friend of yours, look at you and say, "There may come a time when we have to have the conversation"[19]—that really gets your attention, on a personal level. Relating it back to the president: Coming as close as he did to losing the office almost put him emotionally and intellectually on a different level, a different place, where he knew what he had, if anything, was more precious than ever. So his approach was: "Don't get angry. Let's just see what we can get done in the time we've got left."

Riley: Max, you had to deliver the news of impeachment to President Nixon, right? About your vote counts in the House?

Friedersdorf: Well, yes we did. We started counting votes in the House and Senate, and we would give them to him. Of course, they weren't good, but he had a defense mechanism that seemed to dispel anything that we would try to say. I know he really did not realize that he was done until Hugh Scott and John Rhodes and Senator [Barry] Goldwater came down and told him that they couldn't sustain support and they couldn't stop impeachment, and if there was a trial in the Senate, they would lose.[20] But that was very late in the game. We knew from our vote counts that it was true, but I don't think he believed it until he heard it from the leadership and his old friends up there.

I want to mention one additional thing about President Reagan that I think illustrates his personality. As Will [Ball] mentioned, we had really cultivated a close relationship with Tip O'Neill, and even though they both came from similar backgrounds—both second-generation Irish immigrants, Reagan came from a broken home, and Tip grew up in poor circumstances in Boston—one turned extreme right conservative, one left liberal. But there was a magnetism when they were together. Tip, if you remember, in his public statements would be quite critical of President Reagan, and some of them were really nasty, like "I don't think he's right bright, and he doesn't know the issues," and on and on. And somebody invariably would mention those stories to President Reagan in our senior staff meeting in the morning with five or six of us. Somebody would say, "Did you see that?" All President Reagan ever said—I would have expected him to just be furious. But he'd say, "Oh, that's Tip, that's Tip. Forget it."

Neustadt: That reminds me of a very short story I can't resist telling you. I don't believe it has ever been put on anybody's record. At the end of January '82, the Reagans had an absolutely charming luncheon to celebrate Franklin Roosevelt's hundredth birthday. They invited the living secretaries who had worked in the White House at the time, the reporters who'd been there at the time, who were still alive, the people who were still alive who had been in the White House and the government, and the people who had written about him—that's how I got to go there. It was absolutely charming.

It was a lovely lunch, and the president got up and went into the Red Room and spoke to the grandchildren, all of whom had been invited.[21] He said, "People say I'm against the New Deal, but I revered your grandfather. I would never be against the New Deal. I'm just trying to cut back a Great Society." I love that.

Anyway, he gave a totally nonpartisan speech after lunch. There was a large congressional delegation there. Then, when it was all over, he'd gone off, and Mrs. Reagan had to say goodbye to all the guests, and everyone lined up to say goodbye to her. Right behind me was Tip O'Neill with a congressman whose name I've forgotten, I'm sorry to say. And I heard the following conversation. The congressman said to Tip, "Tip, he stole Roosevelt right out from under us." And Tip said, "Well, I guess he had the right. He voted for him four times."

Riley: Frank Moore, I didn't ask you about Jimmy Carter and anger. Did Jimmy Carter have a temper?

Moore: I guess he did. I never saw it. His temper, I guess, took the form more—You could see some in the campaigning, impatience with staying on schedule, a little impatience with people, particularly people he didn't mind offending. But no, I never saw his temper, he never used it with me or in my presence. Now, I've seen it written in some sarcastic marginal notes on memos—they'll all be opened up someday—about a member. He'd make a comment, and I'd get it back, and I'd say, "Ooh, shred this one." I think it took the form of maybe just a cold anger more than a hot temper.

Young: What about the hard times, the hostage crisis?

Moore: He was always just resigned. "We've got to work harder. Have we tried this? Try to do this." It just spurred him to work.

Young: Did he become totally immersed?

Moore: He did. He told me, and I'm sure he's told other people, that the only time during the crisis that the hostages were not on his mind was when he was fly fishing. He said, "The reason is this: When you've got the wind blowing this way, and the water going that way, and you've got a little teeny fly, you cannot concentrate on anything else except putting that fly in front of the fish. Your mind has to be totally on that. The only time the hostages were off my mind was when I was fly fishing," which was usually up at Camp David. Of course I also knew him before he was president. I was his Number Two, and then I was chief of staff while he was governor. I worked for him for thirteen or fourteen years, including the White House—and I never saw it.

Neustadt: Those of you who worked for Reagan or Clinton, are you aware of any differences that might be generic between the first term and the second term—which might apply to more than an individual president?[22]

Friedersdorf: Will and Fred would have more knowledge of the second term, although I was there at the start of the second term. I think the key thing was the change in the chief of staff. Whereas Jim Baker ran such an open shop, and you had [Edwin] Meese and [Mike] Deaver and Baker all pulling in the same harness, and there was no rivalry, no animosity, no jealousy, no envy. They all were doing what they wanted to do and doing it well. The thing worked like a charm. But when that troika split up—which it was bound to, they couldn't keep that up forever—in the second term we got more of a dictatorial chief of staff, and it somewhat destroyed the morale of the staff in the second term. I know it destroyed my morale, and I know it destroyed [Pat] Buchanan's morale and Ed Rollins's, and [Robert] Bud McFarlane was pretty well denigrated. I think the negative things that happened in the second term can be traced back to that change of chief of staff.[23]

Neustadt: But you wouldn't describe that as a change in the president's interest, temperament, concern, manner, or the fact that he couldn't run for office again, or anything like that

Friedersdorf: No, I didn't see anything change there. He still had the same drive, the same interest, the same goals. Like any president, I think he was thinking a little bit about going back to California. I remember one day before a leadership meeting—We always briefed him in the Oval Office, and he would walk through this secretary's office to the Cabinet Room. The leaders were all waiting there for him, and we briefed him, and I could tell he was dragging his feet a little going in there. He really didn't want to.

We walked through the secretary's office, and you could look out to the Rose Garden. It was in April or May, and the flowers and tulips were up, and the birds were singing. There were two or three gardeners out there clipping the trees and trimming the bushes and mowing the grass, and he stopped and looked out there, and he said, "I'd give anything if I could go out there and work with those guys instead of going to this damn meeting." He was getting a little bit tired, maybe.

Ball: To that point, I think Ronald Reagan's Hollywood history, "The show must go on," drove him in a disciplined way that other presidents have not felt bound to do in the regular order. I will always remember going in before a joint leadership meeting that I knew was going to be unpleasant over a contentious issue. As I recall, Senator Byrd had insisted on the participation of other senators who were certain to make the meeting unpleasant. I had relented in a weak moment. So here we come with this cast, and I have to go in and not only explain that the leadership's coming, but that there are going to be some others present. I could tell, he had just slightly this look on his face of discomfort, and as I stepped back, Kathy Osborne, who was then the secretary, walked up and said, "Well, you know, he just finished a root canal."

And I thought, *Holy stars, had I only known.* But anyway, the show went on, meeting took place, and it was unpleasant. I remember a tense moment, I think in that same meeting, he found it necessary to put that puzzled look on his face, and in the midst of a dissertation by a senator who's still serving—so I won't mention who it was—he found it necessary to pull out that hearing aid and dial a number a little bit—

McClure: Which number? Which way?

Riley: We'll never know.

Ball: While students of the presidency may assume that the second term is a time when the energy level begins to decline and the turnover picks up, I think the Cold War made it different in Reagan's second term. He was focused on the negotiations with the Soviets, his meetings with Gorbachev, which became very much personal diplomacy with those two, and the visit by Gorbachev to Washington and their meeting in Geneva. There were a lot of other things going on, but that really drove him right on through the end of his term.

Brain: Bill Clinton, I believe, enjoyed being president up until the very last as they were walking out and playing "Hail to the Chief."

Stein: He looked like he enjoyed it.

Brain: Oh yes. [He had] a session late in December 2000 with the congressional leadership doing the final appropriations package. And in early January, lame duck, new Congress comes in and you have an overlap of two weeks—new Congress, old president. We kicked around having the president call for an increase in the minimum wage just to really stick it to the next Congress. But we couldn't agree with Ted Kennedy on how much, so we couldn't do it, and we didn't. I think Kennedy, [David] Bonior, and others wanted a buck and a half and we, going out the door, didn't think it was responsible to call for more than a dollar. That was the level of activism.

We haven't talked about it, but obviously, the very last day, Clinton was down there doing pardons. A few of them we would rather he had not, and a couple you want to pull back. But still, he took that power of the presidency, and he said, "Now I turn my attention to that." Congress is not involved, it's a power that's inherent only to the president in our system. So he was involved up until the very last moment. In part, it's because he was much younger.[24]

Friedersdorf: How old was he when he left office?

Brain: I'd say fifty-seven.[25]

Friedersdorf: That's interesting. There's a difference between fifty-seven and seventy-five or seventy-seven.

Brain: And he didn't have California to go home to. He couldn't go back to the governor's mansion in Arkansas, which had been home. He had Chappaqua, but that was [not really home].

Riley: Chuck, let me pose one general question out of what you've just said. One of the striking things that we pick up in looking at the last few years of the Clinton presidency is the extent to which there was government by executive order. There was a decision evidently taken at some point that there were things you could do without getting Congress involved. I wonder if you could address that for a few minutes—the politics of doing that. Is it problematic when you decide to do certain things by executive order? Does it create a backlash on Capitol Hill? And, as you're in the process of issuing these orders, are you taking the temperature of Capitol Hill to give the White House feedback as to how much of a stir this is going to create?

Brain: The ones I remember are mostly monuments, declaring national monuments. By law, the president has the authority to do that, and by and large he was declaring monuments that clearly our friends on the Hill were in favor of.

Stein: There were others.

Brain: We did others.

Stein: We did "Roadless."[26] There were a number of environmental orders, and there were workplace orders, too. It *was* a conscious strategy, and it came about because we couldn't get anything passed. We should be very candid about that. The record's clear on it. I don't think it was our fault. It was subsequent to the impeachment proceedings, and even during them I think it was very clear to us that the legislative routes were not open to us.

Riley: Were you actively out trying to determine how they were resonating on the Hill as these decisions were taken?

Stein: We didn't have to determine how they were going to resonate on the Hill.

Brain: We knew our friends would like them.

Stein: We knew who was going to be for them and who was going to be against them, especially on the environmental side. But you have to keep in mind, while we were doing environmentally conscious and sensitive ones, we were also dealing with riders coming from Congress that were the reverse. I think New Source Review was a regulatory, an executive action.[27] It was engaging what I think was perceived to be an effort to hit the environment. This goes back to the Gore issues as well, and the fact that Gore was going to be attacked for environmental stands and there were efforts to roll back all the stuff that he cared about. It was quite conscious. I think it was governed by a lot of circumstances particular to that time. We got no blow-back that wasn't expected. The opposition to it was exactly the opposition anyone would have predicted beforehand. The support for it was exactly the support we knew we had going in.

Thurber: I'd like to follow up on this on the Clinton administration. There's been some measure of the number of pages in the last six months in the *Federal Register*, a measure of all the regulations that went through. Truth in advertising: My wife was the lead attorney at OSHA [Occupational Safety and Health Administration] for health standards, and they had a lot of work to do for the last six months. Did you get together—the legislative shop with the policy people—and decide on the strategy of where you were going to push these new regulations, and also executive orders?

Hilley: Just to set the stage for that and to answer the question about Clinton's second term: His first year, '97, was "balance the budget," and in our policy shops—the policy committee, the National Economic Council, and the various ones in the agencies—we were totally excited [with our success]. Okay, we've got the budget balanced. Now we were running plans: Let's fix Social Security, let's solve that. Let's fix Medicare. There was an ambitious race relations agenda being readied, so the mills at the policy level were hopping, to set the stage for even more efforts.

Then came Monica Lewinsky and the impeachment. And one of the great, unfortunate consequences was that an ambitious agenda—with a president with the energy and the momentum at that time to carry this forward—was quickly taken away from us. At that point we turned to these second-best alternatives on some of the regulatory fronts.

Stein: There was a lot of in-depth analysis of what we could and could not do.

Riley: Was that on policy, or politically?

Stein: Mainly policy. In fact, this was not legislative, so in a lot of cases I wasn't even there. I know that some of it was reaction. By the way, what John described is entirely accurate. When I was going down [to join the White House staff], I thought we were going to reform Social Security and everything else. So the precipitous decline from high expectations to zilch was quite tangible. Over the next year and half to two years, not only were we fighting off impeachment, but we were also fighting off all the kinds of attacks that could be launched below [the level of] impeachment, which governed everything. It governed all the press, it governed all the talk shows, it governed all the discussions, it governed everyone's thought processes. Well, below that Congress could do any number of appropriations riders that did all kinds of stuff that no one was ever going to notice. The number of environmental riders on appropriations bills proliferated after John left, partly because of Gore, partly because the Republicans thought they could get away with it, right?

So the notion of passing things [legislatively] that were positive was beyond the pale. We were too busy fighting off the things that the Republicans were trying to jam down our throats. We tended to succeed in the last month of the year with the summits on the appropriations bills, but, in the meantime, to get some of Clinton's environmental and workplace objectives accomplished, we did it by executive order. And then Bush 43 rolled almost all of them back in his first eighteen months—a little longer than that. They just rolled back New Source Review, for which they'll pay a huge price.

Ball: What about the ergonomic standards?[28]

Stein: Yes, the ergonomics standards. That was one we had to fight every year. Congress continuously put in rollbacks on ergonomic standards.

Neustadt: Let me ask a different question that relates to party differences here. I've read in the last two or three months a number of times that Karl Rove has recommended so-and-so for the Republican nomination for Congress in such-and-such a district. Back in Truman's time, that would have been absolutely anathema because of what had happened to Roosevelt in 1938.[29] One thing we couldn't do was go into primaries. And that logic lingered with the Democrats, although it's also true that Will Rogers said the Democrats are not an organized party, and that might have something to do with it too.

I don't know whether Rove really did, or does, these things, but I wonder, from the representatives of Republican administrations present, whether this was going on, for example, in Reagan's time, Ford's time, or Nixon's.

Friedersdorf: What did Rove recommend again?

Neustadt: Recommending candidates to run in congressional primaries.

Moore: Against incumbents?

Neustadt: To run for nominations. The kind of thing that's commonplace in the UK [United Kingdom], of course, but that's a different system. Once Roosevelt tried a purge in the '38 election, and it flopped, my guy [Truman] would never touch it.

Thurber: May I add three examples of this? [Norman] Coleman in Minnesota, [John] Thune, and this year, [George] Nethercutt in the state of Washington, they were backed by the White House before the primary.[30] That's what you're talking about.

Neustadt: Yes, the White House proposing people as their candidates, proposing them to the local, state, or district party people.

Friedersdorf: That sounds a little bit cheeky to me. I can imagine the national chairman or the chairman of the Republican Congressional [Campaign] Committee or the party itself in various states doing this. Maybe that's accepted now, but I find it a little bit hard to imagine Jim Baker making a recommendation for a congressional district, or John Sununu, or even back farther than that, Cheney and Rumsfeld. I mean, that's not their role, to select political candidates. They're chief of staff of the White House. I think it could cause some trouble out in the boondocks if there are other people getting ready to run and the White House put the stamp of approval on somebody else. I don't think it would sit too well with other potential candidates.

Neustadt: Well, of course, I can't be sure the current administration is actually doing that. I just read what I read in the newspapers.

Friedersdorf: Well, you can't believe everything you read in the newspapers.

Neustadt: I know that.

Stein: They recruited John Thune, there's no question about that. And they certainly talked to Coleman at great length.

Moore: Well, you have certain circumstances like when Senator Muskie resigned his Senate seat to be secretary of state.[31] You had to have a good candidate in Maine. George Mitchell was a sitting federal judge, I believe. And so he had to be persuaded to give up a lifetime seat. Muskie was arranged, and nobody else was going to have it. That's a time when you can [have a would-be candidate] meet with the president, you can urge them to run for this seat. But certainly it's not picking him. It's the party apparatus in the state that says, "This is the best person." I can think of other circumstances where a seat became vacant—a death or a resignation—and the White House, the president or vice president, would be asked to urge somebody to run. But certainly not in a primary against an incumbent. You just don't do that, you stay out of that.

Gilmour: I've taught Dick Neustadt's book *Presidential Power* a number of times, and probably some of you did as well.[32] One of the intriguing theses in the book is that the professional reputation of the president has an important impact on the president's power in Congress. That is, if the president has a reputation for being able to deploy the resources of the office effectively, there is a law of anticipated reactions—people are more willing to cooperate. I wonder if you have experiences that are germane to this thesis, instances of successful deployment of resources that led to greater cooperation—or the opposite, klutziness leading to more difficulties?

Stein: It's almost a law of physics that if you're successful once, you're better off the next time around. But I'm sure you're asking a much more subtle question. The classic negative one is healthcare. Healthcare is thought to be the debacle. The truth is that there was a preliminary debacle. We passed Clinton's budget by the one vote, and I think we made it possible for him to govern. But that was a near-death experience, and it occurred in the first nine months of his presidency.

Hilley: Your ability to deploy resources in this job depends so fundamentally on the cooperation and the quality of the leadership you deal with up on the Hill. The amount of heavy lifting that the leaders have to do on behalf of the president is just absolutely beyond belief. And if you can't count on them to do your work for you, you're just not going to make it. I know about Clinton's first budget bill. Larry and I were in the Senate and saw it first hand. It was down to Bob Kerrey's vote and he had some Svengali out there with Texas boots on telling him how to vote[33]—

Stein: Took him to a movie.

Hilley:—took him to a movie to decide how to vote on the president's most important bill. But without the active intervention of Harry Reid and Tom Daschle to swing that vote and to get Clinton through, and without the time that Mitchell spent rounding up every single vote, [the bill would have failed].[34] I have to say, Tom Daschle [in the Senate] was a marvelous help in my later years at the White House. You just cannot overstate what it takes to get this stuff through, and so much of the resources come from a good congressional leadership and committee structure, because there's no way you do it by yourself.

Ball: The issue in this position more frequently—focusing on the use of presidential resources—is where *not* to apply presidential resources. You have a broad-based agenda, you have a chorus of requests from the Congress and from the executive branch to elevate the importance of this issue and apply the president's time. It is important that the legislative assistants focus their energy and time *just* on major priorities. That entails being a nay-sayer to others in the administration more frequently than being an advocate of elevating the use of the president's time.

McClure: It's also [facetiously] a lot of fun coming into the job where the guy who is the majority leader—or the minority leader in this instance—was a guy that you ran against in the primary for president, Bob Dole. Fortunately, Bob Dole and George Bush developed a wonderful relationship and worked very well together as a part of that process, thanks to Senator Mitchell, nudging us on the other side. He created a world where that had to work together. So thank you guys very much!

Stein: We were helping you!

McClure: I'm going to add another piece to what Will said in terms of managing the president's resources. There's also the issue of using cabinet members or subcabinet members to assist in the process, even though it might have been in a subject area that's not necessarily something that comes under their bailiwick. You then end up having the president and the vice president's time to use when it really, really, means something. Because not only will the members stop talking to us, but they won't talk to anybody else. It's "Okay, I want my call from the president." They want to actually talk to him every time.[35]

Wayne: Ronald Reagan reportedly operated—out of Jim Baker's office—a legislative strategy group in the first term that did, I think, some of the things that Fred was just describing. What happened to that in the second term, and in Bush and Clinton? Did you guys use any of that to orchestrate the day and the administration's efforts on the Hill?

Ball: Yes, in the second term, from '86 to '88, we had a legislative strategy group. Ken Duberstein was the deputy chief of staff and Howard Baker was the chief of staff. It met regularly, not on a daily basis, but we'd have a senior staff meeting on a daily basis, a follow-up meeting with Senator Baker on the schedule of the day, and then we'd have a legislative strategy group on specific issues. So, yes.

Brain: The Clinton model tended to be more "war room": a big effort, pull a lot of resources in together, set up some folks over in the Old EOB [Executive Office Building], and, maybe short of a war room—which developed a reputation and was looked upon with disdain—making sure you had cabinet members working together, coordinating them. As Fred said, if you've got the secretary of agriculture calling Ag [Committee] members, even if it's on an energy matter, it gets their attention. We tended to do it on bigger issues and the highest priorities, less so on a regular basis.

Stein: On a daily basis we did something similar to the legislative study group. We'd have an early morning—7:30 or earlier—message meeting with the press people and the chief of staff and ourselves sitting down there. Then you'd do the chief of staff's meeting, which was more general. And then we would have what we called—for reasons I don't even remember—the budget meeting. It was basically a legislative meeting where you sat there and decided what you're going to do. Then you would spread out into the larger group when you had the assignments.

What was clear to me is something John referred to earlier: The integration of the message stuff with the legislative stuff was fundamental to us and really is something that deserves a lot more discussion in this context because it's crucial. The whole press component as an intermediary between the White House and the Hill is another aspect to this that I don't think we've talked that much about.

Ball: Larry Stein makes a good point about the press and relationships with the press as they affect the legislative process. I would add to what was said a little earlier that it's not uncommon today for members of Congress to communicate with each other through the press. Whereas twenty-five years ago senators might have shared an idea or a thought when they would sit together in the "members only" dining room—and they had lunch on a daily basis—now it seems that in many cases the preferred channel of communication is a leak to the reporter covering that issue. That's really dramatically changed the communications landscape.

McClure: Our legislative affairs office would sometimes use the press as a mechanism to get senators or congressmen on the record about issues that you really, really wanted to get them locked in on. A carefully planted question asked at the right time might elicit the kind of response that you needed to lock somebody down.

Riley: Did you do that very often, Fred?

McClure: Fairly often. It wasn't something that happened every week. All of these circumstances we have discussed vary from issue to issue and level of importance, but it was done with some regularity. The guys in the press would ask us about X. And this was in our independent relationships with them. You might respond by saying, "Why don't you go ask so-and-so Y? You might find out the answer to that question."

Riley: Is it fair to say that each of you studiously avoided having your names appear in the newspapers? Putting together briefing materials on legislative directors is quite a chore because you guys don't leave a long paper trail.

McClure: That's by intention.

Ball: I think we were brought up to understand that if you want to be effective in this business, members have to know that what they say to you is going to be kept in confidence—shared with the president, if necessary—but not be in the paper every day. You would not be able to retain that trust.

Brain: I never thought I was smart enough to be able to figure out the effect of what I was saying to a reporter on the intended target. I'll give you a case—this wasn't me. The White House press secretary is traveling with the president, there's a vote going on, and reporters are saying, "Well, the president really doesn't care about this issue, he's out traveling." The press secretary said, "Well no, the president's engaged, he's making phone calls." "Who's he making the phone calls to?"

So he told them, laid out the names, with one guy in particular: "We've got him very close to making a politically difficult vote." And there it is publicly: The president is pressuring this member to vote. The only way I could think to retrieve this—I just went directly to the member's office. I walked in there, and he just looked at me and said, "You SOB, I knew you'd show up. I was going to yell at you on the phone, but I can't yell at you in person." So there's an example of somebody using the press for one purpose that was completely counterproductive. That's the kind of bank shot that I'm not comfortable with.

Walcott: Along this line, it seems that increasingly in the presidency, issues are approached via a communications strategy, an overall concept of how this thing is going to be sold, which may include congressional relations but certainly isn't limited to it. To what extent do you people have experience with being included in on communications strategy, integrating your activities with what the communications office or the press office is doing to push an issue at the same time?

McClure: Ours was daily. At our senior staff meeting each morning, which was chaired by the chief, it was the seniormost folks. It's the guy who's got communications; it's the press secretary; it's the domestic policy guy, the national security guy, me, and whoever else was in that group. That's where we began the coordination process, what the message was going to be for the day, how it was going to fit in the process. Then, later on during the day, other members of our staff at different levels would participate in the process.

There were other issues, such as clean air, for example, where we were not only building a piece of legislation that we were going to roll out and introduce in Congress, but also trying to get members of Congress to be involved while it was being drafted by us. Part of our strategy in that one was to build the bill around four or five principles, for example. And that was going to be our standard in terms of whether we were going to veto an alternative or accept changes to our bill. So, the public messages were about those four or five principles, and that was the touchstone we used throughout that process.

Friedersdorf: As for taking press calls, in the Reagan administration, first term, if a congressional relations person got a call from the press, they were to refer it to the press office and also let us know that they'd gotten a call so that we could be aware of it.

The second question, about are we included in the communications loop: That was an integral part of the legislative strategy group when it was formed early in the Reagan administration by Jim Baker. That group would be, of course, the chief of staff, congressional relations director, Darman representing OMB, Dave Stockman representing OMB, and Dave Gergen with communications. So that was all coordinated.

In the senior staff meeting in the morning with the president, it would be practically the same group. So there was nothing that we were doing that the communications staff was not aware of. There was nothing the press office was doing that we weren't aware of. Everybody knew where the other office was [on an issue], so it worked pretty well.

Brain: It was very similar for us. There are two points. I think you can overstate the amount of long-range planning. A lot of this work is making it up on a daily basis. You're sitting around at 8:30 and decide, okay, the president needs to go out at 11:00 o'clock and make a statement on this or that. And there are a lot of other forces and interests surrounding the president rather than just what's going up on the Hill, breaking news and whatnot.

But one interesting focal point is the Saturday radio address, which was begun, I think, by President Reagan. To watch that evolve during the week, thinking about it Tuesday—what are we going to do? It changes throughout the week. The great thing about it is it's relatively short, and you don't have to have it final until the president has a mike in front of him. You're live. Sometimes it will change overnight. You might think it's on this, and—oops—it's on that.

Riley: Did those messages resonate with members of Congress? Did they pay attention to them?

McClure: I don't know if they resonate, but members started responding. Whether they respond to the subject matter—which is normally not the case—they started getting their chance to be on the radio, too, so they designate people. The problem is they don't have one person. Do they resonate? It depends on whether the people who hear it on Saturday pick up the phone and make a call or whether they're willing to write a letter or start beating up on somebody because their president said, "You're holding up my judges."

Ball: I think in current White Houses there is, and has been for some time, integration, pretty good integration, with the media communications and legislative professionals using increasingly state-of-the-art techniques. But there is tension in that relationship, and, as practitioners in getting votes, we would find ourselves frequently in disagreement with the communications strategists who, of course—since it's their business—think communications strategy is the answer to all issues. In their view, there was not a single issue that could not be won if Ronald Reagan simply gave an address from the Oval Office in prime time.[36]

Every week someone, a cabinet officer or a senior member of the staff, would say, "This is an important issue, we have to have a presidential address." When you assess the impact of that only on the issue at hand, you find yourself in this position, I think, frequently having disagreement. Though President Reagan developed justifiably a reputation for being a great communicator on TV in that setting, it was not something you would want to put to use too frequently. But, because it was generally effective, it was sought time and time again, even by judicial nominees.

So there is tension there that's probably healthy. When you're down to counting six, eight, or ten votes, there's only so much that a communications strategy is going to do for you—when you get right down to an individual vote of the senators or congressmen.[37]

Brain: With regards to the effectiveness: There was a radio address today, okay fine, will we ever know what it was about? Probably not. We frequently said the amount of work we put into it far surpassed the public reaction to it. But members of Congress, when you're working a big issue, do look at what the president has said and how often. "It can't matter to him. He hasn't said anything about it for three weeks."

McClure: This is especially important when they're your guys telling you that.

Brain: "Well, we're going to say something about it," and that's why maybe the next day at eleven o'clock you say something.

Friedersdorf: I think there have always been leaks up there at the White House. But I think it was perfected by Gergen and Baker during the first term. We would have those legislative strategy meetings, and everybody would be sworn to secrecy, and I'd pick up the *Post* the next morning and there it was, laid out. But they knew how to do it, because the leaks they put out were invariably favorable to us, and they got them printed, so you've got to give them credit for it. They weren't just leaking haphazardly, they were leaking with a purpose.

Knott: The conventional wisdom is that there's been a decline in civility up on Capitol Hill and that in particular it escalated during the Clinton years. I was wondering, particularly Chuck, if you would address this. Is that an accurate perception? And if so, what are the sources of this decline in civility?

Brain: I think that civility might actually be on the rise. Fraternity might be on the decline. Affection. Involvement. You're right. This is the congressional relations side of it, the issue of a stable majority. I grew up on the Hill. I grew up in the '80s, in the last decade of a four-decade stretch. And hell, we knew we were going to be in charge forever. In fact, working for the committee, you could look down the row and you knew sitting there was going to be the next great chairman of the Ways and Means Committee. So let's help him, teach him. Even the chairman never knew that. So you presumed. Translating this to the president's agenda, you had the ability from the Hill, therefore, to work with the president to accomplish his goals because the future of the congressional party didn't depend on it.

We never really talked about it, but the congressional Democratic cooperation with Ronald Reagan on tax reform in 1986 was astounding, a huge victory for President Reagan, which ultimately passed the House of Representatives with very few of his party in support of it. It was passed by Democrats. It changed over in the Senate. In fact, Chairman Packwood and the Republicans were in charge. But that was something where Rostenkowski said to Tip, "Hey, this is our stuff. We've got to do this." It didn't matter if it gave Ronald Reagan a bounce and helped George Bush get elected. It didn't matter, we were just doing it.

But today, you take the margins being so close—I say facetiously, the vote on approving the journal is so important that the speakership depends on it. Maybe the political scientists would say that if the majorities get so close, the middle has to hold, and you'll govern in the middle. No, that's not what happened, in fact. It's the fringes who control. Once you return to a stable majority—and I've got my preferences—then you get into a different system of government, where we're not talking about the future [control of Congress at the expense of the present], because you know you'll be there. If you don't do it this year, you'll do it next year.

Ball: Yes, I think that's an accurate statement. In '86 to '88 we had to work with House Democrats to get anything through there. The Tax Reform Act of 1986 was a good example of that. There was no prospect at the time of Republican control of the House, and dealing with those committee chairmen and the Democratic leadership was necessary to get anything of a revenue measure over to the Senate.

That was a different day. The closeness of the margins today, and the growth and utilization of negative television ads in close districts and close races—and the fact that we're in this perpetual campaign that we spoke about earlier—all have contributed to the deterioration of civility. It makes it very difficult to work across the aisle.

McClure: I'd add a couple of other things: the aggressiveness of Congress when it comes now to issuing subpoenas and wanting to be the investigative czar, if you will. No matter which side they're coming from, they're always aimed at the executive branch. That has increased substantially. It has probably come post-Watergate, but it got into the environmental stuff back during the Rita Lavelle days.[38] It's picked up a sort of steam that has not stopped, which the guys who worked for President Clinton can tell you about and the guys who are now working for this President Bush can tell you about.

On the [loss of] camaraderie, I can at least personally trace it back to the late '80s and the beginning of the Bush administration and take it from that point. Whether it was what happened to Jim Wright, what happened to Tony Coelho, what happened to other members of the leadership in the Congress of the United States, and our former boss, John Tower.[39] The institution is not like it used to be. I guess we can always say that about something we've once done, but when I was there in the '70s it was a totally different institution than when I was dealing with it in the late '80s and early '90s.

Friedersdorf: I take the long view on this civility thing because it seems to me every time there's a big clash up there, they'll say, "This is the most partisan time we've ever had." There are so many stresses, tensions, and conflicts built into the system by the founding fathers and by practice—which is a good thing, I think—that there's always going to be conflict, at times of stress, especially. Impeachment, and war and peace, and some of the fights that Fred just mentioned—you go back to those times, and I guarantee you would find quotes from members saying, "This is the most partisan Congress in the history of the United States." But if you read history, there's nobody getting shot up there, there's nobody getting clubbed like there was in the Civil War, beat over the head with a cane and having fisticuffs occasionally in the lobby.

I can't speak for the Clinton administration, obviously, or the last couple of administrations. I'm sure that there's a lot of incivility. But I would argue that it's not on the increase.[40] I think it's a symptom of the times and the issues that the congressmen and senators are facing.

Wayne: You spoke about press leaks and how that might have hurt you if they indicated that the president was calling someone or something like that. Did any of you have occasion to use the press for the purposes of trying to build support or get legislation through, or getting back at someone who really screwed you?

Friedersdorf: During the Reagan administration—and to a certain extent during the Ford administration—I did give interviews and talk to reporters. I was permitted to do that by the chief of staff because I think he had confidence that I would not say anything that would be in conflict with the president's policy and because I had enough judgment not to say something that would offend a congressman or senator—and to get across the message we were trying to sell. I think that of the other members of the senior staff, Baker was interviewed, Stockman did interviews, and members of the senior staff did interviews. It all depends on the individual. You can't have everybody going out there and being interviewed constantly, but there are certain times in a legislative session when good stories by the congressional relations people help you.

At the other end of the line, you get to know which of those press people you can talk to. There are certain people who call you, and immediately your antennae and your hackles go up: "I can't say anything. I can't even comment on the weather to this person because they're either going to misquote me, or they're going to put this in the worst light." There are others you know that you could be perfectly honest with. We never went off the record. That was a no-no. You either went on the record or you didn't talk to them. But once you knew who the responsible reporters were—and most of them were—you could talk to them. They're trying to get a story, and you're trying to sell a product, and sometimes it comes together nicely.

McClure: The reporters for all the media outlets are hanging out in the same place up on Capitol Hill that the legislative people are hanging out. They're after members to get quotes and comments, and likewise they would be after the legislative folks, in many instances just to find out what's going on. And actually, once you've got the kinds of relationships that Max alluded to and develop them, you found that they could be very helpful to you in figuring out the strategy of somebody else who could potentially be your opponent, or would be your opponent.

Friedersdorf: There's a few of those people probably still there like Tom deFrank of *Newsweek* and Anne Compton of ABC—

Ball: Anne's still there.

Friedersdorf:—and, you know, they were a tool. I consider them tools, because a lot of things I could find out from Tom—

Ball: Good journalists.

Friedersdorf: He would know things that we didn't know. So it certainly wasn't something that we avoided.

Brain: You could talk to them, not as an official White House spokesman for the record, but it was just sharing information.

Ball: I confess I avoided them. You know, you come back from a long day on the Hill and you have fifteen phone slips from members of Congress, ten or fifteen from other executive branch officials and cabinet officers, and ten or twelve reporters. I found a way to put those reporters at the bottom of the stack. I'm sure I paid a price for that. But it's very tough, especially in dealing with the White House press corps. Those are not local folks from the *Greenville News,* these are tough and seasoned reporters. And as Max said, you learn what direction they're coming from. It's a difficult dimension to the job, trying to advance the president's agenda but also to do so through reporters. I was not very good at doing that.

Brain: You asked earlier if there was a topic that we haven't covered, and your saying "coming back from the Hill" reminded me of something: The daily tension in the office, the decision where to be physically.

Riley: Good point.

Brain: I had the job of deputy, House deputy, and then assistant to the president. Quite frankly, in some respects the job of deputy was a hell of a lot better, because I could be on the Hill when I wanted to be 80 percent of the time. If things are nutty at the White House, you just get a car and you go up there, and most of the people are happy to see you. But when you're the assistant to the president, it means you have two places that you have to deal with. You have so much responsibility in the White House. These meetings that we've been talking about—those meetings are going to occur even if you're not there. So they make a policy decision, and you're not there to say, "It's not going to work. It's going to blow up." But yet, one of your strengths is being up on the Hill talking to people. That's where you get the raw data to be able to [judge how the president's program is doing. But if you spend all your time at the White House], then you have senators and members saying, "Where've you been? You don't like us any more? What's wrong?" "Well, I've got these things going on." So that's a real tension.

Friedersdorf: You can sit there in the White House all day long and shuffle papers and never get out of your seat, you can do that. I saw that in the Nixon administration. Bill Timmons got chained to the desk. No fault of his, but he did get chained to the desk. And he got criticized by members. "Where is Bill? Why doesn't he ever come to the Hill?" Well, he had a lot of battles he was trying to fight, and he had to be in the White House.[41]

But I made up my mind that we were not going to get into that trap. We had standing rules that House and Senate staff should go to the Hill by ten o'clock, whether there were committee meetings or not, get up there and go and make the rounds. I made myself go, at twelve noon, no matter how many phone calls, even if Mrs. Reagan was on the line—

McClure: No, oh, c'mon!

Friedersdorf: I would get up and go to the Hill at twelve noon, you know, just to be seen up there on the House floor and Senate floor. As Chuck says, that can make a difference because if they don't see you around there, they feel like the White House is isolated, and they start talking among themselves. You can just walk through the dining room. That's all you have to do.

Ball: That's right. It's all you have to do.

Friedersdorf: It worked pretty good. You torture yourself, because when you come back in the evening, like you say, Will, you've got a stack of phone calls that takes you 'til eight or nine o'clock to return. We had another rule: You couldn't go home until you returned all your phone calls, and you might have twenty-five phone calls. But the beauty of that is after seven o'clock there's damn few people in the office, and you could leave a message that you've returned the call.

Brain: But now there's e-mail.

Ball: Now there's e-mail on top of that. I can't imagine.

Riley: You had a deputy who was responsible for looking after the shop while you were on the Hill. The organization—I'm a little fuzzy, but typically there was somebody who was supposed to stay pretty much anchored in the White House and look after these things, right? Did they just not have sufficient stature to be in the kinds of meetings that you're talking about?

Brain: They did, but they weren't *the* assistant.

McClure: It depended on whether it was an assistants-level meeting. Actually, the person who was the internal deputy on my team—I had three of them during the time that I was there—had the ability to sit in on a meeting and declare for us, if you will, pretty effectively from a legislative affairs standpoint. But there were a lot of those meetings, from judicial selection, to scheduling, to speechwriting, to domestic policy. And that one person had a difficult time making all of those meetings. So it was a pretty busy day.

Friedersdorf: Bill Gribbin was my deputy, and he had tremendous experience on the Senate side, and he was a really well organized person.[42] When I was on the Hill he was always in the White House, and he would cover the key meetings. He didn't go to the Hill that much; he was in our offices practically all the time.

Meese would call the judicial meetings at six o'clock, six thirty, to make sure that we were back from the Hill. Meese would sit there and talk about judges 'til midnight, if you let him. He just loved to talk about judicial appointments and all the qualifications and why the American Bar Association was blocking this one or that one.[43] We're sitting there going half asleep and still hadn't got all the phone calls returned, but he wouldn't have the meetings start until we all got back from the Hill.

Brain: You talk about the continuity in the office, and you mentioned the on-site assistant. I did have that job briefly. One day I was there, and Congressman [Robert] Portman was in and around the White House with some of his friends.[44] And he had had that job, the inside deputy [before he was elected to Congress]. Portman walked into my little cubbyhole, and he said, "Drapes haven't changed." In fact, he turned to his friends and said, "One of those two pillows"—there were two chairs—"has a big yellow stain on the back of it from a magic marker." Sure enough, he went over and picked it up—and this was ten years later. Things don't change.

Riley: Institutional memory?

Brain: Yes.

McClure: He was worthless at that job, by the way. [laughter]

Brain: It was because he was magic-markering.

Riley: With that, then, we'll bring this to a conclusion. Let me once again say how grateful I am to those of you who have come down to tell us your experiences in Washington. It has been a very illuminating experience for us, as well as being extremely enjoyable. I can't think of a group we've met with that we've had more fun with. Too bad that many of the stories that we picked up in the hallways and over dinner last night didn't get on the record, but at least we have them lodged in our memories. Thank you for coming down and being part of this.

Ball: We should thank the Miller Center, too, because this has been an enjoyable opportunity for us.

Friedersdorf: Yes, it's been a two-way learning street. I, for one, enjoyed hearing about the other administrations, the ones I didn't serve in, the ones that came before, and the ones that came after. It's just been like going to school.

Brain: Any time that I have a bad day up on the Hill, should I ever serve again, I'm just going to think of your litany of woes, Max.

EDITOR'S COMMENTARY

During a series of conversations among the cast of academic moderators in advance of this symposium, Professor Richard E. Neustadt voiced concern on several occasions about what he felt would be a tendency among the gathered White House alumni to concentrate their discussions on commonalities at the expense of noting important changes in the job over time. The very nature of the gathering, he understood, would make this inevitable. Having spent years recalling the uniqueness of their work for their president, these former White House aides would, for perhaps the first time, be among the only group of people (notwithstanding its partisan diversity) who truly had a common experience. And that common experience was to be communicated to a group of academic outsiders only partially knowledgeable about their world. Small wonder, under these conditions, that the discussions would gravitate to the similarities about the CL's job. A concern about that bias led Neustadt to open this final session of the symposium by probing about discontinuities.

Although the arc of the symposium's discussions confirmed, in the main, Neustadt's predictions, some important changes in how the White House relates to Capitol Hill did surface. The scope and character of those changes can be more easily appreciated by collecting them for inspection here. Over the symposium's four sessions, one or more of the seven former White House aides highlighted the following as consequential alterations over the last half century affecting how the congressional liaison role is performed:

A marked decrease in the amount of personal time the president can now devote to congressional relations;

The proliferation of congressional affairs specialists throughout the government, each with individualized client interests;

Greater decentralization of the membership on Capitol Hill in the 1970s, followed by an admixture of centralization and continued decentralization in the 1990s;

A commensurate reliance by Congress in recent decades on continuing resolutions and complex omnibus budget bills to make policy;

An increase in the use of (or threatened use of) the filibuster in the Senate, requiring sixty votes to override;

The increased power of the media (especially television) and the influence of the twenty-four-hour news cycle on political behavior in Washington, providing incentives to run "permanent campaigns";

The influence of term-limits on the allocation of committee chairmanships;

An increase in the public contentiousness of judicial nominations, especially at the Supreme Court level, and the complexity of clearance procedures for presidential nominees at every level;

An apparent rise in the prominence of the investigative role of Congress and the use of the subpoena power; and

The death of a "permanent" Democratic majority in the House of Representatives, creating a major source of instability in a place that had for decades been highly stable.

It was also proposed by some that greater partisan rancor and incivility infect Washington today than before, but here opinion was divided. Clinton CL Lawrence Stein endorses the claim of more incivility in chapter 4, as does Reagan's Will Ball in this chapter. But Republican Max Friedersdorf rejects the notion that rancor is worse in Washington now, taking what he calls "the long view on this civility thing. . . . [T]here's nobody getting shot up there, there's nobody getting clubbed like there was in the Civil War, beat over the head with a cane and having fisticuffs occasionally in the lobby." Based on this conflicting testimony, then, it is not possible to establish a consensus judgment from these sources about the path of partisan rancor in recent times.[45]

Even absent concurrence on this one point, however, there remains an impressive array of agreed-upon changes in the environment shaping presidential-congressional relations—thereby influencing the work of the president's CL. With the president's own time commitments more unforgiving than ever before, for example, the CL must take on an even greater share of the burden for managing the president's portfolio in Congress. The proliferation of congressional relations specialists in the executive branch means that the long-standing problem of monitoring departmental and agency freelancing is even more complicated than before. The emergence of an overwhelming media presence in Washington makes it impossible for the CL to undertake his or her work without coordinating the efforts with the communications and press shops, which may mean tacking to the winds of public opinion in some cases when the more efficient course of action within Congress would be a straight-line approach. And this means that notwithstanding some important developments in the post-1994 era to create a more centralized Congress, no CL today is as free as those of Bryce Harlow's generation to work quietly, out of public view, with a few leading figures, with the assurance that their gentlemen's agreements will be accepted by the membership at large.

When the array of confirmed changes is tallied, then, it is actually quite striking that the basic size and structure of the legislative affairs shop has not changed more dramatically than it has over the last fifty years.[46] There has been some modest growth, but nothing commensurate with the altered framework of the CL's responsibilities. It is equally remarkable, given these circumstances, that none of the CLs in attendance at the symposium made the case that a bigger staff is needed. Why? Two possible answers come to mind here. First, perhaps it is the case that the moderately evolved office actually does provide the president with sufficient internal resources to get the job done. These CLs repeatedly told us about a pair of interrelated chores necessary for keeping the job manageable: the requirement of leveraging their power by making proper use of that broader community of executive branch congressional relations specialists, and the need to keep off their plates anything that was not related to the bedrock core of the president's own agenda. The White House congressional relations shop as it stands today may be sufficient for its purposes if it is properly managed along these two key dimensions.

There is, however, another reason why staff growth might not present itself as an attractive option to these CLs: They may consider additional staff counterproductive. Almost to a person, the dimension of the job that these White House alumni warmed to as the most appealing aspect of their work was what Charles Brain called the "sales job." None in this group indicated a particular fondness for the internal management function the job entails—a responsibility that would become more prominent, and more complicated, as the staff grows. Indeed, in this final chapter Brain expressed a decided preference for the Hill work, noting that "if things are nutty at the White House, you just get in a car and you go up there, and most of the people are happy to see you." On the evidence of the symposium, these are people who enjoy the personal engagement of politics and much prefer it to the management of an organization—especially a growing one.

Finally, a corollary point was suggested by Neustadt back in chapter 2: a fear that a bigger operation might actually attract more business. Indeed, one of Neustadt's most trenchant observations in *Presidential Power* was that nobody, even those within the president's employ, sees the president's duties in quite the same way that he does. This means that the existence of a White House staff in any form is not an unalloyed good, because people other than the president can set up shop for their own purposes. Neustadt's student Matthew Dickenson has written extensively on this problem and has recommended as a consequence a significant reduction in the overall size of the White House staff to curtail the problem of political freelancing in the president's name.[47] It is doubtful that these CLs know Dickenson's work, but their impulses about staff growth may well be driven by the very worries that Dickenson, and Neustadt, came to in their careful studies. Having more people involved in selling the president's program on the Hill might, paradoxically, make it more difficult to get that basic job done.

NOTES

PREFACE

1. Details about the Oral History Program's activities appear in Russell L. Riley, "Presidential Oral History: The Clinton Presidential History Project," *Oral History Review* 34, no. 2:81–106, and Russell L. Riley, "The White House as a Black Box: Oral History and the Problem of Evidence in Presidential Studies," *Political Studies* 57, no. 1:187–206.

2. In most interviews only a few brief passages are withheld by the respondent when the document is released. Many of those redactions are to be opened at a later date as designated by the interviewee. In our experience, the vast majority of such passages involve catty or gossipy remarks, made about other personalities during unguarded moments in the interview, which the respondent would prefer not to have publicly known.

3. Frank Moore's oral history with the Jimmy Carter Project and Max Friedersdorf's interview as part of the Reagan Project are already available on the Miller Center's website: http://millercenter.org/academic/oralhistory. Fred McClure's interview with the George H. W. Bush Oral History Project and the Lawrence Stein, John Hilley, and Charles Brain interviews, all of the Clinton Project, will be released on the same website at a future date.

4. In some few instances brief asides have been removed as diversionary, and occasionally some exchanges have been slightly rearranged to improve the flow of the written discussion. In no case has this materially altered the content of the discussions.

CHAPTER 1. INTRODUCTION

1. Anti-Federalist epithet from Herbert J. Storing, *What the Anti-Federalists Were* For (Chicago: University of Chicago Press, 1981), 54.

2. Woodrow Wilson further wrote, "There is no one supreme, ultimate head—whether magistrate or representative body—which can decide at once and with conclusive authority what shall be done at those times when some decision there must be, and that immediately." Woodrow Wilson, *Congressional Government: A Study in American Politics* (New York: Meridian Books, 1956), 184–86 (originally published in 1885).

3. Neustadt's preface is included in the final edition of the book, published as *Presidential Power and the Modern Presidents: The Politics of Leadership from Roosevelt to Reagan* (New York: The Free Press, 1990), xx–xxiv.

4. See Charles O. Jones, "Richard E. Neustadt: Public Servant and Scholar," *Annual Review of Political Science* 6 (2003): 1–22.

Other scholars do note problems in taking such a president-centric view of American politics. A "tandem" (or "shared governance") approach, focusing more on an equal role for Congress, can be found in (respectively) Mark A. Peterson, *Legislating Together: The White House and Capitol Hill from Eisenhower to Reagan* (Cambridge: Harvard University Press, 1990), and Lance T. LeLoup and Steven A. Shull, *The President and Congress: Collaboration and Combat in National Policymaking,* 2nd ed. (New York: Longman, 2003).

5. Charles O. Jones characterizes this reality in slightly different language in a book entitled *The Presidency in a Separated System,* 2nd ed. (Washington, DC: Brookings Institution Press, 2005).

Most of what I say here about presidential-congressional relations is relevant to most of American history. During crisis periods, at which time the government moves to an alternative footing under presidential direction, the realities are a bit different. In such cases, for relatively brief times, congressional deference to presidential direction becomes the norm.

6. CL is the shorthand reference insiders use to refer to the congressional liaison.

7. Although Harlow is sometimes seen as taking a relatively modest view of the president's engagement in the legislative arena—Stephen J. Wayne holds that "Eisenhower and his staff tried to avoid alienating Congress. They deferred to the Democratic leadership"—his fundamental characterization of the CL as a bridge builder holds true universally, regardless of the president's degree of assertiveness in trying to steer Congress. (Harlow worked, too, it should not be forgotten, for Richard Nixon.) The very essence of the job is the effort by one branch to shape the behavior of another, notwithstanding their constitutional separation. How aggressive, or accommodationist, a White House is in pursuing this effort (or, to further the metaphor, how much artillery they roll across the bridge) is a separate matter. Stephen J. Wayne, *The Legislative Presidency* (New York: Harper & Row, 1978), 145.

8. See, for example, James Sterling Young and Russell L. Riley, "Party Government and Political Culture," paper presented at the September 1990 annual meeting of the American Political Science Association, San Francisco.

9. The phrase "separated institutions sharing powers" is also Neustadt's (*Presidential Power,* 29, 32–34).

10. See discussions headed "Cabinet Officers in Congress" in *Congressional Globe,* 38th Cong., 2nd Sess., 1865, 419–48.

11. Committee on Political Parties, American Political Science Association, *Toward a More Responsible Two-Party System* (New York: Rinehart, 1950); Lloyd Cutler, "To Form a Government," *Foreign Affairs,* Fall 1980, 126–43. Another idea for reform—a legislative-executive council comprised of senior members of those two branches for purposes of establishing a consensus national agenda—appeared in Wilfred E. Binkley, "The President and Congress," *Journal of Politics* 11 (February 1949): 79.

12. A valuable anthology addressing this same question is James A. Thurber, ed., *Rivals for Power: Presidential Congressional Relations,* 2nd ed. (Lanham, MD: Rowman & Littlefield, 2002).

13. See Charles M. Cameron, *Veto Bargaining: Presidents and the Politics of Negative Power* (Cambridge: Cambridge University Press, 2004); John B. Gilmour, "Institutional and Individual Influences on the President's Veto," *Journal of Politics* 64, no. 1 (February 2002): 198–218. More broadly on formal powers, see Kenneth R, Mayer, *With the Stroke*

of a Pen: Executive Orders and Presidential Power (Princeton: Princeton University Press, 2001).

14. "All that [a veto] would do would make the next budget negotiating session impossible. As a matter of fact, there wouldn't be one. They'll just say, 'We'll bring you what we feel like.' That's not my style," Bush said. Stephen Dinan and Donald Lambro, "Spending Plan Draws Immediate Ire on Hill," *Washington Times*, http://www.washtimes.com/national/20050208–121658–7204r.htm (accessed on March 29, 2009). This style changed somewhat with the altered partisan majorities on the Hill resulting from the 2006 midterm elections.

One summary of veto information can be found on the American Presidency Project website, http://www.presidency.ucsb.edu/data/vetoes.php (accessed 5 January 2009).

15. For more on SAPs, see C. Lawrence Evans and Walter J. Oleszek, "Herding Cats: Presidential Coalition Building in the Senate," in Thurber, ed., *Rivals for Power*, 172–77.

16. Neustadt, *Presidential Power*, 29–49.

17. On NAFTA, see Bob Woodward, *The Agenda: Inside the Clinton White House* (New York: Simon & Schuster, 1994). Truman quoted in Neustadt, *Presidential Power*, 10.

18. Nigel Bowles, *The White House and Capitol Hill: The Politics of Presidential Persuasion* (Oxford: Clarendon Press, 1987), 92–114.

19. Major Archibald Willingham Butt, *Taft and Roosevelt: The Intimate Letters of Archie Butt, Military Aide* (Port Washington, NY: Kennikat Press, 1971) 1:51.

20. On the *Sequoia*, see James P. Pfiffner, "The President's Legislative Agenda," *Annals of the American Academy of Political and Social Science*, September 1988, 29. O'Brien quoted in Kenneth E. Collier, *Between the Branches: The White House Office of Legislative Affairs* (Pittsburgh, PA: University of Pittsburgh Press, 1997), 73–74. On Gingrich, see Elizabeth Drew, *Showdown: The Struggle Between the Gingrich Congress and the Clinton White House* (New York: Simon & Schuster, 1996), 331–32.

21. On the value of the president's time, see Neustadt, *Presidential Power*, 130–34.

22. While this can be a blessing for a president, it can also be a curse. Presidents need people who can pass along bad news and let them know when they or their policies are in trouble. So the awe-inspiring aspect of the Oval Office can disserve a president who wants to hear dissenting voices.

23. See Kenneth Bradshaw and David Pring, *Parliament and Congress* (Austin: University of Texas Press, 1972).

24. The general political context is important for understanding the obstacles to party unity. Under conditions of crisis, especially wartime, party unity for the president's programs is typically much easier to reach than under peacetime circumstances.

Although these discussions occurred in the broad wake of the 9/11 attacks, it is clear that the participants did not view the extraordinary congressional acquiescence to the leadership of George W. Bush as a permanent condition. Indeed, the symposium was, under the circumstances, remarkably free of reflection on that wartime environment and how it altered political behavior in Washington. For the long historical view on this phenomenon, see Clinton Rossiter, *Constitutional Dictatorship and the Modern Democracies* (Princeton: Princeton University Press, 1948). The Jeffersonian-era quote appears in James Sterling Young, *The Washington Community, 1800–1828* (New York: Columbia University Press, 1966), 165.

25. George Lardner, "Phil Gramm: Risk-Taking Striver Sometimes Stumbles," *Washington Post,* February 7, 1996, A01. George C. Edwards III, *Presidential Influence in Congress* (San Francisco: W. H. Freeman, 1980), 205.

26. Neustadt, *Presidential Power,* 36.

27. Collier, *Between the Branches,* 15.

28. Tom Korologos quoted in Elisabeth Bumiller, "Delicate Diplomacy for This Guest List," *New York Times,* February 21, 2005, A-13, emphasis added.

29. For further details on the life of the CL, see the description in Bradley H. Patterson Jr., *The White House Staff: Inside the West Wing and Beyond* (Washington, DC: Brookings Institution Press, 2000), 114–28. See also Gary Andres and Patrick J. Griffin, "Successful Influence: Managing Legislative Affairs in the Twenty-first Century," in Thurber, ed., *Rivals for Power,* 141–62.

30. Kenneth E. Collier writes, "Without the trust of the president, it is difficult, if not impossible, for the liaison staff to credibly negotiate with Congress" (*Between the Branches,* 31).

31. For commentary on the role of the chief of staff in relation to Congress, see Terry Sullivan, ed., *The Nerve Center: Lessons in Governing from the White House Chiefs of Staff* (College Station: Texas A&M University Press, 2004), 33–35.

32. On the broad problem of presidential relations with the executive branch, see Richard P. Nathan, *The Administrative Presidency* (New York: John Wiley & Sons, 1983); Hugh Heclo, "One Executive Branch or Many?" in Anthony King, ed., *Both Ends of the Avenue: The Presidency, the Executive Branch, and Congress in the 1980s* (Washington, DC: American Enterprise Institute, 1983).

33. There is an Office of Cabinet Affairs in the White House, usually staffed by an assistant to the president, to facilitate coordination with and oversight of the cabinet. See the description in Patterson, *The White House Staff,* 330–39.

34. Abraham Holtzman, *Legislative Liaison: Executive Leadership in Congress* (Skokie, IL: Rand McNally, 1970), 4. Holtzman goes so far as to say that the original development of departmental "legislative liaison must be recognized as a developmental step in the strengthening of the presidency and the political leadership of the executive system as a whole" (p. 5). So the original intent was evidently to help, not hinder, presidential relations with Congress. See also Collier, *Between the Branches,* 51–55.

35. Quoted in Neustadt, *Presidential Power,* 37.

36. This element of Clinton's negotiating style is addressed in John Harris, *The Survivor: Bill Clinton in the White House* (New York: Random House, 2005), 214–17, 420–21.

37. A slightly expanded version of this story appears in the Max Friedersdorf Interview, Miller Center, University of Virginia, Ronald Reagan Oral History Project, October 24–25, 2002, 59–60. There he recounts that Nancy Reagan had grown distraught because Senator Strom Thurmond had talked his way past security to visit with the seriously wounded president.

38. Raymond Moley makes a claim that *he* tended to fill the congressional liaison role for FDR, although it is not clear that others accorded him primacy in that role. See Moley, *The First New Deal* (New York: Harcourt, Brace & World, 1966), 239. Moley provides an interesting account of Roosevelt's own relations with members of Congress at pp. 233–36.

39. Holtzman, *Legislative Liaison,* 2–3. See also Richard E. Neustadt, "Presidency and

Legislation: The Growth of Central Clearance," *American Political Science Review* 48, no. 3 (September 1954): 641–71.

40. Wayne, *The Legislative Presidency*, 38.

On the origins of the CL office, see the discussion in Collier, *Between the Branches*, 29–56. Standard works of scholarship (in addition to Collier) to be consulted on the emergence and development of the congressional liaison function include Jon Bond and Richard Fleisher, *The President in the Legislative Arena* (Chicago: University of Chicago Press, 1990); Bowles, *The White House and Capitol Hill;* George C. Edwards III, *At the Margins: Presidential Leadership of Congress* (New Haven: Yale University Press, 1989); Holtzman, *Legislative Liaison;* Peterson, *Legislating Together;* and Wayne, *The Legislative Presidency.* See also James Sterling Young, "Working Paper: The White House and Congress: A Study of the President's Liaison Staff, 1953–63," typescript, June 1967, editor's personal copy.

Collier concludes that Eisenhower's propensity to delegate also was reflected in his decisions about the proper handling of congressional relations (*Between the Branches*, 35–40).

CHAPTER 2. THE JOB DESCRIPTION

1. Philip Samuel Hughes (1917–2004) was for many years the assistant director for legislative reference of the Bureau of the Budget and later went on to become the first director of the Office of Federal Elections at the General Accounting Office. Elmer Boyd Staats (1914–) was a longtime staff member at the Bureau of the Budget, where he twice held the position of deputy director (1950–53 and 1958–66).

2. Bryce Nathaniel Harlow (1916–87) worked for President Dwight Eisenhower for the entirety of his two terms and was deputy assistant to the president for congressional affairs from 1958 to 1961. He later held the post of counselor in the Nixon White House. Wilton Burton (Jerry) Persons (1896–1977) was deputy assistant to President Eisenhower from 1953 to 1958 and then succeeded Sherman Adams as assistant to the president (chief of staff) until the close of Eisenhower's second term. He previously directed the legislative liaison operation of the Department of Defense in 1948 and 1949. Gerald D. (Jerry) Morgan was a special and administrative assistant to President Eisenhower from 1953 to 1955, special counsel to the president in 1955–58, and deputy assistant to the president from 1958 to 1961.

3. Bryce L. (Larry) Harlow (1949–) served in the Reagan administration in the White House congressional liaison office and headed legislative affairs for the Office of Management and Budget. He later was an assistant secretary of the treasury for legislative affairs for President George H. W. Bush.

4. Kenneth E. Collier also quotes this passage and attributes it to a speech Harlow delivered in Nashville in 1973. See *Between the Branches: The White House Office of Legislative Affairs* (Pittsburgh: University of Pittsburgh Press, 1997), 1–2, and 291 n. 3.

5. Charles O. Jones outlines a more elaborate job description in *Separate but Equal Branches: Congress and the Presidency*, 2d ed. (Chappaqua, NY: Chatham House/Seven Bridges Press, 1999), 180–87.

6. Moore and his troubles were the subject of no fewer than three major

Washington Post profiles in the year following Carter's election. See Mary Russell, "Hill Democrats Unhappy with Carter's Emissary," November 5, 1976, A1; Spencer Rich, "Shakedown Cruise: Carter's Hill Liaison Had Rough Sailing but Frank Moore Sees Smoother Seas," February 25, 1977, A2; Judy Bachrach, "'I Love Those People on the Hill,'" November 3, 1977, B1. See also Eric L. Davis, "Legislative Liaison in the Carter Administration," *Political Science Quarterly* 94, no. 2 (Summer, 1979): 287–301.

7. Dan Tate (sometimes identified as Dan Tate Sr. to distinguish him from Dan Tate Jr., who worked in congressional relations for the Clinton White House) was on Frank Moore's staff as head Senate liaison for President Carter. Wendell Hampton Ford (1924–) was a Democratic Senator from Kentucky who served from 1974 to 1999.

8. Charles O. Jones has observed that congressional liaison work in the Carter White House "was a sensitive and difficult task, since the president was not inclined by his nature or personal preference to respect the work engaged in by his own [liaison] staff. The lobbyists were in daily contact with those whose business it was to strike bargains and make compromises, rather than, in the president's words, to do 'what is right.'" Notwithstanding those sentiments, Moore did merit, along with national security advisor Zbigniew Brzezinski, a daily slot on the president's schedule (Jones, *Separate but Equal Branches*, 181, 187). Jones offers further details about the Carter congressional liaison shop in *The Trusteeship Presidency: Jimmy Carter and the United States Congress* (Baton Rouge: Louisiana State University Press, 1988), chap. 5.

9. The federal government was shut down twice near the end of 1995, both times because of disputes between the Clinton White House and the Republican Congress over the federal budget, leaving much of the national government without the funds to continue operations. Congressional Republicans suffered a loss of public confidence because of perceptions that they had forced the shutdown for political ends.

10. Leon Edward Panetta (1938–) was a Democratic member of Congress from California who later became the first director of the Office of Management and Budget for President Clinton. He then served as Clinton's second chief of staff (1994–96). Erskine Boyce Bowles (1945–) was Clinton's third chief of staff (1997–98). Previously, he had directed the Small Business Administration (1993–94) and served as deputy White House chief of staff (1994–95).

11. Press profiles of Friedersdorf as CL include Judith Miller, "Reagan's Liaison Chief on Capitol Hill to Focus on Harmony as His Priority," *New York Times*, January 6, 1981, B8; Helen Dewar and Lee Lescaze, "Reagan Hill Team Gets Rave Reviews," *Washington Post*, March 17, 1981, A5; Curt Suplee, "The Capitol Connection: Max Friedersdorf, Reagan's Savvy Man on the Hill," *Washington Post*, June 29, 1981, C1.

12. The very existence of a regularized program of legislative initiatives from the White House is a relatively recent historical phenomenon. See Richard E. Neustadt, "Presidency and Legislation: Planning the President's Program," *American Political Science Review* 4, no. 4 (December 1955): 980–1021. See also Andrew Rudalevige, "The Executive Branch and the Legislative Process," in Joel D. Aberbach and Mark A. Peterson, eds., *Institutions of Democracy: The Executive Branch* (Oxford: Oxford University Press, 2005), 419–51; Stephen J. Wayne, *The Legislative Presidency* (New York: Harper & Row, 1978), 101–38; and Paul Charles Light, *The President's Agenda: Domestic Policy Choice from Kennedy to Carter* (Baltimore: The Johns Hopkins University Press, 1982).

Thomas Christopher Korologos (1933–) served in the Nixon and Ford administrations as deputy assistant for legislative affairs and was later appointed by President George W. Bush as ambassador to Belgium.

13. Clark MacGregor (1922–2003) was a Republican member of the House of Representatives (1961–71) from Minnesota, joining President Nixon's congressional relations staff after leaving Congress.

14. Wallace Foster Bennett (1898–1993) was a Republican member of the Senate from Utah (1961–75). Donald Henry Rumsfeld (1932–) had served in the House of Representatives from Illinois (1963–69) before joining the Nixon administration as director of OEO in 1969. He later served as White House chief of staff under President Ford and was secretary of defense for Ford and President George W. Bush.

15. Nixon's emphatic charge to his legislative affairs specialists no doubt derived in part from his own personal distaste for asking members of Congress for their support. This was a job for staff. See Jones, *Separate but Equal Branches,* 143–47.

16. The partisan balance was 53–47 for the Republicans before the 1986 midterm election, moving to 55–45 for the Democrats afterward. The majority leader post went from Robert Dole of Kansas to Robert Byrd of West Virginia.

An up-to-date copy of Rumsfeld's observations can be found at the website http://www.rumsfeldsrules.com/.

17. President Johnson, like his predecessors and one successor, used a recording device for some of his phone calls and Oval Office conversations. Nixon's voice-activated system provided his critics the ammunition they needed, in his own voice, to force his departure from the presidency. The recording system was unplugged by the White House once its existence was discovered by Watergate-scandal investigators.

Information on the LBJ tapes, including links for listening to many of them, can be found on the website of the Miller Center's Presidential Recordings Program: http://millercenter.virginia.edu/index.php/academic/presidentialrecordings/pages/tapes_lbj (accessed May 4, 2007).

Richard Brevard Russell (1897–1971), Democratic senator from Georgia, served in the Senate from 1933 to 1971. Everett McKinley Dirksen (1896–1969) served as a Republican member of the Senate from 1951 to 1969. For the last ten years of that time he was the Senate minority leader.

18. George Pratt Schultz (1920–) was secretary of state under Ronald Reagan from 1982 to 1989. He previously had served in the Nixon administration as secretary of labor (1969–70); director of the Office of Management and Budget (1970–71); and secretary of the treasury (1972–74).

19. James Addison Baker III (1930–) was White House chief of staff in President Reagan's first term. He later served as Reagan's secretary of the treasury (1985–88) and as secretary of state for George H. W. Bush (1989–92).

20. Charles O. Jones refers to this as the "avoidance of mischiefs" that detract from the president's core concerns (*Separate but Equal Branches,* 199–200).

For more on the executive branch's nonpresidential liaison operations, see G. Russell Pipe, "Congressional Liaison: The Executive Branch Consolidates Its Relations with Congress," *Public Administration Review* 26, no. 1 (March 1966): 14–24; Thomas P. Murphy, "Congressional Liaison: The NASA Case," *Western Political Quarterly* 25, no. 2 (June 1972): 192–214.

21. John Henry Sununu (1939–) was White House chief of staff for George H. W.

Bush from 1989 to 1991. Richard Gordon Darman (1943–2008) was director of the Office of Management and Budget for Bush from 1989 to 1993.

22. Howard B. Paster was President Clinton's first congressional liaison, serving in that capacity throughout 1993.

23. Charles O. Jones explains that Moore's job was more complicated than most, partly because of President Carter's commitment to the idea of "cabinet government," which had the effect of licensing departmental lobbyists to greater independence (*Separate but Equal Branches,* 179).

24. The Office of Cabinet Affairs tends to White House relations with members of the president's cabinet. See Bradley H. Patterson Jr., *The White House Staff: Inside the West Wing and Beyond* (Washington: Brookings Institution Press, 2000), 330–39.

25. "To coordinate the efforts of the White House and departmental liaison staff, the Legislative Council was created. The council met on Saturday mornings for several years and provided an opportunity for information sharing and strategic planning" (Collier, *Between the Branches,* 53).

26. The needle exchange issue rose to the presidential level in Clinton's second term. The debate was between those who were against needle exchange, because they believed that it tacitly encouraged drug use, and those who promoted exchange as a public health issue, a way to control needle-borne illnesses such as AIDS.

27. General Barry Richard McCaffrey (1942–) was director of the Office of National Drug Control Policy under President Clinton from 1996 to 2001. Donna Edna Shalala (1941–) was President Clinton's secretary of health and human services for the entirety of his presidency, 1993–2001.

28. Lawrence Francis O'Brien Jr. (1917–90) headed congressional affairs for Presidents Kennedy and Lyndon Johnson from 1961 to 1965. He was also a longtime Democratic party activist, serving terms as chair of the Democratic National Committee.

29. Tip O'Neill (1912–94) represented Massachusetts, as a Democrat, in the House of Representatives for thirty-four years and was Speaker of the House from 1977 to 1987.

According to Eric L. Davis, "In the elections of 1972, 1974, 1976, and 1978, 303 new members of the House were elected, and sixty-one freshman senators went to Washington. . . . A majority of the Democratic members of the 95th House sworn in along with Jimmy Carter in January 1977 [had] never had the experience of serving in Congress while a Democrat occupied the White House" ("Legislative Reform and the Decline of Presidential Influence on Capitol Hill," *British Journal of Political Science* 9, no. 4 [October 1979]: 466).

30. William Robert Poage (1899–1987) represented Texas as a Democrat in the House of Representatives from 1937 to 1979. He chaired the Committee on Agriculture beginning in 1967 until he was removed by a vote of the party caucus in 1975. Thomas Stephen Foley (1929–) represented the state of Washington as a Democrat in the House from 1965 to 1995. He was Speaker of the House from 1989 to 1994. From 1997 to 2001 he served as the ambassador to Japan, appointed by President Clinton.

31. Felix Edward Hébert (1901–79) served, as a Democrat, in the House of Representatives from Louisiana from 1941 to 1977. He chaired the Armed Services Committee from 1971 to 1975. James Claude Wright Jr. (1922–) represented Texas in the House from 1954 to 1988. He served as a Democratic Speaker of the House from 1987 to 1989,

when he was removed from office because of an ethics investigation into his financial integrity. Phillip Burton (1926–83), a Democrat, represented California in the House from 1964 to 1983. Robert Carlyle Byrd (1917–) served in the House from West Virginia from 1953 to 1959 and currently holds the record for the longest service in the Senate, beginning on January 3, 1959, and counting. Byrd, a Democrat, held the post of Senate majority leader from 1977 to 1981 and again from 1987 to 1989.

For a discussion tracking the change from centralized to decentralized power in Congress, see Roger H. Davidson, "The Presidency and Three Eras of the Modern Congress," in James A. Thurber, ed., *Divided Democracy: Cooperation and Conflict Between the President and Congress* (Washington: Congressional Quarterly, 1990), 66–70.

32. The book is Michael Grunwald, *The Swamp: The Everglades, Florida, and the Politics of Paradise* (New York: Simon & Schuster, 2006).

James C. Free was a member of President Carter's congressional relations staff, working on the House side under William H. Cable. Tom Bevill (1921–2005), a Democrat, served in the House from 1967 to 1997. He took a special interest in water projects, most prominently the Tennessee-Tombigbee waterway in his home state of Alabama.

On the politics of the Corps of Engineers, see John A. Ferejohn, *Pork Barrel Politics* (Stanford: Stanford University Press, 1974). On the more general presidential problem of tight links between the bureaucracy and Capitol Hill, see Barry R. Weingast, "Caught in the Middle: The President, Congress, and the Political-Bureaucratic System," in Aberbach and Peterson, *Institutions of Democracy*, 312–43.

33. John Goodwin Tower (1925–91), a Texas Republican, served in the Senate from 1961 to 1985. He was nominated by President George H. W. Bush to the position of secretary of defense, but controversy over his personal life led to a refusal by the Senate to confirm the nomination.

34. Will Ball had formerly been secretary of the Navy himself, under President Reagan.

35. The Congressional Budget and Impoundment Control Act was passed in 1974. Through this legislation Congress sought to limit the perceived excesses of President Nixon in impounding funds Congress allocated but the president did not wish to spend. The act also created a unified budget process for Congress.

John Cornelius Stennis (1901–95) served in the Senate, as a Democrat from Mississippi, from 1947 to 1989. He chaired the Armed Services Committee for more than a decade. Edmund Sixtus Muskie (1914–96) was a Maine Democrat who served in the Senate from 1959 to 1980. He left the Senate during the final year of the Carter presidency to become secretary of state.

36. Charlene Barshefsky was the U.S. Trade Representative for President Clinton.

37. James H. Rowe Jr. (1909–84) was administrative assistant to President Franklin D. Roosevelt from 1939 to 1941 and also worked in FDR's Justice Department.

38. Frederick J. Lawton (1917–1963) worked in the Bureau of the Budget and on Capitol Hill during the Roosevelt years. He became budget director under Harry Truman, serving there from 1950 to 1953.

The Fair Labor Standards Act of 1938 provided for a national minimum wage, overtime pay protection, and strict regulation of child labor.

39. Thomas Gardiner Corcoran (1900–81) was an administrator in Franklin

Roosevelt's Treasury Department and then special assistant to the president. Nicknamed "Tommy the Cork" by FDR, he was for many years one of the president's chief sources of political advice and intelligence.

40. Truman did have two assistants for dealing with members of Congress, but they helped "with the more routine political chores such as minor appointments, tickets to the Army-Navy football game, autographed pictures of the president, and the like." Wayne, *The Legislative Presidency,* 141.

41. For details on the Visitors Office, see Patterson, *The White House Staff,* 400–403.

42. Indeed, patronage was once so important to congressional relations that Lawrence O'Brien held the personnel and legislative affairs jobs simultaneously during the Kennedy presidency (Collier, *Between the Branches,* 59, 74–76).

43. For example, James A. Farley headed up Franklin Roosevelt's New Deal patronage operation as postmaster general. Details of his activities can be found in his aptly titled *Behind the Ballots: The Personal History of a Politician* (New York: Harcourt, Brace and Company, 1938). See also Scott C. James, "The Evolution of the Presidency: Between Promise and Fear," in Aberbach and Peterson, *Institutions of Democracy,* 20–21.

44. William E. Timmons (1930–) was assistant to the president for legislative affairs from 1969 to 1974, serving both Richard Nixon and Gerald Ford. Clark MacGregor (1922–2003) served as a Minnesota Republican in the House from 1961 to 1971 and then went into the Nixon White House to hold several positions, including a post in Nixon's congressional affairs operation.

45. Jack Bascom Brooks (1922–) served in the House of Representatives, as a Texas Democrat, from 1952 to 1995. He was the longtime chair of the Government Operations and Judiciary Committees, successively.

Ball's comments were made before events in the George W. Bush presidency created a new conflict between Congress and the White House over this very issue of staff testimony on Capitol Hill.

46. When the president travels for partisan political purposes as the head of his party, the White House has to make a determination to this effect so that the party can be billed for the cost of travel.

47. The matter of patronage appointments, and the engagement of members of Congress in the process, is one of the core jobs of the CL. Indeed, one of President Eisenhower's main reasons for setting up the office in the first instance was to create an institutional buffer between himself and patronage-seeking legislators. See James Pfiffner, "The President's Legislative Agenda," *Annals of the American Academy of Political and Social Science,* September 1988, 23, 28.

48. Wilbur Daigh Mills (1909–92) was a Democratic member of the House of Representatives from 1939 to 1977. The Arkansan was a longtime chair of the Ways and Means Committee. John David Dingell Jr. (1926–) is a Democratic member of the House from the state of Michigan. He entered the House in 1955 and was a longtime chair of the Committee on Energy and Commerce.

49. Gramm-Rudman-Hollings (after its legislative sponsors, Phil Gramm, Warren Rudman, and Ernest Hollings) is the informal name for the Balanced Budget and Emergency Deficit Control Act of 1985. This legislation was intended to bring under control a quickly growing federal budget deficit by requiring automatic spending cuts if

Congress and the president did not reach a set of agreed deficit targets. Core portions of the act were found to be unconstitutional by the U.S. Supreme Court in the 1986 case of *Bowsher v. Synar.*

The Budget Enforcement Act of 1990 was a key component of the Omnibus Budget Reconciliation Act of 1990, signed into law by President George H. W. Bush. Provisions of the Act superseded Gramm-Rudman-Hollings by establishing caps on discretionary spending and setting up pay-as-you-go (PAYGO) rules for program spending.

50. The Contract *with* America was a governing program some members of the Republican party generated before the 1994 midterm elections to describe what they would do as a governing party were they given majority status by the electorate.

51. Newton Leroy Gingrich (1943–) represented Georgia in the House of Representatives from 1979 to 1999 and is largely credited with orchestrating the Republicans' return to control of the House, after forty years of Democratic rule, in 1994. He served as Speaker from 1994 to 1998, resigning from his seat over ethics questions and the party's unexpectedly poor showing in the 1998 midterm elections.

52. George John Mitchell (1933–) served as a Democratic member of the Senate from 1980 to 1995, representing the state of Maine. He was Senate majority leader from 1989 to 1995. He later served as President Bill Clinton's special advisor on Ireland, and in that position he helped broker the Good Friday Accords in 1998. Thomas Andrew Daschle (1947–) represented South Dakota as a Democrat in the Senate from 1987 to 2005. He was the Democratic Party leader in the Senate, serving terms as both majority leader and minority leader, from 1995 to 2005.

53. Gingrich deserted President George H. W. Bush over Bush's decision, in 1990, to accept tax increases as part of a major budget negotiation with congressional Democrats, intended to arrest growing budget deficits. An account of this story is provided in John Robert Greene, *The Presidency of George Bush* (Lawrence: University Press of Kansas, 2000), 85–88.

54. On this point, see Joseph A. Pika, "White House Boundary Roles: Marginal Men Amidst the Palace Guard," *Presidential Studies Quarterly* 16, no.4 (Fall 1986): 700–15.

55. Clinton's aggravations with the quality of his early staff work can be seen episodically in George Stephanopoulos, *All Too Human: A Political Education* (Boston: Little, Brown and Company, 1999), and Bob Woodward, *The Agenda: Inside the Clinton White House* (New York: Simon & Schuster, 1994).

56. Senator Robert Byrd is a jealous guardian of Senate prerogatives, and during the first year of the Clinton presidency he refused to bend in certain instances that might have helped the White House with its early initiatives. Most prominently, Byrd indicated firm opposition to an idea floated in 1993 that the administration's major health care reform effort be included in the budget reconciliation process, which would have avoided the threat of opposition filibuster. The so-called Byrd Rule is intended to limit the uses of the reconciliation process strictly to budgetary issues, and Byrd insisted that a major health reform measure was extraneous.

57. On Carter, see Charles O. Jones, *Separate but Equal Branches*, 116–18. In the Clinton administration, George Stephanopoulos, in particular, was a lightning rod for criticism that Clinton was being overly influenced by people whose world views were shaped by Capitol Hill Democrats. Al Gore reportedly chided him at one point:

"George, I'm going to have to find some scientific procedure to get that [Dick] Gephardt DNA removed from you" (quoted in Stephanopoulos, *All Too Human,* 204).

58. These were the core members of Bill Clinton's original economic team in 1993. Gene B. Sperling was deputy director of the National Economic Council (and later became its director). Sperling had also been the 1992 campaign's chief economic staff member for Clinton. Robert Edward Rubin was the first director of the National Economic Council (and later succeeded Lloyd Bentsen as secretary of treasury). Lawrence Henry Summers was initially undersecretary of the treasury for international affairs and was later deputy secretary and then secretary of the treasury.

59. James Ralph Sasser (1936–) represented Tennessee as a Democratic member of the Senate from 1977 to 1995 and served as chair of the Budget Committee during President Clinton's first two years in office. From 1995 to 2001 Sasser was ambassador to the People's Republic of China.

60. Abraham Alexander Ribicoff (1910–98) was a Democratic senator from Connecticut who served from 1963 to 1981. He earlier had been governor of Connecticut and secretary of health, education, and welfare under President Kennedy.

61. If all members voted, a relatively rare occurrence, 146 was the magic number.

62. Brain's reference is to a slew of contested media reports that came out shortly after President George W. Bush took office, claiming that the out-going White House staff had trashed the facilities and in many cases had removed the *W* from the computer keyboards as a practical joke. The General Services Administration later concluded that no substantial vandalism had, in fact, occurred.

63. Nicholas E. Calio (1953–) held the position of assistant to the president for legislative affairs under both Presidents Bush, first from 1992 to 1993 and then from 2001 to 2003. He had planned to participate in this symposium but had to withdraw at the last minute.

64. Richard F. Fenno Jr. lists reelection as the first of three basic goals for members of Congress, followed by influence within the House and good public policy (*Congressmen in Committees* [Boston: Little, Brown and Company, 1973]).

65. Richard Joseph Daley (1902–76) served as mayor of Chicago for twenty-one years from 1955 to his death in 1976. He was also the boss of the city's Democratic machine and a force in Illinois and national politics. Frank Annunzio (1915–2001) served as a Democratic member of the House of Representatives from Illinois from 1965 to 1993. He chaired for four successive congresses the Committee on House Administration.

66. Richard Brevard Russell Jr. (1897–1971) was a Democratic member of the Senate, from Georgia, who served from 1933 to 1971. He was the longtime chair of the Armed Services Committee and a powerful member of the Senate's Democratic leadership.

67. Walter Franklin George (1878–1957) served as a Democrat from Georgia in the Senate from 1922 to 1957.

68. Theodore Fulton "Ted" Stevens (1923–) served in the Senate from Alaska, as a Republican, from 1968 to 2009. He chaired the Appropriations Committee for most of the period from 1997 to 2005 and throughout his time in Washington was a fierce defender of his state's claims to federal dollars. His loss in the 2008 election followed felony convictions on corruption charges, later voided and dismissed.

69. "Mountaintop removal" refers to an aggressive form of coal mining that involves blasting mountaintops away to access coal beneath the surface. The practice is strongly opposed by environmentalists. During the Clinton years, Senator Byrd tried to insert a provision into a federal appropriations bill protecting the right of coal companies to conduct mountaintop removal. Although President Clinton at one point had pledged support to Byrd's action, ultimately he signed the bill without Byrd's rider.

70. See Nigel Bowles, *The White House and Capitol Hill: The Politics of Presidential Persuasion* (Oxford: Clarendon Press, 1987), chap.7; Rudalevige, "The Executive Branch and the Legislative Process," 439–40.

71. William Hubbs Rehnquist (1924–2005) was appointed by President Richard Nixon to serve as associate justice of the Supreme Court in 1971. He later became chief justice during the Reagan presidency and served in that capacity until his death. Antonin Gregory Scalia (1936–) was nominated by President Reagan to serve on the Supreme Court and confirmed by the Senate in 1986.

72. David Hackett Souter (1939–) was nominated to the Supreme Court by President George H. W. Bush and became an associate justice in 1990. Clarence Thomas (1948–) was also nominated by President Bush 41, and moved onto the Court as an associate justice in 1991 after a contentious but successful nomination fight.

73. Robert Heron Bork (1927–) was a conservative legal scholar and appeals court judge nominated by Ronald Reagan to the U.S. Supreme Court in 1987. Democratic opponents mobilized an aggressive public campaign to discredit Bork and deny him the seat, resulting in a failed nomination.

74. Howell Thomas Heflin (1921–2005) served in the Senate from Alabama, as Democrat, from 1979 to 1997. He was a member of the Judiciary Committee and a former chief justice of the Alabama supreme court (1971–77).

75. See Walter Oleszek, "CRS Report for Congress: Proposals to Reform 'Holds' in the Senate," RL31685 (Washington: Congressional Research Service), updated December 20, 2007.

76. See Gregory A. Caldeira and John R. Wright, "Lobbying for Justice: Organized Interests, Supreme Court Nominations, and the United States Senate," *American Journal of Political Science* 42, no. 2 (April 1998): 499–523.

77. Clement Furman Haynsworth Jr. (1912–89) was a federal judge nominated by President Richard Nixon in 1969 to the Supreme Court seat then being vacated by Associate Justice Abe Fortas. Haynsworth's nomination failed on the Senate floor, victim to charges of financial impropriety and racism. George Harold Carswell (1919–92) was then nominated by Nixon and also was defeated on the Senate floor. Nixon finally succeeded in placing Harry Blackmun in that seat.

78. A thorough accounting of the chief of staff's role in the modern White House, including congressional relations work, appears in Terry Sullivan, ed., *The Nerve Center: Lessons in Governing from the White House Chiefs of Staff* (College Station: Texas A&M University Press, 2004).

79. Sununu was forced to resign from the chief of staff's job for the first President Bush in 1991. The most proximate reason was a flap over his use of an official vehicle to attend a stamp collectors' auction, but Sununu had angered many people in Washington over time because of his blunt operating style.

80. Harold Robbins "Bob" Haldeman (1926–93) was Richard Nixon's chief of staff from 1969 to 1973, when he resigned over the Watergate scandal. Haldeman had a reputation as a tough and ruthless manager. Richard Bruce "Dick" Cheney (1941–) was White House chief of staff for President Gerald Ford from 1975 to 1977. He later served as a member of Congress from Wyoming, secretary of defense under President George H. W. Bush, and vice president with George W. Bush.

81. Alexander Meigs Haig Jr. (1924–2010) was Richard Nixon's final chief of staff. Haig previously had a distinguished military career, and he later went on to become secretary of state under Ronald Reagan. Donald Henry Rumsfeld (1932–) served as White House chief of staff under Gerald Ford. Prior to that time he had been a Republican member of Congress from Illinois and ambassador to NATO. He later served as secretary of defense under President Ford and the second President Bush.

82. Donald Thomas Regan (1918–2003) served as White House chief of staff under Ronald Reagan. He came to the post in 1985, in a job swap with James A. Baker, from his position as secretary of the treasury. Robert Joseph Dole (1923–) served as a Kansas Republican in the Senate from 1969 to 1996. He was the Republican leader in the Senate from 1985 to 1996, evidently in a majority capacity at the moment Friedersdorf describes here.

83. Kenneth M. Duberstein (1944–) was Ronald Reagan's chief of staff in 1988 and 1989. He had a previous stint as head of congressional liaison under Reagan. Howard Henry Baker (1925–) was a longtime Republican senator from Tennessee who served as White House chief of staff for President Reagan in 1987–88. Baker's primary task was restoring confidence and good operations to a White House rocked by the Iran-Contra scandal. Baker later served (2001–2005) as ambassador to Japan under President George W. Bush.

84. Wayne, *The Legislative Presidency,* 149–50.

85. Mark A. Peterson takes that point to its logical conclusion and asks, "How presidential is the president's program?" He finds that the very process of taking into account congressional opinion while crafting the White House program makes of it a shared product (*Legislating Together,* 40).

86. Harlow quoted in Collier, *Between the Branches,* 6.

87. See Peterson, *Legislating Together,* 104–17.

88. A corollary worry also arose among some scholars and practitioners about the basic health of the executive. For not only did the president now have to navigate through a more complicated environment on Capitol Hill, he was also confronted with a vastly more hostile investigative climate in Washington, as well as more frequent assertions of congressional prerogative in reaction to Nixon's excesses in Watergate and Vietnam. One of the most prominent of these worriers was Richard Cheney, whose later vice presidency was famously devoted to correcting for these enduring imbalances. See Charlie Savage, *Takeover: The Return of the Imperial Presidency and the Subversion of American Democracy* (New York: Little, Brown and Company, 2007).

CHAPTER 3. THE PARTISAN DIMENSION

1. "The problem with only utilizing roll call voting data, the current approach to analyzing presidential influence [including the *Congressional Quarterly* scores]," writes Terry Sullivan, "is that it lacks any of the dynamic possibilities necessary to track changing positions *during* the legislative process" (Sullivan, "Wrong Questions, o-Questions, Legitimate Questions, Reasoned Answers: Affirming the Study of Temporal Path," *American Journal of Political Science* 35, no. 3 [August 1991]: 732). See also Andrew Rudalevige, "The Executive Branch and the Legislative Process," in Joel D. Aberbach and Mark A. Peterson, *Institutions of American Democracy: The Executive Branch* (Oxford: Oxford University Press, 2005), 429–32.

2. See Norman J. Ornstein and Thomas E. Mann, eds., *The Permanent Campaign and Its Future* (Washington: AEI Press, 2000).

3. On the possible contingencies associated with united and divided control of the government, see Charles O. Jones, *Separate but Equal Branches,* 2d ed. (Chappaqua, NY: Chatham House/Seven Bridges Press, 1999), 28–33.

4. These two positions—on welfare reform and movement toward a balanced budget—found President Clinton at odds with significant voices within his own party. Clinton twice vetoed welfare reform proposals in his first term before signing one just months before the 1996 election. His action alienated some Democrats, who accused him of caving in to the Republicans. Similarly, some White House aides and Democratic members of Congress registered strong objections in that same general period when Clinton offered an administration budget proposal that embraced the goal of a balanced budget. Some of the president's partisans thought it better to allow the Republicans, who controlled Congress, to endure the pain of budget austerity without the cover of presidential support.

5. For a scholarly assessment of Clinton's presidency that tracks with Hilley's assessment, see Jones, *Separate but Equal Branches,* chap. 11.

6. The possibility of legislative productivity in times of divided government is the core theme of David R. Mayhew, *Divided We Govern: Party Control, Lawmaking, and Investigations, 1946–1990* (New Haven: Yale University Press, 1991).

7. The Senate did not adopt all the items of the Contract with America enacted by the House.

8. For a detailed accounting of the government shutdown, see Elizabeth Drew, *Showdown: The Struggle Between the Gingrich Congress and the Clinton White House* (New York: Simon & Schuster, 1996), and David Maraniss and Michael Weisskopf, "*Tell Newt to Shut Up!* (New York: Touchstone: 1996).

9. Chester Trent Lott (1941–) began serving as a Republican member of the Senate from Mississippi in 1989. He became majority leader on the occasion of Bob Dole's resignation in 1996 and served in that capacity until 2002, when he resigned the leadership post in controversy over statements he made praising Senator Strom Thurmond's Dixiecrat past.

10. The Health Insurance Portability and Accountability Act, known more commonly by the names of its two Senate cosponsors (Senators Edward M. Kennedy [D-MA] and Nancy Kassebaum [R-KS]), allowed Americans to change jobs without risk of immediately losing their health insurance or coverage for preexisting conditions.

11. Richard Keith Armey (1940–) served in the House of Representatives, from Texas, from 1985 to 2003. He was the Republican majority leader from 1994 until the end of his tenure.

12. President George H. W. Bush found bipartisan support in 1990 for legislative initiatives resulting in successful amendments to the Clean Air Act and the adoption of the Americans with Disabilities Act (ADA), which outlawed discrimination against persons with disabilities. See John Robert Greene, *The Presidency of George Bush* (Lawrence: University Press of Kansas, 2000), 74–76.

A political battle over the fate of anticommunist Nicaraguan forces had been at the heart of pitched political battles between congressional Democrats and the White House during the Reagan years, ultimately leading to legal and institutional disputes such as the Iran-Contra Affair. Early in the Bush 41 presidency, the administration reached agreement with the Democrats in Congress to provide a large sum of humanitarian aide to Latin America as a way to stop arming the conflict.

13. Charles O. Jones agrees with McClure's assessment of the early Reagan presidency in *Separate but Equal Branches,* chap. 9. Richard Fleisher and Jon R. Bond's statistical analysis leads them to suggest, however, that Reagan actually underperformed in 1981 (and beyond). "Assessing Presidential Support in the House: Lessons from Reagan and Carter," *Journal of Politics* 45, no. 3 (August 1983): 745–58.

14. Ford actually served on the Appropriations Committee for some twenty-two years, from 1951 to 1973.

15. Stuart E. Eizenstat (1943–) was President Carter's chief domestic policy advisor. He later held several key subcabinet posts in the Clinton administration.

President Carter produced a comprehensive set of energy proposals that occupied much of his congressional affairs efforts in 1977. See Charles O. Jones, *The Trusteeship Presidency: Jimmy Carter and the United States Congress* (Baton Rouge: Louisiana State University Press, 1988), 135–43.

16. See Jones, *Separate but Equal Branches,* 163.

17. Robert Henry "Bob" Michel (1923–) served multiple terms in the House of Representatives from Illinois. He was the Republican minority leader from 1981 to 1994.

18. See Russell L. Riley, "Party Discipline," in George Thomas Kurian, ed., *The Encyclopedia of the Republican Party* (Armonk, NY: M. E. Sharpe, 1996), 152–56.

19. Stein's comments here confirm that Publius's intention—to tie the incentives of place to the self-interest of the officeholder—has worked as planned. See *The Federalist Papers,* No. 51.

20. Gallup polls of Bush's approval in 2002 ranged from 83 percent at the very beginning of the year to 61 percent at year's end. His numbers steadily declined through the 70s during the first half of the year and through the 60s in the second half. Gallup numbers available at http://www.pollingreport.com/BushJob1.htm (accessed September 3, 2008).

21. Dick Morris (1948–) is a political consultant who had a longtime association with Bill Clinton, reaching back to Clinton's governorship in Arkansas. Morris was a controversial figure in large part because of his unusual willingness to work for both Democrats and Republicans. Morris was not involved in the 1992 presidential campaign with Clinton but was invited by the president to consult again after the midterm loss of Congress in 1994. The term "triangulation" is often associated with Morris. It refers to a

political strategy of avoiding associations with the political left or right, or Democrats or Republicans alone, in the interest of finding a middle way politically, appealing to centrists of both parties.

22. Harry Leroy "Lee" Atwater (1951–91) was a Republican political strategist renowned for his partisan instincts and hardball style. He advised both Ronald Reagan's and George H. W. Bush's political campaigns and served as chair of the Republican National Committee under the latter, before his untimely death. Ed Rollins (1943–) was also a Republican political consultant with close ties to Reagan. His stock in the party fell, however, in 1992 when he managed Ross Perot's insurgent third-party campaign for the presidency.

23. An office of political affairs is now a standard feature of every White House's organizational chart.

24. Leslie Aspin (1938–95) was a Wisconsin Democrat who served in the House of Representatives from 1971 to 1993. For several terms he chaired the Armed Services Committee. He left that post to become Bill Clinton's first secretary of defense in 1993—a position he held for one year.

25. Carter actually trailed all but one Democratic senator and all but twenty-two House Democrats in their districts (Jones, *Separate but Equal Branches*, 64).

26. Negotiations for the 1990 budget deal, which caused President George H. W. Bush to reverse a campaign pledge not to raise taxes, included a series of confidential, high-level meetings at Andrews Air Force Base with these congressional leaders. See the description in Greene, *The Presidency of George Bush*, chap. 6.

27. Karl Christian Rove (1950–) was deputy chief of staff to President George W. Bush and was his longtime chief political advisor.

28. See Eric L. Davis, "Legislative Reform and the Decline of Presidential Influence on Capitol Hill," *British Journal of Political Science* 19, no. 4 (October 1979): 470–71.

29. Richard Craig Shelby (1934–) is a member of the Senate from Alabama. He served four terms in the House and was initially elected to the Senate as a Democrat. He switched parties shortly after the 1994 midterm elections gave control of that body to the Republicans.

An energy tax was a key component of President Clinton's major 1993 budget package. It was initially designed as a tax based on BTUs, to broaden its scope and its usefulness as an environmental protection measure. Ultimately, Congress was unwilling to accept the BTU basis, and the White House substituted for it a gasoline tax.

30. James Merrill Jeffords (1934–), of Vermont, served as a member of the Senate from 1989 until 2007. He came to Washington as a moderate Republican, but in May 2001 he upended a narrowly divided Senate by leaving the party in protest over the leadership of George W. Bush. He declared himself an independent, voting with the Democrats on organizational matters and causing the Senate to revert to Democratic rule.

31. Larry Lee Pressler (1942–) served in the Senate from South Dakota as a Republican from 1979 to 1997. Prior to that time he spent two terms in the House. Pressler chaired for a time the Committee on Commerce, Science, and Transportation.

32. William Philip Gramm (1942–) represented Texas in both the House of Representatives and the Senate. He came to Washington as a conservative Democrat but became

a strong supporter of Ronald Reagan. He provided the Reagan White House early intelligence on the confidential discussions of congressional Democrats as they attempted to develop a strategy for countering Reagan during his first year as president. When the Democrats tried to punish Gramm by altering his committee assignments, he resigned the seat, returning to Texas to campaign for it as a Republican. He won, and soon thereafter, on the strength of this maverick behavior, was elected statewide to the Senate in 1984. See Ross K. Baker, "Party and Institutional Sanctions in the U.S. House: The Case of Congressman Gramm," *Legislative Studies Quarterly* 10, no. 3 (August, 1985): 315–337

33. David Alan Stockman (1946–) served as a Michigan Republican in the House of Representatives from 1977 to 1981. He was designated at a very young age to head the Office of Management and Budget under President Ronald Reagan, filling that post from 1981 to 1985. Kent Ronald Hance (1942–) served from Texas in the House of Representatives from 1979 to 1985. Charles Walter Stenholm (1938–) represented Texas in the House from 1975 to 2005. Both were conservative Democrats who often sided with the Reagan administration.

Boll Weevils is the nickname used for an informal group of conservative southern Democrats (from the so-called Cotton Belt) who often voted against the party's more liberal leadership in support of Republican presidents or policies. The term had special currency during the Reagan presidency because of that White House's reliance on them.

34. One of President Carter's chief foreign policy initiatives was the controversial decision to grant greater control of the Panama Canal to the Panamanians. He succeeded in getting the Senate to confirm his actions but did so at a tremendous political cost. See George D. Moffett III, *The Limits of Victory: Ratification of the Panama Canal Treaties* (Ithaca: Cornell University Press, 1985).

35. See Russell L. Riley, "Party Government and the Contract with America," *PS: Political Science and Politics* 28, no. 4 (December 1995): 703–707.

Richard Andrew Gephardt (1941–), a Democrat, was a longtime member of the House, representing Missouri, from 1977 to 2005. He was the party's minority leader from 1995 to 2003. During much of his career he was viewed as a likely presidential contender, openly running, unsuccessfully, for the party's nomination in 1988 and 2004.

36. Hubert Horatio Humphrey (1911–78) was vice president of the United States under Lyndon Johnson and the Democratic Party's 1968 presidential nominee, losing to Richard Nixon. He also served in the Senate, from Minnesota, from 1949 to 1964 and again from 1971 to 1978. He was generally considered to be one of the party's most consistently liberal voices.

Gypsy Moths are the functional opposite of Boll Weevils. They are moderate or liberal Republicans, usually from the Midwest or the Northeast, who are inclined to vote with Democrats.

37. Les Francis worked briefly for Representative Norman Y. Mineta (D-CA) before joining the Carter congressional affairs staff in 1977. He subsequently became a deputy White House chief of staff for Carter.

38. Patrick J. Griffin headed the congressional affairs office for President Bill Clinton from January 1994 to February 1996.

39. See Terry Sullivan, "Explaining Why Presidents Count: Signaling and Information," *Journal of Politics* 52, no. 3 (August 1990): 939–62. For a detailed discussion of the Eisenhower White House's vote counting process, see Richard S. Conley and Richard M. Yon, "The 'Hidden Hand' and White House Roll-Call Predictions: Legislative Liaison in the Eisenhower White House, 83d-84th Congresses," *Presidential Studies Quarterly* 37, no. 2:291–312.

40. The Department of Energy was created during the Carter presidency in 1977. The Department of Education followed in 1980.

41. John Otho "Jack" Marsh (1926–) was a member of the House of Representatives from Virginia from 1963 to 1971. He served as secretary of the army from 1981 to 1989. During the Ford administration, Marsh was counselor to the president, with cabinet status.

42. Clifford Philip Case (1904–82), a New Jersey Republican, served in the House of Representatives from 1945 to 1953 and in the Senate from 1955 to 1979.

43. John Hubbard Chafee (1922–99) was secretary of the navy under Richard Nixon and then represented Rhode Island in the Senate from 1976 to 1999. Chaffee was a liberal Republican who was an unreliable vote for the Republican presidents with whom he served.

44. The majority and minority leaders—Democrat and Republican—in both chambers.

45. Anne Wexler was assistant to the president for public liaison under President Jimmy Carter. She set up a prominent lobbying firm in Washington after the Carter years, specializing in grassroots mobilization and political coalition building. Her work for NAFTA would have been on behalf of either Bush 41 or Clinton. Wexler's public liaison work is detailed in Jones, *The Trusteeship Presidency*, 93–98. See also Kenneth E. Collier, *Between the Branches: The White House Office of Legislative Affairs* (Pittsburgh: University of Pittsburgh Press, 1997), 189–95; Mark A. Peterson, "The Presidency and Organized Interests: White House Patterns of Interest Group Liaison," *American Political Science Review* 86, no. 3 (September 1992): 612–25.

46. President George W. Bush's administration, with leadership from Vice President Richard Cheney, engaged multiple representatives from the oil and gas industry and other commercial interests in the development of a prominent energy initiative in 2001. The privileged access of these private interests in closed-door meetings for purposes of crafting a bill raised charges of influence peddling from critics of the Bush White House.

47. George Corley Wallace (1919–98) was a four-term governor of Alabama whose conservative influence on national politics in the 1960s and 1970s made him a frequent presidential contender as a third-party candidate and as a Democrat. He was crippled in an assassination attempt in 1972 as he campaigned in Maryland for the Democratic nomination. He ran again in 1976, losing the nomination to Jimmy Carter.

Erwin C. Hargrove writes that "Carter pledged to support the creation of a Department of Education in responding to a written question from the National Education Association *Reporter*," something that took place *after* Carter had secured the nomination and was not much emphasized by the campaign. He subsequently hedged on the commitment during the general election season because it was in tension with his broader interest in consolidating executive departments. See Hargrove, *Jimmy Carter as*

President: Leadership and the Politics of the Public Good (Baton Rouge: Louisiana State University Press, 1988), 60–61.

48. In 1979, President Carter pressed through Congress a bipartisan plan to rescue the Chrysler Corporation from severe financial distress, resulting in federal aid of approximately $1.5 billion.

49. See Brendan J. Doherty, "The Politics of the Permanent Campaign: Presidential Travel and the Electoral College, 1977–2004," *Presidential Studies Quarterly* 37, no. 4 (December 2007): 749–73.

50. The Caribbean Basin Initiative was a set of bilateral trade arrangements generated in the early 1980s, under President Reagan, to create closer U.S. ties to Latin America and the Caribbean. The initiative was one component of the administration's larger effort to draw the region away from communist influence. The Tax Reform Act of 1986 was one of the administration's signature second-term efforts.

Samuel Ichiye Hayakawa (1906–92), a California Republican, served in the Senate from 1977 to 1983. Lloyd Millard Bentsen Jr. (1921–2006), a Texas Democrat, served in the Senate from 1971 to 1993. He was his party's vice presidential nominee, paired with Michael Dukakis, in 1988, and he was secretary of the treasury from 1993 to 1994 under President Bill Clinton.

51. Gillespie V. "Sonny" Montgomery (1920–2006), a Mississippi Democrat, served in the House of Representatives from 1967 to 1997. He was the longtime chair of the House Veterans' Affairs Committee.

52. Howard Worth Smith (1883–1976), a Virginia Democrat, served in the House of Representatives from 1931 to 1967. He had been a Virginia state judge before election to the Senate. He served as a longtime chair of the Rules Committee.

53. Claude Denson Pepper (1900–89), a Florida Democrat, served in the Senate from 1936 to 1951 and subsequently in the House from 1963 until his death. For six years he chaired the House Rules Committee.

54. The Senate typically operates on the basis of unanimous consent, so other formal rules are superfluous.

55. Lisa Kountoupes was deputy assistant to the president for legislative affairs for President Clinton, working primarily with the House of Representatives. She came to the White House from a three-year stint as assistant director for legislative affairs at the Office of Management and Budget.

56. Professor Gilmour explores the subject of veto threats in "Institutional and Individual Influences on the President's Veto," *The Journal of Politics* 64, no. 1 (February 2002): 198–218.

57. On the exercise of the presidential veto, see Charles M. Cameron, *Veto Bargaining: Presidents and the Politics of Negative Power* (Cambridge: Cambridge University Press, 2000); Robert J. Spitzer, *The Presidential Veto: Touchstone of the American Presidency* (Albany: State University of New York Press, 1988); and Richard Abernathy Watson, *Presidential Vetoes and Public Policy* (Lawrence: University Press of Kansas, 1993).

58. David Edward Bonior (1945–), a Democrat, represented Michigan in the House of Representatives from 1977 to 2003. He was the Democratic Party whip during the entirety of the Clinton presidency.

59. Clinton actually had two vetoes overridden: the first was on the Securities Litigation Reform Act, coming in December 1995 during a contentious time of government shutdowns; the second related to military base closures in November of 1997. Mitchel A. Sollenberger, "CRS Report for Congress: President Clinton's Vetoes," Washington: Congressional Research Service, updated April 4, 2004, available at http://www.rules.house.gov/Archives/98–147.pdf (accessed September 5, 2008).

60. Stephen J. Wayne provides some historical background on this topic in a chapter describing White House–OMB interaction in *The Legislative Presidency* (New York: Harper & Row, 1978), 70–100.

61. Friedersdorf's numbers were corrected from slightly different figures in the original transcript.

Michael Joseph Mansfield (1903–2001), a Montana Democrat, served in the House of Representatives from 1943 to 1953 and then in the Senate from 1953 to 1977. He was Senate majority leader from 1961 to 1977. Samuel Taliaferro Rayburn (1882–1961) represented Texas in the House from 1913 to 1961. He served as a Democratic speaker of the House for ten terms. Carl Bert Albert (1908–2000), an Oklahoma Democrat, served in the House from 1947 to 1977. He served three terms as speaker of the House, the last ending in 1976. These three are giants of the mid-twentieth-century Congress.

62. Pietro Vichi "Pete" Domenici (1932–), a New Mexico Republican, was first elected to the Senate in 1972. He has served as chair of the Senate Committee on Energy and Natural Resources and has written two books on nuclear power. William Blaine Richardson (1947–) is a New Mexico Democrat. He served fourteen years in the House and became ambassador to the United Nations in 1997 under President Bill Clinton. In 1998 he was designated by Clinton to be secretary of energy. He later was elected governor of New Mexico.

63. In 1984, President Ronald Reagan addressed the United Nations International Conference on Population in Mexico City, were he proclaimed a ban on U.S. funding for international family planning efforts that provided or advocated abortion services anywhere in the world. This became known as the Mexico City policy. President Clinton suspended the policy when he took office. Several times during Clinton's presidency the issue became the focus of congressional activity, with conservatives attempting to overturn Clinton's executive order removing the ban.

64. George C. Edwards III, *At the Margins: Presidential Leadership of Congress* (New Haven: Yale University Press, 1989), 46, 185, 213.

65. It is worth considering the possibility that these assembled practitioners actually overstated their reservations about single-party control of the government as a way to emphasize an important point about the *limits* of partisanship to a scholarly community well known to advocate the virtues of the political party. But the absence of dissent among the group on this point is worth noting.

66. Edwards, *At the Margins*, 47.

67. Also on this general topic, see Kent R. Weaver, "The Politics of Blame Avoidance," *Journal of Public Policy* 6, no.4 (October–December 1986): 371–98.

CHAPTER 4. BICAMERALISM

1. See Ross K. Baker, *House and Senate* (New York: W. W. Norton, 1989).

2. Howard E. Shuman wrote in 1957, "The rules of the Senate of the United States are only 40 in number and comprise only 49 of 832 pages of the Senate manual. Yet when literally invoked they can bring Senate business to a standstill. They are most often ignored or circumvented by unanimous consent in order that the Senate may operate conveniently as a deliberative and parliamentary body. To pass legislation when they are invoked is a formidable enterprise" ("Senate Rules and the Civil Rights Bill: A Case Study," *American Political Science Review* 51, no. 4 [December 1957]: 955).

3. Suspension of the rules is a special procedure in the House typically used to pass noncontroversial measures. A vote to suspend requires a two-thirds majority of the members voting.

4. Political scientist Gary C. Jacobson confirms Stein's assertion, writing that "Polarization in Congress has outstripped polarization in the electorate." See "Party Polarization in National Politics: The Electoral Connection," in Jon R. Bond and Richard Fleisher, eds., *Polarized Politics: Congress and the President in a Partisan Era* (Washington: CQ Press, 2000), 28.

5. Richard F. Fenno Jr. confirms this assertion, writing that "senators do not specialize as intensively or as exclusively in their committee work as House members do" (*Congressmen in Committees* [Boston: Little, Brown and Company, 1973], 172).

6. Lyndon Johnson believed that a president has "got just one year when [members] treat you right, and before they start worrying about themselves. . . . The fourth year is all politics" (quoted in Harry McPherson, *A Political Education: A Washington Memoir* [Boston: Houghton Mifflin Company, 1988], 268).

7. J. Dennis Hastert (1942–), an Illinois Republican, was elected to the House of Representatives in 1986. He served as speaker of the House from 1999 to 2006. Nancy Pelosi (1940–), a Democrat, was elected to the House from California in 1987. She rose to the speakership—the first woman to do so—in 2006.

8. Friedersdorf seems to have misremembered the specific context in this instance. President Nixon, for whom he also worked, vetoed an emergency medical services bill on August 1, 1973. Nixon later signed a version promoted by then Congressman Gerald Ford.

9. James Danforth Quayle (1947–), an Illinois Republican, served in the House from 1977 to 1980 and in the Senate from 1981 to 1989. He was elected vice president on the ticket with George H. W. Bush in 1988.

10. David Hampton Pryor (1934–) an Arkansas Democrat, served in the House from 1966 to 1973. He was Arkansas governor from 1975 to 1979 and held a seat in the Senate from 1979 to 1997.

11. Daniel David Rostenkowski (1928–) served in the House from Illinois from 1959 to 1995. A Democrat, Rostenkowski was a longtime chair of the House Ways and Means Committee. He lost his seat over a scandal concerning misuse of office funds and was ultimately convicted of mail fraud. President Clinton pardoned him in 2001.

12. Walter Frederick Mondale (1928–) served as vice president of the United States with Jimmy Carter. He previously had been a member of the Senate from Minnesota,

from 1964 to 1976. The figures on Mondale's service have been corrected from the original, which were overstated. Although Mondale served twelve years, this number includes two partial terms and one full one.

13. Lawton Mainor Chiles Jr. (1930–98) represented Florida as a Democrat in the Senate from 1971 to 1989. He subsequently served two terms as governor of that state. Charles Harting Percy (1919–) served from 1967 to 1985 in the Senate, representing Illinois as a Republican.

14. On April 20, 1999, two students of Columbine High School near Denver, Colorado, went into the school heavily armed, killing twelve students and wounding many more before committing suicide.

15. See "Remarks Announcing Senate Minority Leader Dole's Endorsement of the Intermediate-Range Nuclear Forces Treaty," December 17, 1987, available at http://www.reagan.utexas.edu/archives/speeches/1987/121787d.htm (accessed September 5, 2008).

Mikhail Sergeyevich Gorbachev (1931–) was general secretary of the Communist Party of the Soviet Union from 1985 to 1991 and president of the Soviet Union in 1990 and 1991. He presided over the breakup of the Soviet Union and was awarded the Nobel Peace Prize for his efforts to end the Cold War in 1990.

The East Room of the White House is an expansive internal chamber in the main residence, usually reserved for large gatherings and ceremonial occasions.

16. Richard Moe became chief of staff for Vice President Walter Mondale; Michael S. Berman became Mondale's counsel and deputy chief of staff; James A. Johnson became Mondale's executive assistant and later managed the 1984 presidential campaign. Joseph Lester "Jody" Powell was a longtime Carter aide who served as White House press secretary; Hamilton Jordan was a key Carter advisor who became chief of staff in the middle of Carter's single presidential term.

17. Bertram Carp was deputy assistant to the president for domestic affairs and policy in the Carter White House but previously held a senior position on Mondale's personal staff in the Senate. Eliott R. Cutler was associate director for natural resources, energy, and science at OMB and at other times was a Mondale political advisor.

18. The Roosevelt Room is a meeting room, just off the Oval Office in the White House, that is commonly used for senior staff and cabinet meetings.

19. On the politics of conference, see Steven D. Van Beek, *Post-Passage Politics: Bicameral Resolution in Congress* (Pittsburg: Pittsburg University Press, 1995); Lawrence D. Longley and Walter J. Oleszek, *Bicameral Politics: Conference Committees in Congress* (New Haven: Yale University Press, 1989).

20. Albert Conrad Ullman (1914–86) was a Democratic member of the House of Representatives from Oregon, serving from 1957 to 1981. He chaired the Ways and Means Committee during the Carter years. Russell Billiu Long (1918–2003), a Louisiana Democrat and son of the famous southern populist Huey Long, served in the Senate from 1948 to 1987. He was a longtime chair of the Senate's Finance Committee, in which capacity he would have frequent occasion to be paired with Ullman in conference.

21. In the fall of 2003 Congress was debating a massive energy bill, which included tax breaks for producers and subsidies for ethanol, among other things. A conference committee report was produced and then filibustered to death by the Senate. A similar measure then passed and was signed into law by President George W. Bush in 2005. By

"the tax bill" Ball evidently is referring to President Bush's second major round of tax cuts, which passed in 2003.

22. John Sidney McCain III (1936–) is a Republican senator representing Arizona. He was first elected in 1986 after serving two terms in the House of Representatives. He was the Republican Party's nominee for president in 2008, defeated by Barack Obama.

23. Leading up to the year 2000 (Y2K) there was great concern among some experts and public policy makers about the chaos that might be caused because the world's computer systems were unprepared to read internal computer calendars showing "00." Preventive steps were taken at great cost to avoid that scenario. The date largely passed without incident.

24. The question at issue with ANWR was whether portions of the refuge would be opened up to oil drilling and further exploration. This was a hotly contested issue pitting environmentalists (a largely Democratic constituency) against those interested in increasing domestic energy production (largely committed to the Republican Party).

25. Richard Darman's own account is found in his memoir, *Who's In Control? Polar Politics and the Sensible Center* (New York: Simon and Schuster, 1996).

26. A line-item veto would permit the president to delete objectionable details of a piece of legislation without killing the entire bill. The language of the U.S. Constitution makes this problematic in the American model. See, for example, Mathew Thomas Kline, "The Line Item Veto Case and Separation of Powers," *California Law Review* 88, no. 1 (January 2000): 181–232.

27. Howard Morton Metzenbaum (1917–2008), an Ohio Democrat, served in the Senate in 1974 (filling an unexpired term) and again from 1976 to 1995. Metzenbaum was usually a dependable nemesis of Reagan on Capitol Hill.

28. A more positive assessment of White House engagement with interest groups appears in Mark A. Peterson, "The Presidency and Organized Interests: White House Patterns of Interest Group Liaison," *American Political Science Review* 86, no. 3 (September 1992): 612–25.

29. William S. Broomfield (1922–) is a Michigan Republican who served in the House of Representatives from 1957 to 1993. Elford Albin Cederberg (1918–2006) served in the House from 1953 to 1978. Charles Ernest Chamberlain (1917–2002) also served as a Michigan Republican from 1957 to 1974.

30. Robert Paul Griffin (1923–) served as a Michigan Republican in both the House (1957–66) and the Senate (1966–79).

31. President Ford died after this symposium, on December 26, 2006. Eighty-four-year-old William Broomfield collapsed at Ford's state funeral in the Capitol rotunda.

32. James Sterling Young, *The Washington Community, 1800–1828* (New York: Columbia University Press, 1966). It should be noted here that in the Washington of Young's period, members of the political community tended to reside in boarding houses that were segregated along geographical lines. Therein, "Senators and Representatives mixed freely, bridging in their extraofficial life their constitutional separation in official life" (p. 98).

33. George C. Edwards III, *At the Margins: Presidential Leadership of Congress* (New Haven: Yale University Press, 1989), 188.

34. For a classic treatment of the phenomenon of expanding conflict to create a

better balance of competitors, see E. E. Schattschneider, *The Semisovereign People: A Realist's View of Democracy in America* (New York: Harcourt Brace, 1975).

CHAPTER 5. WORKING WITH AND FOR THE PRESIDENT

1. Birch Evans Bayh (1928–) is an Illinois Democrat who served in the Senate from 1963 to 1981. Frank Forrester Church (1924–84) was an Idaho Democrat who served in the Senate from 1957 to 1981. Henry Martin "Scoop" Jackson (1912–83) represented Washington State in the Senate from 1953 to 1983. Morris King Udall (1922–98) represented Arizona in the House, as a Democrat, from 1961 to 1991. In 1976 Humphrey was back in the Senate representing Minnesota. Edward Moore Kennedy (1932–2009), a Massachusetts Democrat and youngest brother of the former president, entered the Senate in 1962.

2. On the situation Carter inherited, see Eric L. Davis, "Legislative Reform and the Decline of Presidential Influence on Capitol Hill," *British Journal of Political Science* 9, no. 4 (October 1979): 465–79. See also Charles O. Jones, *Separate but Equal Branches: Congress and the Presidency*, 2nd ed. (New York: Chatham House/Seven Bridges, 1999), 90–93.

3. Zbigniew Kazimierz Brzezinski (1928–) is a Polish-born foreign policy specialist who served as Jimmy Carter's national security advisor. Stansfield Turner (1923–) was an admiral in the U.S. Navy and from 1977 to 1981 held the position of director of the Central Intelligence Agency (CIA), appointed by Jimmy Carter.

4. Norman Yoshio Mineta (1931–) served in the House of Representatives, from Hawaii, from 1975 to 1995. He later was to become secretary of commerce during the Clinton presidency and secretary of transportation for George W. Bush.

The USS *Sequoia* was the presidential yacht, first used as such by Herbert Hoover. Jimmy Carter had it sold at auction during his term as a sign of fiscal discipline and his commitment to reining in the imperial aspects of the presidency.

5. Charles O. Jones has called Lyndon Johnson's method of working with Congress a "majority leader style of building coalitions" and further says of it: "Such complete management of congressional relations, however, demands a great deal of the president's time. It so happens that President Johnson wanted to use his time in this way" (Jones, *Separate but Equal Branches*, 143). Not everyone else does.

6. The ABC television news program *Nightline*, hosted by Ted Koppel, began during the Carter presidency as a nightly broadcast to update the country on the day's developments in the Iranian hostage crisis. It long outlasted that particular event, becoming a fixture of evening political coverage for a generation.

7. This California governor is Ronald Reagan, who sought the Republican presidential nomination in 1976 over the incumbent Gerald Ford.

8. Caspar Willard Weinberger (1917–2006) was President Reagan's secretary of defense from 1981 to 1987. Alexander Meigs Haig Jr. (1924– 2010), a former four-star general, was Reagan's secretary of state in 1981 and 1982. In the confused aftermath of Reagan's shooting, Haig publicly claimed that he was in charge of the White House because of the president's disability. James Scott Brady (1940–), Reagan's presidential

press secretary, was seriously wounded and permanently disabled in the same shooting incident as the president on March 30, 1981.

9. James Strom Thurmond (1902–2003) served in the Senate from South Carolina from 1954 to 2003 except for a brief period in 1956 when he vacated the seat voluntarily. Thurmond originally came into the Senate as a Democrat but switched his allegiance to the Republican Party in 1964.

10. A crucial part of the Reagan-era defense buildup was the placement of new cruise missiles in Europe. This effort generated heated protest in Europe among those who believed that these additional nuclear weapons were unnecessarily provocative and raised the level of danger for nuclear conflict.

Margaret Hilda Thatcher (1925–) served as Britain's Conservative Party prime minister from 1979 to 1990. She and President Reagan became fast allies.

11. Clark McAdams Clifford (1906–98) was a longtime Democratic Party activist and consultant to presidents beginning with Harry Truman. He served for a time as secretary of defense for President Lyndon Johnson.

12. See Richard E. Neustadt, *Presidential Power and the Modern Presidents: The Politics of Leadership from Roosevelt to Reagan* (New York: The Free Press, 1990), 114.

13. The exchange occurred at a Republican candidates' debate in New Hampshire during an argument about which candidates would be allowed to participate in the debate. Reagan had responded angrily to the moderator's direction to a sound engineer to turn his microphone off.

Reagan summarily fired striking air traffic controllers rather than giving in to their collective demands.

14. Friedersdorf's first reference is probably to the November 1981 vote to authorize the sale of five sophisticated AWACs aircraft to Saudi Arabia, over strenuous Israeli objections. Reagan won the vote in the Senate 52–48 in what was deemed to be a test of his competence in foreign policy making.

Reagan's major trouble with his colon began in 1985, so Friedersdorf may have misspoken here. In his separate oral history as a part of the Miller Center's Ronald Reagan Oral History Project, Friedersdorf recounted basically the same story, but then simply said that Reagan "was not feeling well for some reason." One possible explanation is that this event takes place not too long after the failed assassination attempt. Max Friedersdorf Interview, Miller Center, University of Virginia, Ronald Reagan Oral History Project, October 24–25, 2002: 67.

Mark Andrews (1926–) served a single term in the Senate (1981–87) from North Dakota. He had previously served in the House of Representatives from 1963 to 1981. Robert William Packwood (1932–), Republican, served as a member of the Senate from Oregon from 1969 to 1995.

15. Harold Eberle was a Republican activist who had several legislative affairs jobs in the Nixon and Ford administrations. Henry Alfred Kissinger (1923–) served as national security adviser for President Nixon and then secretary of state under Presidents Nixon and Ford, for a time simultaneously holding the national security adviser's post. It seems likely that he was serving only as national security adviser during the episode mentioned here, as Ford's service as minority leader ran from 1965 to late 1973 and Kissinger was sworn in as secretary of state on September 22, 1973.

16. This reference places Stein's start date at mid-January 1998, when the story of the president's relationship with a former White House intern first appeared in the press.

17. George Robert Stephanopoulos (1961–) was one of Bill Clinton's chief campaign advisers in 1992, and from there he took a series of senior positions in the Clinton White House, including communications director and counselor. He left the White House at the end of the first term. On the confidential testimony of other aides serving Clinton at the time, the president often used Stephanopoulos as an outlet for venting frustration over such things as bad press coverage.

18. Paster and Griffin were Clinton's first two CLs. Paster served the first year and Griffin until 1996 .

19. "The conversation" would be the one encouraging Clinton to resign.

20. Hugh Doggett Scott Jr. (1900–94), Republican from Pennsylvania, served in the Senate from 1959 to 1977 after multiple terms in the House. John Jacob Rhodes (1916–2003), an Arizona Republican, served in the House of Representatives from 1953 to 1983, including eight years as minority leader. Barry Morris Goldwater (1909–98) served as a Republican in the Senate from Arizona for five (nonconsecutive) terms. He was also the Republican Party nominee for the presidency in 1964.

21. The Red Room is a small parlor in the public portion of the main White House building, often used for small dinner parties or other intimate gatherings.

22. Charles O. Jones observes that "it has been a characteristic of all administrations that [congressional] relations deteriorate over time" (*Separate but Equal Branches,* 110). For more on the political calendar and the dynamics of legislative effectiveness, see Mark A. Peterson, *Legislating Together: The White House and Capitol Hill from Eisenhower to Reagan* (Cambridge: Harvard University Press, 1990), 118–27.

23. The demoralizing developments in the second term are usually associated with Donald Regan, the first-term secretary of treasury who left that job to become the second-term chief of staff. Regan insisted on closely guarding access to the Oval Office himself, which chafed those accustomed to a more open relationship with Reagan.

Baker, Meese, and Deaver—dubbed the "Troika"—constituted the primary leadership structure of the first Reagan White House. Baker was chief of staff, notwithstanding the fact that he was a relative newcomer to the Reagan network. Edwin Meese III (1931–), a longtime Reagan staffer, was counselor to the president and later designated attorney general. Michael Keith Deaver (1938–2007) was deputy chief of staff, and generally was charged with keeping Reagan's image.

Patrick Joseph Buchanan (1938–) is a longtime conservative activist who served as Reagan's communications director from 1985 to 1987. Ed Rollins (1943–) is a political operative who was Reagan's national campaign director in 1984 and then became deputy chief of staff for governmental and political affairs, leaving in October of 1985. Robert Carl "Bud" McFarlane (1937–) was President Reagan's national security adviser from 1983 to 1985. He was deeply enmeshed in the Iran-Contra affair and convicted of illegal behavior but pardoned by President George H. W. Bush.

24. Clinton sparked controversy on the way out the door of the White House by issuing pardons to 148 individuals on his final day as president. Several of these cases were politically sensitive, and the president bypassed the usual procedures providing for careful Justice Department review in some of the most controversial instances.

25. Clinton actually was fifty-four when he left office in January 2001.

26. Clinton's "Roadless Rule" forbade logging, mining, and other development activity in over forty million acres of undeveloped forestland. The president's initial directive was issued on October 13, 1999, asking the U.S. Forest Service to generate a final plan before the expiration of Clinton's term. That administrative rule came out in January 2001 and was subsequently the subject of court challenges and administrative opposition in the George W. Bush years, ultimately including an effort to completely reverse it.

27. New Source Review was an effort to improve air pollution control by instituting a complex set of regulations for industrial sources of pollution, focused primarily on new equipment. Clinton-era environmental administrators developed a set of comprehensive proposals in 1996 that were the focus of ongoing discussions and debate, unsettled well into the Bush 43 administration.

28. The Occupational Safety and Health Administration (OSHA) attempted during the Clinton years to issue standards to diminish workplace injuries associated with such things as repetitive stress, especially related to eye and lower back injuries.

29. In 1938 FDR attempted to purge the Democratic Party of some of its more conservative elements by campaigning for more progressive candidates over some conservative Democratic incumbents. The effort famously failed.

30. Norman Bertram Coleman Jr. (1949–), a Republican, was elected to the Senate in 2002 when his favored opponent, incumbent Senator Paul Wellstone, was killed in a plane crash weeks before the election. Coleman had reportedly been recruited by the White House to run against Wellstone. John Randolph Thune (1961–), a South Dakota Republican, narrowly lost to Tim Johnson, a Democrat, in the 2002 Senate race there but then successfully challenged Senate minority leader Tom Daschle in 2004, with significant White House backing. George R. Nethercutt Jr. (1944–) served in the House of Representatives from Washington State from 1995 to 2005.

31. This nomination occurred in May of 1980, the same year in which Carter lost his reelection bid to Ronald Reagan.

32. Neustadt, *Presidential Power and the Modern Presidents.* The first edition of this classic text was published in 1960, and it went through several editions before this final 1990 version.

33. Robert J. Kerrey (1943–) represented Nebraska in the Senate from 1989 to 2001. His vote is usually considered the crucial one for Clinton's narrow first-year budget victory.

34. For a brief recounting of the story of Kerrey's vote—and the movie invitation—see George Stephanopoulos, *All Too Human (A Political Education)* (Boston: Little, Brown & Company), 175–76.

Harry Mason Reid (1939–), a Nevada Democrat, was elected to the Senate in 1986 and became the Senate's majority leader in 2006.

35. See Peterson, *Legislating Together,* 168–70.

36. The relationship between Reagan's congressional affairs operation and his use of direct communications appeals to the American people is examined in Kenneth E. Collier, *Between the Branches: The White House Office of Legislative Affairs* (Pittsburgh: University of Pittsburgh Press, 1997), chap. 8.

37. See Lawrence R. Jacobs, "Communications from the White House: Presidential Narrowcasting and the National Interest," in Joel D. Aberbach and Mark A. Peterson, eds., *Institutions of American Democracy: The Executive Branch* (Oxford: Oxford University Press, 2005), 174–217.

38. Rita M. Lavelle was a Reagan appointee to the U.S. Environmental Protection Agency with jurisdiction over the Superfund created to deal with hazardous waste site cleanup. She was convicted of lying to Congress about misuse of Superfund monies and other improper regulatory behavior.

39. Democratic Speaker of the House Jim Wright was forced to resign his office over charges of financial improprieties related to a book deal. Democrat Tony Coelho (1942–) resigned from the House over allegations of financial favoritism in bond trading. Texas Senator John Tower (1925–91), a Republican, was nominated by the first President Bush to the post of secretary of defense, but his former colleagues refused to confirm him because of charges of alcoholism and womanizing.

40. Scholarly support for Friedersdorf's assertion can be found in Kathleen Hall Jamieson and Erika Falk, "Continuity and Change in Civility in the House," in Jon R. Bond and Richard Fleisher, eds., *Polarized Politics: Congress and the President in a Partisan Era* (Washington: CQ Press, 2000), 96–108.

41. It should be noted that one change in the CL's job since its inception is that in the early period, with Harlow, Persons, and even O'Brien, they rarely spent much time on the Hill. See Collier, *Between the Branches,* 62–63.

42. William Gribbin is a Republican Party activist who also had long experience in the drafting of the party's quadrennial convention platforms.

43. A committee of the American Bar Association has for many years evaluated the legal qualifications of nominees to the federal judiciary. The Reagan administration frequently complained about political bias in the ABA's work because that White House disagreed with the association's poor rating of some Reagan nominees.

44. Robert Jones Portman (1955–), a Republican, served in the House of Representatives from Ohio from 1993 to 2005. He had earlier been on George H. W. Bush's congressional affairs staff, and he later held several positions in the George W. Bush administration, including director of the Office of Management and Budget.

45. For extensive discussions of this topic, see Bond and Fleisher, eds., *Polarized Politics.*

46. Kenneth E. Collier writes: "The congressional relations organization created under Eisenhower resembles the office today" (*Between the Branches,* 32).

47. See Matthew J. Dickinson, *Bitter Harvest: FDR, Presidential Power, and the Growth of the Presidential Branch* (Cambridge: Cambridge University Press, 1997); and Matthew J. Dickinson, "The Paradox of Politicization," in Joel D. Aberbach and Mark A. Peterson, eds., *Presidents and Bureaucrats: The Executive Branch and American Democracy* (New York: Oxford University Press, 2005): 135–73

INDEX

Other Books In The Joseph V. Hughes Jr. And Holly O. Hughes Series On The Presidency And Leadership

The Politics of Shared Power: Congress and the Executive, Louis Fisher
Shaping and Signaling Presidential Policy: The National Security Decision Making of Eisenhower and Kennedy, Meena Bose
Games Advisors Play: Foreign Policy in the Nixon and Carter Administrations, Jean A. Garrison
The Managerial Presidency, James P. Pfiffner
Good Advice: Information and Policy Making in the White House, Daniel E. Ponder
Congressional Abdication on War and Spending, Louis Fisher
Vicious Cycle: Presidential Decision Making in the American Political Economy, Constantine J. Spiliotes
Presidents and the People: The Partisan Story of Going Public, Mel Laracey
The Opposition Presidency: Leadership and the Constraints of History, David A. Crockett
The Presidency, Congress, and Divided Government: A Postwar Assessment, R. S. Conley
The White House World: Transitions, Organization, and Office Operations, Martha Joynt Kumar and Terry Sullivan, eds.
Between Law and Politics: The Solicitor General and the Structuring of Race, Gender, and Reproductive Rights Litigation, Richard Pacelle Jr.
The Presidency and Women: Promise, Performance, and Illusion, Janet M. Martin
Out of Touch: The Presidency and Public Opinion, Michael J. Towle
Power and Prudence: The Presidency of George H. W. Bush, Ryan J. Barilleaux and Mark J. Rozell
The Character Factor: How We Judge America's Presidents, James P. Pfiffner
The Nerve Center: Lessons in Governing from the White House Chiefs of Staff, Terry Sullivan, ed.; foreword by James A. Baker III
Nixon's Business: Authority and Power in Presidential Politics, Nigel Bowles
Saving the Reagan Presidency: Trust Is the Coin of the Realm, David M. Abshire
olicy by Other Means: Alternative Adoption by Presidents, Steven A. Shull
Institutionalizing Congress and the Presidency: The U.S. Bureau of Efficiency, 1916–1933, Mordecai Lee
Scripted for Change: The Institutionalization of the American Presidency, Victoria A. Farrar-Myers
The American Campaign: U.S. Presidential Campaigns and the National Vote, second edition, James E. Campbell
Running Against the Grain: How Opposition Presidents Win the White House, David A. Crockett
Intelligence and National Security Policymaking on Iraq, James P. Pfiffner and Mark Phythian
The Leadership of George Bush: An Insider's View of the Forty-first President, Roman Popadiuk
Honest Broker? The National Security Advisor and Presidential Decision Making, John P. Burke

ISBN-13: 978-1-60344-149-0
ISBN-10: 1-60344-149-2